The **Flame Broiled** *Doctor*

FROM BOYHOOD TO
BURNOUT
IN MEDICINE

Franklin Warsh MD

Dr. Franklin Warsh
London, Ontario, Canada
www.drwarsh.blogspot.com

This book is not intended as a substitute for the medical advice of physicians. The reader should regularly consult a physician in matters relating to his/her health and particularly with respect to any symptoms that may require diagnosis or medical attention.

Book Layout © 2015 BookDesignTemplates.com

The Flame Broiled Doctor/ Franklin Warsh. – 2nd ed.
ISBN 978-0-9958232-4-2

Yes, It's A Memoir, But...

WRITING A MEMOIR as a doctor is a hazardous undertaking. There's the ever-present problem of not having all the facts straight, the ever-present risk of pissing off somebody from your past unintentionally, and – most importantly – the ever-present danger of cutting too close to the reality of the patient's story to maintain confidentiality. I ended up perilously close to, if not crossing, all three lines in putting this book together. The downside of writing about your experiences in a town smaller than a metropolis is that it's too easy to figure out who's who.

Accordingly, many minor details in these stories have been changed. Patients' appearances, ethnicities, family structures, and in rare instances diagnoses have been changed to protect their identities.

Names of locations in the second half of the book – Rutherford City, Fort Sussex, and others – are made up. The names of most of my coworkers from that point forward in the book have also been changed.

The section of the book wherein I discuss my time in Public Health describes a conflict between the governing Board of my former workplace and the provincial Ministry of Health. Though the point of the story – namely, a look at how politics and medicine interact – is unchanged, and the dialogue is accurate to my memory, the backstory of the conflict has been reworked.

Now sit back and enjoy the story, free from worry that the book in your hands might be evidence in a lawsuit.

Please accept my resignation. I don't care to belong to any club that will have me as a member.

-*Groucho Marx*

Warts and All

OPEN A NEWSPAPER or read a health care blog on a given day, and you're bound to come across a declaration from a doctor that he or she is quitting medicine. The reasons outlined are many, though the same ones crop up time and again: the hours are brutal, the red tape is onerous, the bureaucrats are in control, or something or other about money. I don't begrudge anyone for their choice to quit medicine. The hours *are* brutal. The red tape *is* onerous. The bureaucrats *are* in control. As for the money? Well, that depends on the time and the place.

I quit medicine at the not-so-ripe age of 42. While some of the stock reasons played a part, except for money, they were overshadowed by the job itself. I spent most of my days as a family doctor, with time in the ER and public health for good measure. I honestly wish that I loved the practice of medicine, or at least liked it on a consistent basis. It would have made life so much easier for my family, my patients, and my coworkers. But twenty years after getting my "golden ticket" into medical school, I'm ready to admit that I didn't belong there in the first place.

It's not that I think I was a *bad* doctor. Most of my patients seemed content to be under my care. I can't be certain, of course, because I never followed my online ratings. My mother once chided me for some unflattering anonymous patient comments, and that was the end of that. Admittedly, my physical exam skills stunk, I wasn't all that conscientious with my continuing education, and I was often browbeaten into ordering tests or medications I shouldn't have. On the flipside, I could boast strong instincts for diagnosis, good communication skills when I needed them, and an admirable sense of the big picture. On paper, I should have thrived in the job. In reality, it was a never-ending cycle of boredom, frustration, anger, and burnout.

Whether close to family or far from family, busy or slow, clinical or administrative, the work just never made me *happy*.

It shouldn't come as a surprise, really. Aren't three quarters of all people unhappy at work? Okay, you say, but that includes huge chunks of the population in some truly awful jobs. You can't honestly expect someone to love emptying septic tanks or scraping roadkill off the streets for a living.

Can I compare medicine to marriage, then? A "lifelong" commitment that nowadays ends half the time in divorce? I don't think the analogy is that far off - you invest years of your life, undergo (sometimes wholesale) personality changes, and there's a constant need to keep things fresh. Since so many marriages end prematurely, can we expect a career to turn out differently?

Maybe I sound like a spoiled kid right about now. Thousands upon thousands of bright, young, altruistic people apply to medical school each year, and only a fraction even make it to the interview. And after amassing the ubiquitous student debts and doing my time in ~~cheap labor~~ residency, I'm doing pretty well. I've never had a problem finding work. There's been enough money to keep me driving a nice car, taking an all-inclusive trip each winter, and even reaching that mythical work-family balance.

So if it wasn't the training - which left its share of scars - or a question of competence or workload or money, why leave?

That's what I hope to explain, to myself if not anyone else. If there's a less selfish aim to the exercise, I suppose it's to shine a light on what still makes little sense to me, this many years after swearing the Hippocratic Oath. It turns out everything I thought I knew about medicine - every preconception, every expectation - turned out to be almost 100% wrong. What I once saw as arcane became utterly mundane, the wonders of the human body not wondrous at all. And for a supposedly human endeavor, people serving people, medicine can be more dehumanizing than jobs working with the inanimate. If you've ever left a hospital ward or doctor's office feeling like less of the person you were when you walked in - and I can only pray it wasn't my office - I hear you.

At times, I was as guilty as anyone of indifference, even cruelty, but it's the systems I worked in and around that defy explanation. The health care systems, or if you prefer institutions, serve their own self-promotion and their own self-righteousness, all at the expense of the patients and caregivers advertised as being at the center of things.

After a time, it wears on you. Put together with the day-in, day-out grind of practice, my periodically wonky health, and the Sisyphean task of meeting the needs of the truly needy, I found myself unable to be of much use to anyone, including my wife and kids. My heart and mind finally cried uncle, and here I am to tell the tale.

Still, my career, brief as it was, wasn't all tragedy. A lot happened between the day of my acceptance and the day I called it quits, some of it as funny as it might be instructive.

This is the book I wish someone had placed in my hand before even applying to medical school. Life as a doctor, warts and all.

CHAPTER ONE

Number 100

THE SUMMER OF 1997 wasn't the worst time to be a 24-year-old geek in Toronto living in Mom's basement. Pentium processors made for excellent computer gaming, enjoyed with friends over dial-up. The OJ trial was in the past, with the more ribald Lewinsky scandal on the way. The Spice Girls dominated pop music, Howard Stern was coming to Canadian radio, and...

Who in hell am I kidding? My life was going **nowhere** in the summer of 1997. I'd spent the two years after finishing my Bachelor's degree doing not that much, at least not that much towards my future. Yes, I'd done a fair bit of volunteer work to buff up my med school application, including a trek overseas as a basic ambulance medic. And I'd been helping my Dad by computerizing the books for his window coverings business, my qualifications for the job being a) the only one in the family able to productively use a computer, and b) having been the Teacher's Pet in my high school accounting class. I stumbled onto one other noteworthy job that year, but let's save that tidbit for now.

Both years since finishing undergrad I'd landed interviews at medical school. That's nothing to sneeze at - people with better grades or resumes than me don't get that far. In the 1996 application cycle, I'd even earned a coveted spot on the Waiting List at one school, albeit not a numbered one (the numbered spots are almost a guaranteed admission, since the superstar candidates get offers from multiple schools). And though I called the Admissions secretary every two or three days, week after week to see if I'd get an offer, it was all for naught.

The 1997 cycle had been more of a letdown. My lone interview was at McMaster, a school renowned for prizing well-roundedness as highly as grades. Good grades I had, but well-roundedness? Sure, I had volunteer work, but casually chatting with the other candidates, a lot of them were finishing Master's degrees. Some had even reaped rewards from their - no joke here - talents. Did I have a chance?

I suppose I must have, to have scored the interview, but I blew it and knew it. I came off cocky and argumentative in the group exercise part of the process. It might have been nerves, more likely being naturally cocky. My personal interview was the last on the day's schedule, and it felt like my spiel on Why I Want to Be a Doctor was one spiel too many for the interviewers that day. No phone call, no wait list, just a flat-out rejection letter. If there was any consolation, it's that McMaster did offer rejected applicants written feedback on their interview performance. I sent off for that information lickety-split. You never know what you'll learn for next time, right?

Still, applying to medical school does not in and of itself create prospects in life, and I needed to figure out what to do next. While my Bachelor's in Math could make me some quick cash tutoring, I needed a solid backup plan for my career. Two of my friends were already in med school, another two were working on MBAs, and no way was I going to spend forever in Mom's basement.

It was a Tuesday morning right at the end of August when the phone rang. I hadn't a clue as to the time, and fumbled to find my glasses in the mess of CD cases and *Magic: The Gathering* cards on the carpet. There was no stomping or hollering from upstairs, which meant Mom had gone to work and my younger sister Amy to the gym. I estimated the time to be somewhere between 8:30 and 9:00, probably closer to the latter. The only call I'd been expecting that day was from Dave, one of my close friends from high school, and the only one not venturing on a second degree. Dave had an excuse to take it slow with his education - he was working to fund his schooling after his parents split - and was going to give me a ride that day to York University to register for classes. Biochemistry seemed a sensible choice for a major - enough of a life science to look good on the med school application, and enough math in the material to play to my strengths.

I hopped upstairs to catch the call on the third ring. "Hello?"

"Hello, is this Franklin?" said a woman's voice.

"Yes, it is," I said. "May I ask who's calling?"

"I'm calling from the McMaster Medical School Admissions office."

"Um, okay." They can't be calling to rub it in. Was I supposed to send a cheque to get that interview feedback?

"As you know," she said, "your name was put on a waiting list for the class entering in September."

"It was?"

The woman on the other end chuckled. "Yes, and I'm calling to let you know that your name has now come up. Are you still interested in attending?"

"Uh...yes?"

Holy shit. I'm in.

LIKE ANY BRAINY big-city secular Jewish boy, I grew up with an impressive but limited menu of career options. At the top of the list, naturally, was Doctor. If I couldn't hack organic chemistry, second choice was Dentist. If I couldn't handle blood, Lawyer. If I wasn't good with people, Accountant. Family Business was a fallback #5, but nobody in the family had built any kind of "empire", and I had neither any passion for business nor a head for making deals. I seem to remember Pharmacist somewhere in the mix of recommended careers - "How hard is it to count pills?" my irascible Nana would often ask - but that one was only pushed on the girls for some reason.

But bright and brainy I was, standing out even amongst the crowd I went to school with, the children of lawyers, psychiatrists, and professors. Granted, my grades couldn't reach the rarefied heights of those on the Asian kids' report cards. Too many hours of Nintendo games and reruns of *Three's Company* saw to that. But I could walk into a two-hour calculus exam with nothing but a pen - I would never sully myself with something erasable - and stroll out forty minutes later having answered every question and double-checked my work. My aptitude for science didn't fall far behind my gift for math, and my essay writing was never less than solid.

Coming into university, I was the Total Academic Package, maybe the best from either side of the family. I was destined to be the family's first doctor. As far as I knew, or at least convinced myself, that was the endpoint.

Get into med school, game over. You win. That part I understood. Medicine was as close as you could get to lifelong job security, if not always in the city of your choice. Your income ranged from respectable to stratospheric, depending on the specialty, although it honestly wasn't about the money in my eyes.

And therein lay the problem. Why *was* I pursuing medicine? I craved the degree, to prove myself to family, friends, and the doubters from times I wasn't on my game at school. A chip on the shoulder and a little ambition can take you pretty far if you have the right skills. I just never put much thought into whether I wanted the job.

IT'S IMPOSSIBLE TO overstate the elation among my family and friends when I broke the news. Mom was effusive, shedding tears in the comfort that she hadn't failed as a parent. My Dad cheered in an excitement the likes of which I'd not seen before or since. And my friends couldn't wait to shell out for dinner, drinks, and a lap dance.

Celebrations aside, classes started in a little over a week. I needed a cheap apartment and a start on what I imagined was a deluge of forms. That meant a day trip to Hamilton, but Mom needed her car for work. A ride in Amy's fuchsia Ford Escort it was. Not the manliest car to be seen in, but it had a CD player.

When we finally navigated the McMaster parking lot and found the med school offices, it was mid-morning. The Admissions secretaries were friendly and welcoming, which was a dramatic change from the perennially grouchy staff of an undergrad office. They wasted no time in getting me oriented to the layout of the school, which took up the lower two floors of a teaching hospital. The building was as utilitarian as any built after the 1950s, more resembling a factory than a place to treat the infirmed. However, someone came up with the clever idea to color-code each corner of the building. It would take effort to get lost so long as you could tell red from yellow. I was escorted

through all the important spots - library, bookstore, student
lounge - then ushered back to the Admissions office for the paperwork.

While I tried to process it all, one of the secretaries noticed
that part of my orientation package was missing.
"Could it have been dropped in the mail?" I asked. "I might
have said to mail it before I decided to drive up today."
"I don't think so," said the secretary. "We wouldn't have sent
it this close to Labor Day knowing you were coming in. I'll call
the Program Coordinator to find out." I was still flabbergasted
by the level of service. Dealing with the Registrar's office as an
undergrad, assuming you were even able to speak with a live
human being, you were always made to feel like a number and
little else. "Oh, hi Debbie, it's Anne in Admissions. Do you remember the hundredth student we let into the program...no, the
one from yesterday, the last candidate from the list...right, him.
His orientation package is incomplete."

After the paperwork was sorted out, I found a steal of a
basement apartment just four blocks from the school. My landlord turned out to be the chap running the medical bookstore -
Bookstore Bert, we called him. It was a basement and I'd be living with a roommate, but the rent included everything, even full
cable. With no significant other nor foreseeable prospects for
one, I'd need something to do after closing the books each night.

But basement or no basement, roommate or no roommate,
girlfriend or no girlfriend, this was med school. I'd made it into
med school.

...as the very last person the school was interested in.

...after they'd exhausted their preferred candidates.

...and the waiting list.

What was that again about a chip on the shoulder?

CHAPTER TWO

Growing Pains

IF MY INITIAL standing in the class wasn't enough to make me feel like I didn't belong in med school, the first semester didn't help. The academic work wasn't a problem. I was a sponge for knowledge, even finding a discipline for study that I never knew as an undergrad. No, it was everything outside the textbooks that proved a mixed bag.

Though I'd like to think otherwise, I was something of a hermit. Admittedly, I've always been reclusive, even now. One is not normally elected Prom King by excelling at math and *Warcraft*. I went back to Toronto most weekends instead of staying to socialize, though that was more about laundry and square meals than disinterest in my classmates. I did manage to make some close friends, though, and even found a measure of popularity as one of the class clowns.

(I had help on that front, courtesy of coming to my apartment one night to the sight of Bookstore Bert's bare behind scurrying away...the mileage on a good story is not to be underestimated.)

That said, I went through a major culture shock. Sometime between the end of my undergrad years and my first day of medical school, university became a lot more expensive and a lot more politically correct. I neither foresaw nor was prepared for it, and didn't know how to handle it. Staff and students alike spoke a low-level pseudo-political gobbledygook I couldn't make heads or tails of: "At the end of the day, we need to frame a person's illness through the clinical lens, but also in the context of their prevailing socioeconomic issues." Huh? What the hell does that even mean? And my go-to solution to awkward conversations, an off-color joke? Went over like a fart in church.

I was a flop at Communication Skills training as well. My default laid-back manner came off as cold and disengaging. I should cut myself a little slack here, because during my very first try with a simulated patient, the woman was mouthing back my words as I uttered them (it was an experience as unnerving as the first time a girl let me get past first base). Since being laid back didn't work, Plan B was to overcompensate. On a later attempt, I tried my best to emulate a teacher that seemed able to *ooze* empathy on command. Suffice it to say I'm a terrible actor, and might as well have interviewed the patient dressed as a Muppet. Once Plan B backfired, I responded to feedback in the least adult way possible, by simply not giving a rat's ass.

None of this lay beyond my personal coping skills. That is, until the stomach pains came along.

IT WAS A DREARY Friday night in October, and almost nine by the time I finished studying and taking notes. With no teaching sessions on Fridays - scratch that, no teaching sessions I attended on Fridays - it was by far my most productive day for studies. Most weeks those studies were done back home, freeing up the rest of the weekend for family and old friends. The rain had been brutal the night before, though, making the trip to Toronto an unsavory idea. A bunch of my classmates had planned a movie night for Saturday, so better to stay and be social, I'd decided.

My stomach had been bothering me for hours, and this particular discomfort was new to me. We all know those bad cramps that crop up now and then, either from eating something we shouldn't or not having enough water. Those cramps last only until your intestines empty out, with or without an accompanying explosion. This wasn't that. It felt like a rodent or house cat was seated behind my navel, scratching at the inside of my belly muscles every three or four minutes. I'd popped a few antacids with no results.

My roommate Marty was puttering around, packing a few things before the three-hour drive to his wife and teenage daughter. Marty entered med school a "mature student", a veteran paramedic by trade in his pre-medicine days. He was now in the third year of a family/emergency medicine residency, with the plan to work the ER of his home town and run a clinic on an

Aboriginal reserve every so often. Marty and I hit it off quickly, and he was as easy a roommate as it gets. If he wasn't in hospital on call, he took off for home as often as possible. I never lacked for quiet study time. Marty ended up being a terrific mentor to me. More than being a damn good teacher, he had some masterful ideas on how to handle the egos and political games that plague every hospital on the planet.

In his back-and-forth from the kitchen to his bedroom, Marty noticed me clutching my belly and groaning in front of the TV. "Don't you look well," he laughed. "Reminds me of that old Monty Python movie. 'Bring out your dead! Bring out your dead!' Can I give you anything, man, seriously?"

"I'm not dead yet," I moaned back in Cockney. "Thanks, guy, but I don't know what the hell this is. Hopefully I'll just have a bout of diarrhea and that'll be the end of it."

"Well doesn't that sound like a great weekend! Have a good one, man!"

I tried to channel-surf as a distraction from the abdominal pangs. Wrestling reruns, Apes movie marathon, early season hockey - nothing to hold my attention. Ten minutes passed before I surrendered and finally decided to open a novel.

The scratching sensation grew more intense, and I soon lost all focus in my reading. I dropped down to on all fours in a cold sweat, like I was reenacting the transformation scene from a horror movie. I crawled in agony to the washroom, barely reaching the toilet in time to vomit everything I'd ingested for the past two days.

I pulled myself upright using the toilet seat as an anchor and staggered to the sink. I was pale but not dizzy. I splashed a few drops of water in my mouth, but thirty seconds later I returned face down to the porcelain. The vomiting slowed down the shredding at my insides, but I could sense the pain still lying in wait to ambush. Not daring to eat or take more than a sip of water to rinse out the bile acids, I lurched my way to bed and passed out in the fetal position, not bothering to turn out any lights.

I woke up early, feeling like a bomb had gone off in my gut but hungry all the same. I wasn't light-headed or bleeding from any orifice, so I convinced myself I made the right call in being macho and avoiding the ER. It was the first time I'd thrown up since I was a little kid, not counting nights when alcohol was the culprit. I inspected the contents of my cupboards, repulsed by the thought of eating what I'd upchucked violently just hours before. I hosed off in the shower and headed out to grab whatever salted-and-fried-potato item I could get my hands on from the nearest fast food joint.

My belly finally settled two hours after filling it with salt, carbs, and grease. Saturday was a complete write-off, as I fell in and out of sleep in front of the TV. Too tired to get up and groom, I never did make movie night after all.

IT COULDN'T HAVE just been a panic attack. Shortness of breath, maybe a chest pain or two, slip a tranquilizer under the tongue, done. No, I had to go through bouts of vicious belly pains, complete evacuation of my intestines - both ends - and every test short of a colonoscopy only to be diagnosed with somatization. Stress. Anxiety. One way or another, the pains originated in my head, not my gut. Not that the diagnosis made them vanish. No, the stomach pains and puking episodes would continue to plague me, before exams, evaluations, residency interviews...twice I missed mandatory sessions and nearly failed a rotation. I no-showed a Clinical Skills exam, languishing for a day in the ER. How I eluded remediation or worse remains a mystery to me to this day.

It couldn't have just been a panic attack.

But it wasn't all bad in my first year. Between a dodgy adjustment period in the fall and a dreadful spring, winter was good to me. The school jumbled up the tutorial groups every three months, and my second group clicked as a study team. Then one day I managed to charm a girl.

Kylea hailed from Thunder Bay, the city on Lake Superior that's a gateway to the northern, "fat part" of Ontario. She was blond, charismatic, outgoing, gorgeous, and an accomplished piano player and competitive singer. No wait list for her, Kylea was solidly in the top 20 candidates (judging by a student number some 80 points lower than mine). No putting myself down or selling myself short, she was simply out my league...which probably explains why I took the liberty of discussing masturbation the first time we happened to be in proximity of one another in the library. Some weeks later, when *she* called to invite *me* to a movie, I asked who else she might want me to contact, assuming it was a group outing she was arranging. Not until after I dropped her at home did she notify me it was a date.

Fellow nerds, take note: math skills do not amount to much in the world of dating. When in doubt, ask someone who's good with people for advice.

IT WAS THE end of the last tutorial group session of first year, and time for the group members to evaluate one another. The spring term was a trainwreck. In contrast to my experience in the winter, this study group had no chemistry whatsoever. For the first time since high school I was truly a complete misfit. The doctor leading the tutorials had a presence about him that stiffened the atmosphere and choked off any semblance of enjoyment. Getting through each session was drudgery, and I never found myself able to make a positive contribution.

We went around the table evaluating each other and my only positive thought was that I had no need to puke that instant. Sure enough, everyone got in his or her best shot when it was my turn. *Alienated yourself from the group... unprofessional...almost deserves to be failed.* It was a blur but not a surprise. I *was* unprofessional and I *didn't* contribute anywhere near what I was capable of.

I never protest in moments like that. The person feeding you shit doesn't care how it tastes. Besides, the last thing I wanted was to risk making the tutor reconsider his decision to let me pass. I swallowed my medicine and cowered out of the room.

As we'd already been dating a few months, Kylea met me to grab dinner and spend the evening together. She asked about my evaluation, knowing full well how shitty the previous few months had gone. I related the experience in broad strokes. She was infuriated at the others on my behalf, showing an unshakeable loyalty I don't thank her enough for even now. But I was too bummed to get angry. Lucky for both of us, the relationship was still fresh. And lucky for me, I suppose, I didn't actually fail, nor get the warning or suspension I'd dreaded for most of first year. I forced myself to get past the day's misery and enjoyed the rest of a romantic night.

CHAPTER THREE

The Long and the Short of it

I SQUEEZED INTO the exam room in silence, trying neither to bump into the old man's family members nor come between doctor and patient. Space gets tighter and tighter the more bodies get packed into an exam room, and an observing medical student is lowest on the totem pole. I was in the dorky short lab coat that identified me as a student rather than a resident, so at least acting invisible didn't count against me. It was week 2 of the second-year elective block, but the first clinic in which I'd shadowed this particular staff doctor. He also happened to be one of the school's administrative bigwigs, so I didn't mind skulking in the corner and keeping my mouth shut.

Actually, Dr. Bigwig was both easygoing and approachable, despite his Proper British Accent and the power that came with his position at the school. Most everybody I met at the Cancer Clinic was amiable, give or take the odd quirk. Part of it must be the personality it takes to work in this field, which at times I've convinced myself I possess. The other part of the equation is that the big pricks in medical school seemed drawn to careers in surgery.

Dr. Bigwig introduced me to the crowd and had the old man stand up and disrobe. "Now, Frank, Mr. Survivor is here in follow-up for cancer of the penis."

Naturally, my eyes flashed to the patient's crotch for a peek. Saggy and grey-haired, as one would expect.

"As you can see," said Dr. Bigwig, "he's had a penectomy, but needs a routine exam to look for recurrence."

Penectomy? As in surgical removal of the penis? My eyes darted back to the old man's nether region. I could almost hear the BOING! of my eyes erupting from their sockets like a cartoon character. It was saggy down there because it was **nothing but his balls.** He had no penis!

I was frozen in an unblinking daze while Dr. Bigwig finished the visit. He gave the old man a quick once-over and some instructions for follow-up that I wasn't conscious enough to process. I followed Dr. Bigwig from the exam room to the working area for the oncologists and nurses. He laid a hand on my shoulder. "It would appear, everyone, that young Frank here hasn't seen a man after a penectomy before."

I was slack-jawed, foraging my brain for any words I could find. No such luck.

Dr. Fancyties, who led my tutorial group in the early days of first year, paused his dictation and grinned. "Didn't you know, Frank? After fifty it just falls off!"

I was still in a fog as the room full of doctors and nurses saw the look on my face and laughed. If I was twenty-five, and expect much less sex when kids enter the picture, how many years did I have left?

SECOND YEAR PROVED to be a major improvement over the first. My fall semester tutorial group fired on all cylinders from day one, a welcome and radical change from what I encountered in the spring. I still had my stomach issues come evaluation time - puking and all - but the sense of non-belonging faded.

And there was a lot of fun to be had. True, social gatherings could turn into bitch sessions about this or that doctor, or this or that rotation, but most of the time it was about finding a laugh where you could. You didn't look for humor because it was "necessary in the face of tragedy or suffering or death" or any other overwrought reason you might glean from novels or movies about med school. Humor was necessary to make the slog of studying your ass off bearable. Yes, the emotionally wrenching moments happened, but not where you expected and never when you were waiting for them.

Because I went to a school with an accelerated, three-year MD program, the big challenge of second year was trying to find a direction for my career. I never gave it much thought before applying to med school, which might be one reason why I never gave a good interview. I'm pretty sure I answered Pediatrics when asked, which is a good default. It's not a big-money specialty like, say, Dermatology, that could set off alarms bells in an interview - how dare this applicant be in it for a guaranteed six-figure income - and who doesn't like kids, right?

There are roughly two dozen medical and surgical specialties, a few dozen more subspecialties, and almost no limit to the directions you can ultimately take your career as a doctor if you have the patience and motivation. As there was no shortage of work for doctors, and a residency spot was guaranteed for every trainee in the country, you would expect second year med students to be sanguine about their career prospects and focus on their studies. You would be wrong.

In fact, the anxiety around landing a residency spot wildly outstripped the neurosis of applying to med school. I was far from the only one going through it, too. At least half the class played a curious game of guess-and-second-guess when planning their elective rotations, all in the name of improving the odds of landing a plum residency. Do I do electives locally, or in other towns? Do I work with the approachable docs, who are likely to write me a glowing letter, or be the zillionth student to work with Dr. Esteemed? Do I summon the nerve to ask for an elective with the Program Director? Do I stick to electives in my desired field, or try to demonstrate a zeal for broad-based learning by picking something unusual? Whether any of this fretting serves a purpose must rank among medicine's greatest mysteries.

At the time, I was pretty set on Internal Medicine. Surgery didn't appeal to me, and my hands were too clumsy and fidgety to make me a fit for the job anyways. Family Medicine didn't seem challenging enough, and the less said about my experiences on the Obstetrics & Gynecology rotation the better. My nose couldn't handle the Pathology lab. I didn't want to spend my life in front of a screen as a Radiologist (as a lifelong couch potato and now writer-blogger, the irony is not lost on me). The Pediatricians I worked with spent at least half their days dealing with ADD or kids that were plainly brats. And there was the old joke about Internists being the smart ones that knew everything and did nothing. If ever there were a more accurate description of me, I hadn't heard it. Fate and karma had a different plan for my career, but all that in due time.

While I earmarked the bulk of my elective time to Internal Medicine rotations, I had long planned on spending time with Marty, who finished residency the previous summer. As per his plan, he divided his time between two ERs and a clinic on an Aboriginal reserve, and was more than happy to have me help out. The ER offered a med student the best per-hour educational yield, although it was an exhausting place to be by hour six or seven of a shift. You would see everything from the life-threatening to the absurd. The ER, for me, will always represent the heart and soul of the health-care experience.

IT WAS EARLY into the overnight shift, and the waiting room of Midland-Penetanguishene ER wasn't busy at all. Though nothing I would see in my month shadowing Marty made the ER stand out, I couldn't shake a sense of doom anytime we went in for a night shift. Penetanguishene was the home of a particularly awful maximum-security prison, a prison housing the criminally insane no less. I suppose keeping an eye peeled for an escaped maniac helps you stay awake through the night, but it's not at all easy on the nerves.

There were a few patients in the less urgent exam rooms, some waiting to be seen, others waiting for test results to come back. Marty was chatting with the Head Nurse over a doughnut. Don't forget to feed your staff, he would tell me, especially on nights. The two were prioritizing the waiting room patients, none of whom had an urgent problem.

Marty squinted at a familiar name on a chart. "This guy's here again? Let's try to get him in and out before he causes trouble." The nurse nodded in agreement and escorted the patient to an exam room. Marty asked me to take the history while he caught up on his charts.

Mr. Triple Crown had a storied past for a small-town guy. He was an inveterate IV drug user, carrying a raft of communicable diseases. Most significantly he had HIV and Hepatitis B and C - the "triple crown" of blood-borne infections, hence the moniker.

He was gaunt, ashen, and on the wrong side of the old Tooth-to-Tattoo Ratio that doctors would use to presage a person's untimely death. (This was a time before the modern popularity of body art rendered the Ratio obsolete). His hospital chart was filled with dictated notes lamenting his no-shows at specialist appointments. Nobody had a clue how advanced his diseases were. Even when he did make his appointments, the state of his veins made drawing blood almost impossible.

Though I was sporting the Official Look of an ER doctor - jeans, scrub shirt, five o'clock shadow - I wasn't yet an MD and made a point of introducing myself as a student. "Hello, sir, my name is Frank. I'm a medical student working here with the doctor. What brings you into the ER tonight?" One of those tips you pick up on early in training: find out what's wrong *tonight*, or you're giving license to a patient to narrate their life's story.

"I think I have another infection," Triple Crown mumbled. "Or maybe it's a blown vein. I hope it's not a clot."

"Is there any redness or pain around the area? Do you have a fever?" I asked.

"Yeah it hurts, but it's been hurt for a while. Only vein I have left." He unbuckled his belt and fumbled with his pants zipper.

I raised a hand to stop the show. "So, the vein you're worried about is on your penis?"

"Yeah, man, only vein I have left."

I drew the curtain closed and handed Triple Crown a gown to change into. "Let's give you some privacy and get you changed, rather than having you just, uh, expose yourself."

I darted to the charting station, more than a little freaked out. "Marty, can I get you to come do this physical exam with me? I'm not sure what I'm looking for, to tell a blown vein from a clot from an infection. Plus, well, it's his dick."

"You don't know what a normal dick looks like?" Marty snickered, rising. We strolled over to Triple Crown's bedside and drew the curtain. "So tell me what's going on tonight."

"Oh, man," moaned Triple Crown. "I've got bad luck. Don't know what I did, but it hurts."

"Were you injecting again?" said Marty without expression. Marty was normally warm and engaging with patients and pushed me to be likewise. He drew a line, though, when the patient was clearly drunk or high. No cruelty, just business. It was jarring for me to see it the first time, until I realized that it wasn't a demonstration of haughtiness or preaching. When the patient is intoxicated, you just can't be sure who you're talking to - the patient or the drug.

"Yeah, but only had one vein left. Man, it's like, sensitive and shit, you know? Hurts."

"I don't doubt it. Let's have a look."

Triple Crown lifted his bedsheet and gown. His body was peppered with old track marks and scars, just like his arms minus the tattoos. His penis lay limp as the rest of him, marbled with white patches where warts or other lesions had been burned off. Triple Crown lifted his shaft like he might animate a marionette, pointing out the vein at the root of his discomfort.

Marty gloved up and motioned for me to join him for a closer look. "You can see where he's injected, but the vein is still intact. There's no redness or drainage, and when I palpate there's no firmness that might indicate a clot." I aped Marty's physical exam for my own learning.

"Well," said Marty, "there's nothing to worry about. No blood clot, no infection. The pain is just the reaction to whatever you injected. Try some ice packs or Advil." We left the bedside and headed back to the charting desk.

"What should I put down as the diagnosis?" I asked. "Painful injection? Injured penis?"

"The guy's injected drugs so many times," said Marty, "he's down to one open vein on his body. Considering where the vein is that he shot up, I would put down the diagnosis as 'hitting rock bottom'."

CHAPTER FOUR

Foreign Relations

I SCARFED DOWN the last bites of pizza as my pager ratcheted up to its max volume on the third set of beeps. I had all of twenty minutes to grab dinner and use the washroom after everyone else signed out for the night. I chugged the last of my Diet Coke and sauntered over to dial the house phone on the wall of the sparsely populated cafeteria. Now late into my final year of med school, I'd already been matched to a residency program. Finding a reason to care about these last few nights on call was becoming a serious uphill battle.

"Oh hi, it's Frank, the clinical clerk on tonight."

"Hello, Frank, it's Dr. Al-Saudi, the resident for General Surgery."

I wound up on call with Al-Saudi at least a half-dozen times on different rotations. His phone greeting never changed in tone, volume, or cadence, no matter how early or late into the shift it was. He was a friendly enough guy, but I couldn't point to a single thing I'd learned while on call with him. I had no cause to complain the previous spring when he was only an intern - interns aren't expected to teach - but I'm supposed to get *something* out of working with senior residents beyond the mindless tasks doctors typically label as *scut work*. Al-Saudi was but one of many trainees from the Arab nations. Their governments fork over outlandish sums of money to have their doctors train in North America. It's a win-win for the home countries and the medical schools, that enjoy a windfall of both cash and warm bodies to fill the call schedule.

Actually, there was one thing I learned from being around Al-Saudi, and that was not to piss him off. A few of my classmates shared stories of times they'd disagreed with him, or nights on call when they felt out of their depth. Invariably, Al-

Saudi had chewed them out and that was the last page they'd get all night.

"What's up?" I asked.

"There's a patient on the ward who is day two post-op complaining of chest pain," said Al-Saudi. "I've already asked the nurses to get an ECG and draw his blood count and cardiac enzymes. Can you please assess him and call me back?"

"Yeah, okay." I headed to the ward to get the scoop from the nurses. The patient had sprays of nitroglycerin without much effect, but his ECG didn't show anything to suggest he was having a heart attack. I had a brief chat with the patient and performed a cursory physical exam. He was uncomfortable but not crashing. The assigned nurse rhymed off other details from his medical history - diabetes, two past heart attacks, early kidney failure - that could portend a complicated night if his pain didn't settle.

The wheels started turning in my otherwise haggard brain. No matter what I've learned about philosophy, ethics, professionalism, and responsibility, I've never escaped the sense that many of life's decisions still boil down to a cartoon angel and devil whispering in each ear. This night, the devil was just a wee bit more convincing. *This could be a complicated night, yes, but who says it needs to be complicated for me?*

I opened my eyes wide and let my jaw tremble. "Okay, so he's had his nitro but still has pain, and he has this complicated history. Did Dr. Al-Saudi leave any other orders?"

"No," said the nurse, "I'm afraid there are no other orders he gave. The bloodwork was drawn, but it'll still take time to get back."

"Did he ask if you thought the patient was safe to be seen by a student? This gentleman is pretty complicated."

"No, he didn't mention that, once I told him the vitals."

I paced a bit and begin rifling through the patient's chart, with a seeming sense of urgency if not a purpose. "This patient's had a pretty big surgery with a complicated history. I'm not sure I feel confident here."

"Oh, I agree," said the nurse. "I'm surprised Dr. Al-Saudi sent you. If you can keep an eye on this gentleman, I'll go page Dr. Al-Saudi to come right away."

"Thanks. I just feel out of my league, you know?"

"I totally understand. I'll be back in a minute."

I checked on the patient while waiting for Al-Saudi. He felt no different in the few minutes I'd been there. He was probably fine, maybe suffering some heartburn or discomfort from the hospital bed, but I wouldn't be sure until the bloodwork was back. Then again, I was damn sure that bloodwork would no longer be my problem in another three minutes.

Al-Saudi stormed onto the ward and pointed at me to step outside the patient's room. He didn't even let me get a word in. "I told you to ASSESS the patient, not to MANAGE the patient! Assess, and call me back, not to treat or manage him yourself! I don't need you here. GO!"

I cowered off the ward to the sympathetic gazes of the nurses, my posture slouched all the way to the stairwell. Not Oscar-worthy, but mission accomplished all the same.

I took a satisfied stroll to the student lounge to catch up on e-mail and my favorite web sites. I savored a peaceful evening of reading in my on-call room, and gave Kylea a shout to say good night. I turned out the light at 11 and settled myself in bed.

I woke up at 6 the next morning, after getting the best sleep imaginable in a hospital on-call bed. Pager never went off once.

AH, CLINICAL CLERKSHIP. The final year or so of medical school that supposedly gets you ready to manage patients on your own. I can't be sure it did anything apart from acclimate my body to the Dickensian conditions of internship, and get me hooked on arrowroot cookies otherwise meant for patients. I'm sure I learned *something* - by osmosis if not didactic lectures - but one night in four without sleep is not a recipe for long-term memory health.

In most ways, clerkship is easier than internship and residency. Nobody expects much of you, so unless you're still in need of reference letters, you're free to meet those low expectations. Teaching sessions abound, affording you chances to get off the wards, don real clothes, and fraternize with classmates. And of course, half of your rotations are elective or outpatient-based, giving you weeks at a time to catch up on sleep.

That said, clerkship does entail the titanic stress of finding and applying to the right residency programs. The plotting and maneuvering that went on in years 1 and 2 take on a new level of urgency as a clerk. Ironically, the students going for competitive (i.e. big-money) specialties almost have it easier. They automatically apply everywhere, and pick a few programs as backups in less competitive fields. The rest of us have to choose wisely. On the one hand, you don't want to apply to programs in cities you have no desire to visit, never mind live in. The costs of flights and hotels add up fast, and jet setting across the country for a pointless interview wastes everyone's time. On the other hand, if you apply to too few programs and blow the interviews, you might end up unmatched to *any* residency. If that happens, you're stuck picking from the B-list of positions offered to foreign med school graduates, rarely in a city you fancied.

For me, clerkship brought into high relief the importance of mentoring in choosing a specialty. Not that a good role model necessarily leads you to the right choice, but a lousy preceptor can make you write off a specialty for all the wrong reasons.

Without a doubt, it was bad preceptors that led me to rule out Psychiatry as a possible career. Given that I'm clumsy with my hands, physically lazy, and low-key in demeanor, I should have had Psychiatry near the top of my list of options. Moreover, I met some terrific teachers in my pre-clinical rotations.

That all changed when I rotated through the wards of the psych hospital. It was a near-constant freak show, and I'm not referring to the patients. Most of my nights on call I was paired with Dr. Slowpoke as a resident. Slowpoke embodied every 1980s stereotype of gay men you can imagine in his mannerisms, which made it a challenge to converse with him seriously. More importantly, though, the guy took FOREVER to assess and discuss each patient. My first night of psychiatry call entailed me sitting in the room as he interviewed a woman for well over two hours. For an encore, Slowpoke took another forty-five minutes to tediously describe every one of the lady's facial twitches and verbal inflections to the staff psychiatrist, all in baroque jargon. By three in the morning of my last night on call with Slowpoke, the person in hospital most at risk of suicide was me.

Slowpoke had nothing on the staff psychiatrists, though. There was Dr. Loudlaugh, who drew me a decision-tree approach to diagnosing mental illnesses, only to slap a copyright symbol on the paper and make me swear an oath not to share his diagram with anyone. Then there was Dr. Magneto, who droned on and on about his research on magnetic fields as an untapped treatment for this, that, and the other. Whether his research ever bore fruit I haven't a clue.

The looniest of the bunch, however, was Dr. Grants. Dr. Grants had only two trains of thought that I could discern. First, that every psychiatric patient was a collection of brain-chemical receptors that he was personally researching. Second, that he had scored gazillions of dollars' worth of grant money to conduct said research. His research funding entered into every...single...monologue I heard from the man - speeches he would deliver whilst prancing around the room, orating with the bombast of a *Superfriends* villain. Whatever credibility Psychiatry earned in my eyes from excellent pre-clinical experiences (and post-*Frasier* television), it stood no chance against the parade of oddballs I met as a clerk.

Kylea and I had been together over a year when clerkship began. I hadn't yet summoned the courage to propose, though my family could see it coming. Once we entered that nebulous phase of a relationship when it's "serious" - probably about the time Bookstore Bert's basement became little more than storage space for me - Kylea abandoned the idea of becoming a surgeon. Surgery is not a career that melds easily with home and family. She eventually came around to Internal Medicine, with the long-term goal of treating cancer patients.

I applied to Internal Medicine as well, as I'd planned through first and second year, but late in the game I stumbled upon Anesthesia. Anesthesia was a field with some fascinating science behind it. It harkened back not only to parts of the med school curriculum I enjoyed but also undergraduate physics. It was heavy on procedures, but they weren't as long or involved the way a surgery could be. Besides, you were typically able to sit down once the patient was asleep and stable, rather than being stuck on your feet for hours to develop varicose veins. The drugs Anesthesiologists use had such wildly cool effects on the patient - amnesia, full-body paralysis - you could almost picture yourself as a wizard out of some fantasy novel or comic book. In case it's not obvious, I found the field really, really fun. I made a series of frantic phone calls and wrote the most desperate letters I could to programs still taking applications.

Not long thereafter, I was headed to the Halifax, on Canada's east coast for an Anesthesia residency, matched with Kylea for a five-year adventure.

"I SWEAR TO fulfill, to the best of my ability and judgment, this covenant." It was surreal. I couldn't believe I was a doctor. Not that I truly was. I had the degree, but all that was good for at the moment was getting my ass kissed at the bank.

"I will respect the hard-won scientific gains of those physicians in whose steps I walk, and gladly share such knowledge as is mine with those who are to follow. I will apply, for the benefit of the sick, all measures which are required, avoiding those twin traps of overtreatment and therapeutic nihilism." My eyes scanned the crowd. Kylea's parents, yup. Okay, spotted my mother...and she was standing next to my stepmother?!? Oh, Jesus. Did they even know who the other one was?

"...I will not be ashamed to say 'I know not,' nor will I fail to call in my colleagues when the skills of another are needed for a patient's recovery." Oh, God, my mother and stepmother were talking. I was so not ready for this. Just breathe and recite the words, I told myself, or you'll have another stomach attack. Breathe and recite the words.

"...Above all, I must not play at God." Really, that was in there? Did the doctors-playing-God cliché come before or after this part of the oath?

"...May I always act so as to preserve the finest traditions of my calling and may I long experience the joy of healing those who seek my help."

Okay, so I graduated. Now came the hard part. I had to survive dinner...with both my parents in the same room for the first time since my Bar-Mitzvah...oh, and my stepmother in the mix...and my future in-laws.

YES, I WAS more than a little distracted while swearing the Oath of Hippocrates. Perhaps it was an omen of things to come, though foresight is a scarce resource for a newly-minted doctor.

Graduation time was a whirlwind, but a fun and exciting one - parties with classmates, planning a move, and of course the family meet-and-greets. I'd met Ann, my future mother-in-law, early in my relationship with Kylea, but this was my first time getting to know Kylea's father Emil. Emil was a construction worker forced into retirement by injuries on the job. He was more curious and shrewd than the typical blue-collar type, and gave the impression that had he been born elsewhere and elsewhen, he'd have ended up with many more years of formal education. My first encounter was a memorable one to say the least. I came by Kylea's apartment a few days before the Oath ceremony, to join the family at dinner. While getting a glass of water, I ran the tap too fast and a made a mess on the floor. Before I could even look for a rag, Emil had raced and retrieved a **single** piece of toilet paper - just one square - from the bathroom and mopped up the mess. Of course, the man was raised in a family of 17 children in the 1940s. I suppose it'd be impossible to avoid learning the importance of thrift in a house that packed.

Ann hailed from Swaziland originally, and had a daughter from a previous marriage in the U.S., my sister-in-law Patience, before moving to Thunder Bay. Ann was a social worker by trade, devoting her career to the developmentally disabled. Deeply devoted to her Christian faith, Ann was in the autumn years of her career and almost as cynical as me.

Emil was a single father to Kylea when he and Ann met. He had adopted Kylea with his first wife, a woman with two children of her own, but that marriage ended while Kylea was still in pre-school. If you're starting to find this confusing, that's because it is. I married into the family over fifteen years ago, and still feel like I need a programme to navigate family gatherings. My own family was much simpler to keep track of. My parents were *very* divorced, having split up when I was still in elementary school. At the tail end of my undergrad days, my father David married my stepmother Maxine, a native of Florida he met through a Kabbalah network - that New Age Jewish mysticism practiced by such religious luminaries as Lindsay Lohan and (not to be confused with the Virgin Mary) Madonna.

My mother Ruth was a supply teacher when I was a kid, but went back to school after the split from Dad to become an optician. Keeping the house up with Amy and me left her little time for a social life while we were still young and dependent. A few men came into her life over the years, but she never took the plunge to remarry. Like everyone on her side of the family tree, Mom was wickedly smart, albeit without a hint of my cockiness. She also shared the family's caustic and often tasteless sense of humor. I've been told more than once that conversations around our dinner table were traumatic to genteel outsiders.

The star of graduation week was my 90-year-old grandmother, whom Dad flew in from overseas for the festivities. Despite advancing age and looming heart problems, she was as effusive and cheerful as ever around us. Kylea and her family found her absolutely adorable, language barrier be damned. It would be the last time I'd see her, though she lived to be just shy of 100.

A somewhat nerve-wracking dinner - for me, at least - with both sets of in-laws was the plan for graduation night. While wine got me through dinner painlessly, the night set the stage for future family gatherings. Mom hit it off with Emil and Ann right away, so much so that they were clearly going to be partners in crime in pushing for grandchildren. It would be some months before Dad was as comfortable around them, though I'd bet it was Mom's presence that made things awkward.

The Main Event of graduation time, though, was the engagement party Dad threw for Kylea and me to close out the weekend. He had invited my entire social circle *and* his. After schmoozing and posing for pictures until my smiling muscles ached, I came to the painful conclusion that it's impossible to feel like an adult around your parents' friends. My age and the number of degrees I'd accrued meant nothing - it still felt like I belonged at a folding table in the corner, wolfing down chicken fingers instead of whatever the grownups ate. Moreover, being addressed as Doctor (or "doc-*TAH*" by Dad's more stereotypically Jewish friends) still sounded weird, like patronizing words of encouragement from a tipsy aunt.

Still, I'd made it to and through medical school, fulfilling The Dream for myself and the family. The next five years would be exhausting, but I'd get through them just as I did the last three, and I was no longer going at it alone. I had much to be proud of, and a life to look forward to.

What I didn't foresee was the detour through hell along the way.

CHAPTER FIVE

The Lowly Intern

DR. FIXTICKER SAT up to deliver his feedback. "When I came on service in the unit this week, the nurses came up to me and said, 'there's a BIG problem with the new intern'."

Great. Dr. Fixticker was an approachable staff person and decent teacher, but he never saw fit to tell me any of this until my end-of-month evaluation? I'd worked myself hard on the CV-ICU, the intensive care unit for heart surgery patients. The days started at 6am, ended somewhere around 7pm, and any thought of leaving early after a night of sleepless call was a fantasy. I was the only MD in the unit for hours at a time while the staff docs and senior residents were in the operating room, with minimal teaching and barely a clue as to what I was doing.

My stint on the CV-ICU capped off a spectacularly shitty three month start to residency. My first two months had been a rotation in Anesthesia. I enjoyed it, but proved hapless at some of the most basic procedures like starting an IV line. I struggled to click with my staff supervisors, who had none of the patience for an underperforming intern that they might extend to a clinical clerk.

At least Halifax was an easy town to adjust to. We found a terrific apartment just blocks from the waterfront, and walking distance from the teaching hospitals we'd be rotating through. There were any number of great shops and restaurants in the avenues around us, though we had no expectation of time to enjoy them. Every other weekend one or both of us was trapped in hospital, which meant our "free" weekends were eaten up by grocery shopping and a relentless pursuit of sleep.

"The nurses said you argued with them about routine orders," Fixticker continued, "you were away from the unit for large chunks of time..."

"With all due respect, sir," I pleaded, "I was only ever in the study room after rounds, right there in the back corner of the unit. The nurses knew that, and could knock on the door at any time. Never once did I not answer a page or come when asked." The feedback was already in writing. Why was I wasting my time arguing? "There was *one* bad incident with the patient who had the GI bleed, but I was called on it by the resident on the consulting service. As I understood, it was addressed then and there." Actually, it wasn't that things were addressed so much I was dressed down.

"I didn't hear about that," said Fixticker. A few seconds of uncomfortable silence elapsed, and I hadn't a clue if that portended an even lousier evaluation. "Look, I didn't observe these problems with you, so I can only go by what's told to me, and almost none of it was positive. I didn't hear enough to fail you on the rotation, but I can only give you a marginal pass. I'll also have a talk with your Program Director, to see if he thinks you would benefit from some sort of remedial training in professionalism." More silence. "Do you have any thoughts or feedback on the experience you'd like to share?"

My thoughts? Like my first week, when your colleague didn't teach a damn thing to a clueless, off-service intern, nor see fit to tell a patient's family that their loved one would be a vegetable once off the ventilator? Or my second week, when your other colleague swore like a frat boy all day, and insulted an Allied Health professional to her face? Was that a new-fangled method of teaching how to manage ICU patients?

Terrific. It was first year med school all over again, and the rules for me were the same as they ever were. "No, sir." I signed the evaluation and backed out of the office without a word. I craved food in my grumbling belly and a real night of sleep.

I was in something of a daze, ambling home in the twilight. It was mostly from exhaustion. Still, Fixticker's speech played on repeat in my cranium. It wasn't that I felt sorry for myself, although I suppose I did to a degree. It was that I just could not figure out what the lesson was. Was I doomed to muddle along, just like I did in med school? Thrive on some rotations and just survive others, no matter how hard I worked? Was it going to be five years of this?!?

I kept quiet about the evaluation to Kylea over dinner that night. She'd been in the ER that month, and was just as dog tired as me. I took a bath to settle my nerves after the meal, blowing bubbles at our cats for a juvenile laugh.

I sank into the warmth of our bed when the answer hit me: the nurses. Senior residents were sometimes around, sometimes not, and staff doctors flickered in and out of sight. But the nurses were always around, always watching, always talking. How could I win them over?

I'd never have the gravitas of an alpha-type, the doctor who can impose his or her will at the utterance of a word. I wasn't vicious enough to inspire fear full-time, even if I wanted to. And I was too moody and introverted to pull off a sunny, bubbly disposition - the proverbial life of the party - for more than a day at a time. What was left?

Suck up. Kiss ass. Swallow every nugget of shit thrown at me and call it steak. Be a servile lapdog for everyone I would work with, and a dancing poodle for everyone else...The Lowly Intern they expected me to be.

IT TOOK EFFORT to be a sycophant. It wasn't that I was disrespectful by default, or at least I don't think I was - you're never an objective judge of your shortcomings. Rather, I think the problem was that I lacked the tact to mask my impatience with people that rubbed me the wrong way. Given the hundreds of people staffing a hospital, it's impossible to avoid oil-and-water working relationships now and then. No doubt the ballooning deficit of sleep that went along with life as an intern only made things worse.

Still, I found a way to pull it off. I parroted whatever I heard from my superiors and rubber-stamped every nurse's requests. After a few weeks of my new persona, I'd earned more credibility than I was accustomed to on the wards. More importantly, I didn't crave sedatives at evaluation time anymore. The shtick would outlive its usefulness by the following spring, as the months of training made a decent clinician of me.

I wouldn't blame you for questioning my judgment at this point, or at least my sincerity. Would it not have made more sense to work on being a better person, a better communicator, someone more mindful of his impact on others? I'm sure it would. But with all the life changes - living with Kylea, new city, juggling finances without parental support - I had yet to find my identity as an adult, never mind finding Buddha.

I wish I didn't have to devote so much energy into becoming someone I really wasn't while on the job. Some doctors did it so effortlessly, flipping their "empathy" and "professionalism" switches on and off at will. Others were just born communicators - Kylea a perfect example - and didn't need to change a thing from the way they relate to anybody. For me, it was a trial-and-error blend of my natural personality with whatever mentor or fictional character the situation demanded. I'm naturally a cynical, sarcastic misanthrope. It took most of my time at med school to evolve into a passable communicator with patients, let alone staff. Between the grunt work of internship and chronic fatigue, meditating my way to better personhood simply wasn't in the cards. In the end, insincere obsequiousness beat out self-improvement as a way to get through the day.

Not that my suck-up act was a cure-all to the gulag of internship. Peace with the nurses or not, internship still stunk...figuratively *and* literally.

IT WAS SOMETIME after midnight when the page came. I'd been on the General Surgery service for three weeks, and knew better than to bother hitting my call room. If there was sleep to be had, it wouldn't be until at least two, and that was only if both the ward and ER were unusually quiet. This was a mandatory out of town rotation in Saint John, New Brunswick. It had so far had been a net positive after my disastrous stint in the CV-ICU. True, Kylea and I badly missed our individual-pocket-spring-coil mattress, holed up as we were in the mildew-y apartment complex earmarked for nursing students, medical students, and residents. But I was hours away from Halifax doctors that thought less than the world of me, out of sight and hopefully out of mind.

The page came from the OR rather than the ward - my senior resident, wrapping up an urgent surgical case. I took a few breaths to try and slow my accelerating pulse. Even after weeks on service with him, he still scared the daylights out of me. He was nearly a foot taller and at least three stones heavier than me, and inspired enough fear that working on his team made me wonder if the title of General Surgeon described a field of medicine or military rank. The staff surgeons all sucked up to *him*.

His real name didn't matter. I just called him Doc Vader. "Oh, hi, it's Frank from General Surgery."

"Frank, you busy?" blurted Vader. A man of few words.

"No, the ward's quiet. What's up?"

"We have a consult waiting in the ER."

"Did you want me to get started? What's the presentation?" Most ER consults to surgery were straightforward, not counting the traumas – gall bladders, intestinal bleeding, appendicitis.

"No. It's an abscess I need to drain and pack. I'll meet you there in five." Would you mind, Frank? I could use a hand if you're not too busy.

"Sure," I said. "Be there in fi--" Click.

I made a pit stop on route to the ER. It was a risky step if I hoped to avoid Vader's disapproving glare. Every morning I'd arrived on the ward with five minutes to spare before rounds started at 6:30, but every morning I'd joined rounds three minutes late, once my colon decided it needed to clear the deck of my breakfast. Without fail Vader would roll his eyes at me as I scrambled to catch up. I hoped to avoid the same fate on call, but you never knew how long these consults could take. The last thing I wanted to bear was standing for an hour or longer with a full bladder.

Vader beat me again, but I was spared any look of displeasure. "The patient's in Treatment Room 2. It's a perianal abscess. The nurse is getting the tray ready for us."

My fear and wisecracks aside, Doc Vader earned every shred of respect he was accorded. He was never anything less than

100% professional with anyone, and the guy was indefatigable. Other Surgery residents give up and change specialties, after so many hours in hospital wears down the immune system. Vader thrived on it. I would kill for the stamina, never mind the motivation or interest.

The patient was already prone with backside exposed when we strolled in the room, and an imposing, chunky backside it was. The largest of said chunks resembled a ripe hothouse tomato - red, firm, ready to burst - and it was the object of attention this night. Vader had a brief exchange with the patient, double-checking the man's history and outlining details of the procedure. The patient, who'd had a painful and miserable week, gave Vader the go-ahead. Vader applied the drape and injected some local anesthetic. A minute later, he made a half-inch incision to express some pus.

And I was smacked in the face with an ungodly stench...the pungency of pus and the foulness of feces, pounding in my nostrils at the slightest inhalation. I recoiled, desperate to stay standing.

Vader didn't flinch. Satisfied that he relieved the immediate pressure, he extended the incision, exposing another cup's worth of pus to mop up.

The smell erupted through the room. My sinuses flooded with the odor, as though the blood flow to my brain was undergoing dialysis with stool. I tried mouth-breathing to cope, rewarded only by my inner voice screaming 'this tastes like shit!' with no exaggeration.

I hearkened back to my high-school chemistry class, when the teacher had us turn the acid responsible for the smell of rancid butter into oil of wintergreen. Your nose will get used to the smell, he reassured, and it won't bother you after a few minutes.

High school teachers clearly don't spend much time near perianal abscesses, because this smell wasn't going anywhere. Struggling to stay conscious and avoid adding to the bouquet by puking, I tried to brainstorm an excuse to leave the room or at least open the door.

Beep, beep, beep. Could it be? I stood still, pretending to keep my focus on the patient.

BEEP, BEEP, BEEP. I silenced the pager. It was the ward. "You going to answer that?" said Vader.

"It's the ward," I said. "It was quiet before we came down here, so I doubt it's urgent." The Law of the Lowly Intern reads the same as the Law of Inertia. Do as you are doing unless redirected by an external, unbalancing force, such as the Titan of Olympus masquerading as my senior resident.

"I just need to pack the wound and clean up. The floor's your priority. I'll call if something comes up." My cue to flee the scene.

I breathed deeply on the dash upstairs to the ward. The nauseating mélange of fragrances in a hospital – body odor, vomit, hand sanitizer - never smelled quite so sweet.

CHAPTER SIX

Howard

THE CANCER WARD of Toronto's Sunnybrook Hospital was as serene as any health care facility I'd seen in years. No monitors flashing or beeping, tasteful sun-bathed sitting areas - it was much more than the pretense of warmth you see in so many clinics and hospitals, and welcoming for patient and visitor alike. I'd probably be proud to work there, if only I were there that day for work.

As interns, Kylea and I were allotted four weeks of vacation for the year, but it was scheduled as a single block with no choice to spread out the time. Two of those weeks were spent in Barbados, where we married in the company of family and old friends, baking in the sun and away from the encroaching damp cold of an Atlantic Canada winter. With the honeymoon over and only two days left before Kylea and I were to fly back for winter on the wards, this was my only chance to see Howard. The melanoma that was excised years prior came back with a vengeance, and what treatment he'd been through wasn't doing much.

Howard was, strictly speaking, my oldest friend. I'm three days older than him, and our moms hit it off on the maternity ward. We were frequent preschool playmates, and spent Sundays in the summer picking grass on the soccer field. We lost touch once in school, reconnecting now and then at summer camp, on the Bar Mitzvah circuit, or over a beer in the days we were undergrads.

We ended up roommates with two mutual friends in 1996, in Israel as volunteer ambulance attendants. Three of us were there to pad resumes for med school applications. Howard was there to have a good time. And have a good time we did.

Howard was by far the most outgoing guy I'd ever met, and a gifted schmoozer. On the Israel trip we'd gotten lost one afternoon, sneaking around an archaeological site we had no business violating. We stumbled onto a corporate party in the middle of nowhere, and within no time Howard had scored us a three-course dinner and a ride home.

Within two minutes of meeting Howard you were his friend...not in a glad-handing, business-network, social-climber sense, but a genuine friend. He came by it naturally, judging by the many members of his family that were always a joy to be around.

I hadn't seen Howard since the summer before med school. As these things go in early adulthood, we each had family we were obliged to make time for, and we each had closer friends. Still, the great thing about your old buddies is that one night over a drink or two is all you need to catch up. There would always be nights to grab a beer with Howard.

Kylea and I knocked on his door and Howard's mom embraced us in a warm greeting. I introduced Kylea to everybody, and Howard cut off debate with his nurse about his afternoon pills to invite the both of us to sit on the bed.

I did my best not to gawk before opening my mouth. Howard had lost a ton of weight, though he wasn't quite what I'd label cachectic. His eyes were sunken, his face thin but not skeletal, and...Jesus, I was examining him like a patient.

Kylea and I took our seats and I launched right into small talk. I described our wedding and honeymoon, trying to convey the better stories. I whined about life as an intern, relating what I saw on the wards to our misadventures on the ambulance. That led to a few more tales of "Frank's faux pas" – screw-ups that predated my domestication into husband material.

Kylea expression showed a clear annoyance with my transparent tap dance around the elephant in the room. "So Howard, how are you?" she finally said.

I was grateful to Kylea for breaking the tension. She was the budding oncologist and a better communicator than me anyways, even if the guy in front of us wasn't an old friend. Howard seemed relieved to speak openly as well, and he was candid about his disease and decline. He was taking each day as it came rather than getting hung up on his prognosis. Managing his symptoms without being stoned 24/7 was a delicate art, but he was surrounded by family and friends to lend a hand. He harbored no denial of how grave his condition really was, and lamented that he'd never know the joys of married life or parenthood. I'm not arrogant enough to think that this was the only time he'd had this conversation, so I listened without inserting wisecracks.

The conversation eventually circled back to funny stories, as Howard grew sleepy and it was time for us to go. I gave him a hug but could not stop myself from adding in a "guy's backslap" while fighting back tears. I suppose it was a show of denial. There would always be nights to grab a beer and catch up, right?

CHAPTER SEVEN

The Dead of Winter

IT WAS MID-DECEMBER and my first night of call on the Internal Medicine service. What was left of my honeymoon tan would be gone by the morning, supplanted by bags under the eyes and - if I were lucky - a little bedhead. The first few days were a nasty reminder of what caring for complex patients can entail. It took less than twenty minutes after morning rounds to review each Surgery patient with the charge nurse. If none of the surgical cases were interesting enough to scrub in on, I had a decent chunk of time each morning to grab a coffee and read emails before the post-ops and discharges demanded my attention. Managing just five Medicine patients took me all fucking day, with scarcely a minute to empty my bladder.

And these folks were in a miserable state. Two were nursing home residents with urinary infections. They would be ready for discharge by week's end. The chronic patients were a different story altogether. There was Vented Vic, a man in his 60s with advanced emphysema. He ended up on a ventilator during a vicious bout of pneumonia but lacked the lungs to resume breathing on his own. There he sat, all day, every day, unable to speak through his tracheotomy. Each morning the team rounded on him to see how he feels, and each morning he mouthed the words "not too bad" right back. He'd spend the rest of his days cooped up in that room. If he avoided sucking a drug-resistant "superbug" into his lungs, that meant he could linger for months.

Vic's roommate, Renal Ron, had nothing going for him apart from 11% function in one kidney. His care needs were too heavy to go home safely, and even a nursing home couldn't handle him on the brink of dialysis, such as he was. He, too, was most likely in hospital to the bitter end.

My third long-term patient was Elsie. She was a sweet old thing who couldn't stop bleeding from her upper GI tract. No matter what we tried - meds, endoscopies, transfusions - she was good one day and puking blood the next. A lifetime of alcohol left her body unable to fix itself.

I got a page from upstairs as the dinner hour approached. For some nonsensical reason, the two Medicine wards in the Halifax hospital were three floors apart, and the intern on call covered both while the senior handled ER consults. I suppose a jaunt up or down the stairs can boost your energy at two in the morning, without the aggravation of tremors or toilet trips that follow a cup of coffee. Still, it was a pain.

The page was from Kylea, finishing her day shift on the upstairs ward. Until then we'd been able to coordinate our schedules, working different services but on call the same nights. Not so this month, when we were on the same service in the same hospital (on different wards was probably for the best - I always looked lazy by comparison). Almost every day for two months, one of us would be on call and sequestered in hospital, or post-call and somnolent. Not a good recipe for post-honeymoon bliss.

Rather than use the phone, I jogged upstairs to bid her a good night in person. "You rang?" I asked playfully.

"I did," said Kylea, "and not just to say goodnight. I need to tell you about one of my patients, Mr. Huffnpuff. You'll probably get called about him. He's got fibrosis of the lungs and is basically end-stage. If he dies, he's down as a no-code, so you don't need to panic. But he tends to get these spells of distress now and then with his breathing. If he does, he usually settles with a few milligrams of IV morphine, maybe 3 or 4."

"Why not just leave a prn order?" *Pro re nata*, doctor-speak for 'as needed'.

"Nurses can't give narcotics by IV push. You'll actually have to get up from your chair." We said a proper goodnight and Kylea headed home. I went back downstairs to finish the last of my day's work and drop some stuff in my call room.

The wards were relatively quiet through the evening, and I fielded the typical calls about late-day test results and requests for sleeping pills. Around ten I headed to the call room. I'd hoped to brush my teeth and lie down for a snooze when I was paged from the upstairs ward.

"Hi, it's Frank, the intern on call."

"Hi, doctor. I'm one of the nurses here on 7-Medicine. We have a Mr. Huffnpuff here, and I'm not sure if you're familiar with him..."

"Actually, I took handover on him earlier! Is he having one of his breathing spells?"

"Yes he is. Do you mind coming to assess him?"

"No problem. Can I get you to draw up a syringe with 5mg of morphine? As I understand he shouldn't need it all, but you never know."

I marched upstairs to 7 and strutted to the nursing station. There's no better feeling as an intern than walking into a situation secure in your knowledge of what to do. God knows there were not many of those moments in my first six months on the job. The nurse pointed out Huffnpuff's room and handed me the morphine syringe.

Huffnpuff's breathing was shallow and rapid. You could hear his wheeze from halfway down the hall, but once inside the room there was an audible gurgle as well. His eyes were rolled halfway back, and he didn't flinch as I announced myself or put my stethoscope on his chest. His lung fields were as wretched as I'd heard. His inhalations sounded like snow on and old TV, his exhalations like a beginner on the trumpet.

I found an alcohol swab to wipe an IV port and pushed 3mg of morphine as per Kylea's suggestion. His labored breathing stilled almost instantly. Five seconds. Ten seconds. Thirty seconds. Whoops.

The nurse strolled into the room. "Doctor, did the morphine settle him down?"

"Oh, he's settled down, all right." I rested my stethoscope on his chest again, more than a little nervous. Nothing. Did I just do what I think I did? "Uh, I think I killed him."

The nurse picked up on my anxiety and shook her head. "No, doctor, we've expected this for days now. I'll call the family in right away."

I lost all sense of time going through the ritual of pronouncing Huffnpuff dead and dealing with the paperwork. Patients died on me as a med student and on my earlier rotations, but never...how to put it...by my own hand? Some minutes later, as I was finishing up my notes, two women charged onto the ward towards me.

"Is he dead?" the younger one said frantically.

"I'm Frank, the doctor on call. Thank you for--"

"Is he dead?" she repeated.

"Yes, and I'm so--"

"Thank God." She breathed a sigh of relief and hugged her kin. "We've been waiting for this for days."

"I, uh, was told that a few milligrams of morphine..."

"Thank you. It doesn't matter. Thank you." Both women shook my hand in gratitude, then a nurse guided them into Huffnpuff's room.

CIRCLING THE DRAIN.

That's the doctor's unofficial metaphor for the inpatients on a medical ward - the decrepit and moribund folks too sick to live their lives, but too stable to die anytime soon. They aren't like heart patients, that hum along fine until a clogged artery kills them abruptly. They aren't like cancer patients, that reach a predictable end of weakness and wasting. They just bide their time, bouncing from home to hospital to home again. We change one drug to treat one symptom and add new drugs to treat the side effects of the first. Get the lungs a little clearer, make the kidneys a little wonkier. Get the urine to flow more freely, make the memory a shade hazier. On and on we tinker, on and on they linger.

Circling the drain.

I bitched and moaned in private all through my Surgery rotation because it was unbearably exhausting. However much I admire surgeons' dedication, I'm mystified that they don't consider the insane hours a deal-breaker. That being said, the work wasn't all that bad. The patients might be at death's door, or the surgery a technical challenge, but the problems were concrete, the questions straightforward. Do we operate or not? Can we re-sect the mass or not?

The Medicine ward raised a far less distinct set of questions. Not so much clinical dilemmas, like what test to order or what medication to add. The answers to those are found easily enough in medical journals or the experience base of your superiors. No, it was more the unsettling sense that treating the chronically ill as we do borders on absurd, even inhumane. But on the flipside, if we decide that we shouldn't be in the business of keeping people alive at all costs - yes, only after we consult with the patient and his or her family - why have medical wards at all?

I don't mean to be flippant or nihilistic, recognizing that's how it might come across. In some ways, I guess, these philosophical musings might be little more than a smokescreen, a cover-up for the more selfish opinion I had of the Medicine wards.

And it was selfish. Because so many times, in the middle of the night, in the depths of winter, apart from my wife and friends, desperate for sleep and a sit-down meal, there I was. Paged to the bedside of an irretrievably sick old man or woman. Trying to preserve a life so wretched, you'd be arrested for foisting it on an animal. And no matter how tightly this one clutched his chest, or how frantically that one gasped for air, I could summon no enthusiasm, nor empathy, nor even pity. The only way I felt those nights was *angry*. Angry to be answering calls for laxatives instead of having dinner with my wife. Angry to be guzzling coffee or cola as a substitute for sleep. Angry to smell nothing but piss and shit and death, day after day after day.

Everyone promised things would get better. I'd eventually get sleep and have time for a family. I'd eventually be free from a millstone of debt. Eventually.

THE END OF two months on Medicine was almost in sight. I was on service in the city's older hospital, which should have been a blessing but was anything but. On the plus side, many of the patients were stable, hanging around for nursing home beds to open. It made the workload less intense, and I could find time here and there to collect my thoughts and return emails.

The downside was that stable patients meant no senior resident on the team. It was just me and three clinical clerks under the attending, Dr. Rolex (the watch came courtesy of a drug company, back when that sort of thing still happened). Rolex had an old-school approach to teaching, weaving current evidence with anecdotes and clinical pearls, and he engaged the patients with enthusiasm. But right after morning rounds he all but vanished for the day, and wouldn't return pages for hours.

I was in over my head once again, this time supervising students. I suppose it wasn't as unsafe as an intern running an ICU, but I had neither the knowledge base nor teaching skills to supervise clerks. Blind leading the blind, as they say.

It had been a surprisingly quiet Sunday on call. Rolex zipped through rounds in under an hour. Nobody was fit to go home, and the last open bed had been filled three days prior. Factor in the low acuity of most of the patients, and the result was an afternoon of blissful boredom and catnaps. Kylea was on call in the other hospital, a good deal busier than me. She would page me when she had some time, no doubt after nightfall.

The serenity was broken up just before dinner, as the nurses asked me to assess Mr. Nastykin's complaint of leg swelling. He was a cranky fart in his mid-70s, admitted two weeks earlier for pneumonia and mild heart failure. His clinical course had been uncomplicated, and he would have been discharged if not for his children. Nastykin had three daughters in to visit him each day, and each day they identified some deficiency in their father's care that precluded his discharge home. All three of them were demanding, even rude, but the oldest was a world-class bitch. NOTHING seemed to please the woman, no matter how far her father came along. She reserved a special vitriol for the medical team. Since every effort is made to shield students from abusive patients, and Dr. Rolex was never around, I ended up the prime target of her diatribes.

There was something about the Nastykin family dynamic that just didn't add up. Patients and their families get angry with hospital workers all the time, but you can generally blame it on one or more of ignorance, bad communication, and unrealistic expectations. None of that applied with the Nastykin family. The daughters seemed educated, we kept them apprised every step of the way, and the old man's condition was only on the upswing.

I examined Nastykin's leg. It was swollen and painful to touch. Could be an infection, could be a blood clot, I thought. Either way, he wouldn't be going home. I ordered some blood tests, set him up for an urgent ultrasound in the morning, started him on a blood thinner, and bemoaned my karma in advance of his daughters' visit.

Soon thereafter I was summoned to the ALC floor, or alternate level of care. The patients on that ward were medically stable, waiting for home care supports or admission to a nursing home. I was called when Ms. Elderly went non-responsive.

Once upon a time, Ms. Elderly was a nurse, and a globetrotting one at that. She devoted her life to her work and her students, foregoing marriage and kids. She eventually retired, of course, and heart failure brought her into hospital. I reviewed her chart and did a cursory physical exam. She was breathing but comatose. She most likely had a stroke, but it was academic at that point - she'd declared her disinterest in batteries of tests or the heroics of defibrillators and ventilators. I called her next of kin, a nephew from out of town, relating the details of her condition. He confirmed Ms. Elderly's prior wishes, and assumed responsibility for whatever would be needed in the coming days.

The ward nurses paged me back downstairs to have a look at The Mechanic. The Mechanic was in his mid-60s, admitted some weeks earlier for a flare-up of emphysema. He had been holding his own, but was something of a trainwreck before getting in the door - two prior heart attacks, the emphysema, and years of heavy drinking. Socially he wasn't much more fortunate than he was physically. If he had any family, he was estranged from it, and his next of kin on the chart was a neighbor.

The Mechanic was on high-flow oxygen, but it exhausted every muscle of his upper body to breathe. Puffers, pills, masks of medicated mist - nothing would open his airways that day, and his blood oxygen level was starting to fall. He wasn't terribly alert as I examined him, which could have been exhaustion or his high-dose sedatives. I found nothing of note on exam. I rifled through his latest test results, looking for something I could treat that might help the poor guy. No luck. I paged Dr. Rolex, who agreed with my assessment: The Mechanic was trying to die, and nothing at our disposal would stop him.

I wolfed down a microwave dinner in the resident's lounge, trying to forget about the rather morbid horserace-to-death I'd just kicked off. I was about to take a few minutes to browse my favorite web sites when the nurses paged me back to the ward. Two of Nastykin's daughters were in for their visit. I sauntered back to Nastykin's room.

The oldest daughter accosted me at the door as her sister stripped off Nastykin's bedsheet. "Can you explain this?!?"

"Yes," I said, my voice already defeated. "I was called a few hours ago to have a look at your father's leg, which the nurse noticed was swollen."

"You didn't notice the swelling when you did rounds this morning? Or yesterday?!?"

"Your father's been admitted for his lungs, and he's been getting better. No, we didn't check his legs, and he didn't mention it this morning."

"Well, there's no way he can go home like this," said the middle daughter.

Why didn't he speak for himself when they were around? Weird. "He'll have an ultrasound in the morning," I said. "If it's not a blood clot, there's a good chance he can go home in the next day or so."

"And if it is a blood clot?" said the oldest. "How long will he be staying then?"

"I can't answer that," I said. "The blood specialists have a protocol in place for patients with blood clots. We'll call them for a consult tomorrow and see what happens from there."

"Why weren't we called about the change in his condition?"

"I'm sorry about that. I was called about emergencies with two other patients, and just didn't get the chance." Christ, lady, you've been here every day like clockwork.

"Didn't have a chance to call?!? The nurses said you were at dinner!" Shit.

"Again, I am sorry I didn't call. You've been reliable with visiting your father every day. I just assumed--"

"And if we didn't come in? It's Sunday evening. Our sister isn't here. Now we have to interrupt **her** family dinner, because **you** couldn't be bothered to show us basic courtesy!"

What the...? "Excuse me," I fired back, my patience fleeing the scene. "Your father is not the only patient I'm responsible for, and--"

"No! YOU listen! Of all the doctors we've dealt with in this hospital, you have been the rudest, most arrogant, and disrespectful..."

My blood boiled as the woman's rant morphed into Charlie-Brown's-teacher-speak. She was all but incoherent to me, as I needed every ounce of concentration to stay my temper. To hell with this. I turned and marched out of the room, rather than risk saying something that would tarnish my already-spotty record. I invited the nurses to page me for anything urgent, and left the ward with Nastykin's daughters still barking at my back.

I plopped down on my call-room bed and whipped my stethoscope across the room. I was supposed to roam around a hospital for another four years, sleeping in call rooms instead of my bed, treating half-dead derelicts, swallowing shit from their families - *and* staff for that matter - all for what? Bragging rights? A big house and a nice car?

Devoid of caring, my inner voice screamed with rage.

I need to get the fuck out of here.

CHAPTER EIGHT

A Change in the Forecast

THE MEDICINE ROTATION broke me. I was exhausted, demoralized, bitter, and fed up. I'd relax for a night, only to wake up flooded with guilt for being insensitive towards the sick. I might very well have been depressed through all of it - Howard's death certainly set the stage for it - but it's impossible to say in hindsight.

Perhaps more than anything, I felt lost. The prospect of many more months of Medicine and Intensive Care over another four years of an Anesthesia residency was as nauseating as it was scary. For most of my life, I was fine with delayed gratification, with biding my time. The Medicine rotation tore that notion to shreds. The hospital was morphing into a trigger for every negative emotion, from despondence to dread to deep, visceral rage. The entire idea of becoming a doctor to "help people" seemed fraudulent. The families demanded we help, but the patients lay beyond it. We - the so-called healers - could order tests and play around with medication all the live-long day. The patients still died, or at best went home to languish. This was a dream job?!?

It's easy for an outsider or someone who's long past it to make the case that it gets better. And they'd be 100% right...it **does** get better, by almost every measure imaginable. But on those long, brutal nights, when your eyes won't stop twitching and watering from the fluorescent lights denying you sleep, when your loved ones and your happiness feel a thousand miles away, words of encouragement mean nothing. Unable to see past the misery of the hospital, I longed for an escape, for light at the end of the tunnel. But an escape to what?

After Medicine I rotated through the ER. It was a welcome break from the wards I'd been confined to for months. No 30+ hour shifts, no interminable rounds, no daily dissertations to write on patients waiting to die. Just assess the patient, treat the patient, then discharge or call a consult. I didn't see myself destined for a career in the ER - the shift work was family-unfriendly and I was much too fond of sitting - but the variety and brevity of the patient interactions were a breath of fresh air.

I made the jump to Family Medicine, with an intent to pursue additional training in low-risk Anesthesia. The Anesthesia Program Director did his best to try and talk me out of it, but the horse had left the barn by the time I'd made the decision. Though with Family/Anesthesia I'd never find work in a big-city hospital, a career bouncing between the OR and perhaps the ER of a community hospital somewhere seemed like a decent compromise.

A *compromise*. Only someone with a doctor's ego would label a career in Family Medicine with additional skills training to be a compromise. To a normal, sane person, the job description reeked of achievement and prestige, of academic excellence and community service. In fact, most specialists I've met have a deep admiration for the work that family doctors do.

For whatever reason, though, family doctors are the Rodney Dangerfields of medicine - they don't get no respect - self-deprecating to the point of comedy. It's not even the discrepancy in pay that relegates family practitioners to second-class-citizen status among doctors. Heck, business-savvy family doctors earn more than their colleagues in not-so-lucrative specialties.

Maybe it's that the training is years shorter, and there's essentially no competition for the residency spots. Maybe it's that specialists have the inside track on research money, and all the esteem that follows. Maybe it's a fundamental personality difference between those destined for specialties and the rest of us. Whatever the root cause, the discipline of family medicine suffers from a serious inferiority complex.

So there I was, diving into a field of medicine that offered early salvation from residency, left with a lingering sense that I was a washout. Still a "doc-*TAH*", still Living the Dream, but a rung or two down the ladder of expectations.

At least the worst of my internship year was behind me. There would be long nights of call on Obstetrics and Pediatrics in the coming months, but neither rotation promised the soul-sucking gloom of the Medicine wards. Life-threatening moments for new moms and kids, uncommon as they were, were handled strictly by senior residents and staff.

Many nights sequestered in hospital, hours of anticipated down time, eyes too bloodshot to read...was there way to make those nights on call turn a profit?

IT WAS A SLOW night on Labor and Delivery. Okay, scratch that. It was a typical night on Labor and Delivery, but there were two clinical clerks on call instead of the usual one. Both clerks were ultra-keen to take part in deliveries, a role I was more than happy to offload. It's one thing to catch the baby of a woman you've followed all through pregnancy - that can be a terrific moment to share with a family you've grown to know. It's a different thing entirely to meet a total stranger in the delivery suite. "Here's my vagina, steer clear of the poop!" If you didn't know, bowel movements during delivery...yes, shit happens.

I was killing time in the nurse's lounge. I could have headed to the resident's lounge to watch TV or play FreeCell, but I felt lazier than usual that night. One of the nurses was finishing her supper.

"It's Frank, right? Were you the resident that reads Tarot cards?" she asked.

"I am! And I'm cheap--only five dollars." Yes, I was a Tarot reader - certified no less, after taking a course at the local community college. It was a spectacular investment, netting me anywhere from thirty to fifty bucks a night on call. What with 100% of my salary earmarked for rent and interest payments, it was the perfect way to finance a DVD collection. The Pediatrics rotation in particular was a windfall - I'd do kids' readings for free (stripping the deck of all the sad or scary cards), and the nurses lined up to open their wallets to me. Had I been a less faithful husband, I imagine some nurses would have opened more than their wallets, but that's speculation on my part.

The nurse shuffled the deck and I spread the cards in the standard layout. Given the overlap in card interpretations, a Tarot reading tells a highly malleable story. The nurse's reading, however, was odd. Few of her cards had happy, generic meanings. "This is unusual," I said.

"What is it?" she asked.

"There's almost nothing here about money or home life. Your mind is...you're distracted. There's romance, passion, but nothing positive about home or family."

"Really?" She grew nervous, fidgeting in her seat.

"There's temptation, a sense of something forbidden." I pointed to the cards that represented the present and recent past. "These cards, all three of them...they most commonly point to an affair."

The nurse went red, rose from her seat and shut the door. She sat just to my left and whispered, "The cards are true. I don't believe it."

"Go on," I said. This is awesome.

"I've...I mean...one of the obstetricians and I...can you keep a secret?"

"Of course I can." This is SUPER awesome.

She spilled the beans - ALL the beans - on herself, her staff Obstetrician lover, and miscellaneous dirt on a handful of her colleagues. My mind flashed back to all those corny 1980s medical movies, and season after season of *St. Elsewhere* and *ER*. For years I'd figured the nonstop sex depicted in those shows was just titillation to hook the viewer. Apparently I was way off. Anything shy of an actual porn *severely* understates the regularity of trysts among hospital staff.

As I lay in my call bed staring at the ceiling, I couldn't help but second-guess the decision to change residency programs. People always told me that I had a trustworthy look. If I could have found a way to stomach four more years of farting around the hospital, how much money could I have made off blackmail?

CHAPTER NINE

Backs to the Wall

TIME FOR A POP quiz! Name the three specialties of medicine that pay the most for malpractice insurance.

Okay, I have no idea where you might live or whether such a factoid has crossed your mind, so I suppose it's on me to cough up the answers. The doctors that pay the most for malpractice coverage, by far, are Obstetricians, for what I hope are obvious reasons. #2 is Neurosurgery - it really *is* brain surgery - a field with disastrous patient outcomes even when things go right. #3, though, is a three-way tie, between General, Cardiac, and Orthopedic Surgeries.

If you can't quite figure that one out, I don't blame you. General Surgeons treat colon, breast, and other cancers. They're also the ones to stanch the bleeding in your belly if ever you're in a catastrophic accident. It makes sense that they would pay high malpractice premiums. Likewise, Cardiac Surgeons operate on the most indispensable organ in the body. But Orthopedics? Who dies of a broken bone or a bum knee? Don't Urologists, Ophthalmologists, and other surgeons operate on body parts that are at least as critical as our bones? On its face, the high cost of an Orthopedic Surgeon's malpractice insurance almost looks unfair.

Almost.

Here's the truth: despite the same education as every other doctor, Orthopedic Surgeons have a reputation for being the "dumb jocks" of the medical profession. The label is not entirely undeserved. An hour in the Orthopedics residents' lounge is like a visit to a high school locker room, complete with high-level debate of which nurse would be better in bed - the one with all the piercings or the one with the animal-print panties. The Orthopod's instruments are glorified carpentry tools, and their surgeries can resemble playtime with a Meccano set. Still, should that make them more likely to face a malpractice suit?

Maybe it's that the inelegant history they take from a patient - "So it appears you fell" - is a toxic addition to a lousy bedside manner that follows from insanely long hours. Maybe it's because there's some truth to all the urban-legends out there, like the one about an Orthopedics resident charting "VSS, wound looks good" - VSS being medical shorthand for 'vital signs stable' - on a dead man.

Whatever the cause, it can make for awkward interactions between Orthopods, their patients, and especially other doctors. I have my own theory as to why. See, most of us got the grades to land a spot in medical school by being unabashed nerds. And if there's one lesson that came through loud and clear from the 1980s comedy I grew up with (and, quite frankly, my own life), it's that nerds and jocks belong in very different worlds.

BY THE FALL of 2001, I had settled into life as a Family Medicine resident. It took a good three months after my time on the Obstetrics ward to start feeling human again - sleeping in my own bed more often than not, rediscovering leisure, and reconnecting with friends and family - but I still had some ways to go before I was free from the shackles of 30-hour shifts in hospital.

Second year Family Medicine residency was less about preventing an imminent death than acquiring the knowledge needed to deal with patients in the real, outpatient world. As any health care professional will tell you - doctor or not - musculoskeletal problems are near the top of the list of what you can expect to see every day. Sprains and strains, rusty knees, bad backs...these are bread-and-butter complaints you need to be efficient at dealing with. The only way to gain that kind of experience is to rotate through Orthopedics, and it's a preposterously busy rotation.

It was nearly 1:30 in the afternoon in the outpatient Orthopedics clinic. Nobody had paused for more than a sip of coffee, and the waiting room was still jammed with patients booked into the morning. Christ, how many people do they see in the run of a day? Most of the patients were there for fracture follow-up, with a sprinkling of consults for creaky joints or bad backs.

As the off-service resident, I couldn't hope to match the speed of the Orthopedics residents or staff, so I did what I was told and tried not to slow the team down. The follow-ups, particularly those for post-surgery checks, didn't add much to my skills or knowledge base, so I was delegated to see the new patient consultations.

The first consult was Mr. Achyspine, a 50-something year-old man with back pain. Achyspine fell from a ladder while playing handyman a few years prior, and never got over the injury. He tried physiotherapy, massage therapy, chiropractors, nerve blocks, pills, and injections. Nothing was much of a help. He waited six months for his imaging tests, and nearly a year for the consultation appointment. In the meantime, his life went down the toilet, as he left his job as a painter, lost his house, emptied his savings, and ended up on welfare.

I took Achyspine's history and performed a perfunctory exam within the limits of what his pain allowed. "I don't want to make you too uncomfortable poking and prodding. Dr. Vertebrae will examine you in greater detail once he comes into the room."

A few minutes later I caught up with Dr. Vertebrae in the staff area. He was a nationally renowned spine surgeon, a Big Fish with piles of international accolades. I related the patient's story while Dr. Vertebrae examined his X-ray and CT scans. He asked no questions and followed me into the exam room.

I was about to introduce Mr. Achyspine when Dr. Vertebrae blurted out, "I can't do anything for you."

"I'm sorry?" said Achyspine.

"I can't do anything for you," repeated Dr. Vertebrae, shaking his head.

"Well, what should I do? Go back to a chiropractor? Is there a medication I can take?"

"Talk to your family doctor," said Dr. Vertebrae. "Whatever will help."

Dr. Vertebrae strode out of the room just like that, and the door shut behind him before I could even take a step to follow.

Achyspine and I eyed one another in a painful silence.
"Uh...sorry," I muttered, retreating out to the hallway.

For all the fuss about ombudspersons and whistleblowers, it's
not often you come across a truly egregious fuck-up that someone won't at least *try* to remedy in good faith. Much more
common is the situation like the one with Achyspine, when you
witness a superior acting like a first-rate prick. There are guidelines and training programs for how to handle Disruptive
Physician Behavior - jargon for "doctor throws a tantrum" - and
it's easy enough to suck up to a staff doc on an ego trip. But I
could never figure out how to handle bad manners towards the
patient. What's a resident - a junior, off-service resident with a
spotty record of his own - supposed to do? Tattle-tell to my Program Director? The Chief of Staff? Would I be reporting
anything to these administrators that they didn't already know?

The next consult for me was Mr. Sadsack, a guy younger but
even more pitiful than Mr. Achyspine. Sadsack injured his back
five years earlier in a car accident, and spent as much time
fighting insurers and lawyers as he did trying to manage his
pain. He had his entire stack of reports and documents in his
lap, and pushed the pile at me as I introduced myself. The papers were in an entirely random order, some upside down, most
with the funk of old cigarettes.

Sadsack started blubbering within seconds of beginning his
story, and it proved nearly impossible to tease out the pertinent
details. I tried to pay careful attention at first, but my rumbling
gut and the smell of stale tobacco soon overtook my powers of
concentration. I shifted to somewhat terse close-ended questions and rushed through the physical exam. I suppose it begs
the question of how much a poor bedside manner might simply
follow from the doctor being hungry, but I doubt it's as important as fatigue.

When I left the exam room I couldn't help but feel sorry for
Sadsack. He was clearly miserable, and though I'm not Nostra-
damus, I was pretty sure he wouldn't be offered surgery. Seeing
as how he'd waited almost two years for the consultation, I

wanted to get the poor schmuck something more than the in-and-out treatment.

I presented the story to the Dr. Bonesetter, the Orthopedics fellow, who was more gregarious and engaging with patients. As a fellow, Bonesetter functioned as more or less an independent consultant in clinic. He could assess, treat, and discharge patients entirely on his own. Dr. Vertebrae need only join in if spinal surgery were recommended.

Bonesetter listened to me attentively, and pored over Sadsack's films. He walked me through some of the key things to look for on imaging. "Anything to find on exam?" he asked.

"Not really," I said. "His strength and reflexes were okay. Range of motion was terrible. Honestly? You could sneeze in his general direction and it would put his back into spasm."

"Do you think he's faking? said Bonesetter.

"Faking? No. Putting on a show? Maybe, but I don't think so. He was sent here by his family doc, not an insurance company or Workman's Comp. This is probably what he's like all the time."

"Okay. Let's go have a look at him."

Sadsack was circling the exam room chair, breathing heavily and clutching the brace on his back as we opened the door. Bonesetter invited him to take a seat again, but Sadsack waved it off. "It's a flare from the exam. I'll be okay to sit in a minute," he said. "Or did you need to examine me as well?"

"Frank here told me how uncomfortable the exam was, so I don't need to recheck you," said Bonesetter. "I've also reviewed your imaging. Unfortunately, I don't think we can really offer you a surgery that will help your pain."

Sadsack collapsed into the patient chair. "What are you saying? I have to live like this forever?" Tears started streaming down his cheeks again.

"You seem depressed," said Bonesetter.

"Wouldn't you be?!?" hollered Sadsack. "I've lived with this for more than five years!"

"Is your depression being treated? I'd be more worried about your depression right now than a back operation," said Bonesetter.

"I've tried anti-depressants before," said Sadsack, deflated and facing the floor.

"What about Paxil?" said Bonesetter. "Have you tried Paxil? That's supposed to be a good medication. I'm not a psychiatrist, but I could give you prescription of Paxil to start."

Sadsack buried his face and cried in silence.

We left the room and Bonesetter shrugged his shoulders. "You never want to operate on a guy like that," he said. "He wants a settlement more than pain relief." Bonesetter fired a glance at the clock on the wall. "Listen, it's getting on past two and I think it's only follow-ups in the afternoon clinic. Grab some lunch and see if anything needs to get done on the ward."

Thank God.

I gathered my lab coat and stethoscope to dash off for a bite. As I walked away, I overheard Drs. Vertebrae and Bonesetter compare notes on the consults, laughing their asses off.

CHAPTER TEN

Fifty Shades of Grey

THOUGH NOT A BREEZE, second year residency passed by at a faster clip than internship. By the time winter was coming to its end, I found myself on Geriatrics, the last of my off-service rotations. After that, I'd have six straight months of Family Medicine with the big licensing exam wedged somewhere in the middle. It was something of a challenge to pace myself with the exam prep. Cramming was out of the question - there was simply too much I needed to retain - but getting fed up with studying too early was a genuine risk to my odds of passing.

I couldn't have asked for a better schedule to wind down residency. I was done with in-hospital call and shift work. The pages might still come through the night, but they'd be coming to me in my own bed. I dreaded the thought of going back to nights in a call room for a third year, but that was a worry for another day.

Call me crazy, but the Geriatrics ward was kind of fun, and not only because the call was light. The patients were all at some stage or another of dementia, but they weren't all that unwell medically. Some were going through stroke rehab, some were undergoing intensive assessment, and some were just hanging around until a nursing home bed freed up. Not that dementia isn't an awful, awful condition I wouldn't wish on anyone, but the care of these folks was more about making sure they were safe than keeping them alive at all costs.

The patients that happened to be on the Geriatric unit when I rotated through were also an entertaining bunch. Each day I enjoyed a cordial chat with Philosopher Phil, a chap with alcoholic dementia. There's something marginally less awful about alcoholic dementia. It lacks the insidious progression of Alzheimer's disease, and patients with alcoholic dementia tend to blurt out genuinely amusing gibberish. I recall one day when Phil tried to reach his bank manager with a dead hospital phone. When his efforts proved fruitless, he regaled me with his thoughts on life and God that might as well have been delivered while gargling.

Phil was only the warm-up act for rounds on the 3M room, though. No, it had nothing to do with corporate sponsorship. The 3M room housed three of the long-term ladies with Alzheimer's disease - Muriel, Merle, and Myrtle.

Muriel was in her late 70s, the resident social butterfly of the ward. She was outgoing and chatty. Tragically, the only things she was capable of saying, outside of the basics, were the expressions "too true" and "six of one, half dozen of the other". Then again, you'd be surprised how deep you can go in a conversation with that limited a vocabulary before someone catches on.

Merle was Muriel's partner in crime. If the ward wasn't secured, the two of them would escape the hospital in a heartbeat. Not that they'd have been overly hard to spot, at least not Merle. Despite being 81 years old, Merle had a monstrous but benign cystic growth in her abdomen. As a consequence, the only clothing that fit her was maternity wear. Ever spied an octogenarian looking nine months pregnant? Then tried to look away?

Poor Myrtle. Myrtle couldn't take part in her roommates' hijinks. She was at the end stages of her disease, no more independent than an infant. She was also 104, which caused no end of grief for the hospital's prehistoric computers. Under a two-digit birth year system, Myrtle showed up as a preschooler. Normally a patient that elderly and enfeebled wouldn't even qualify for admission to the ward, but Myrtle had a disruptive grand-niece next-of-kin that burned bridges with every nursing home in the time zone. The Medicine ward was overfull, scrambling to look after patients admitted to their service but still on ER gurneys. Geriatrics was the only place Myrtle could go.

It was a banner day for the 3M room, because this was the day they got a new roommate, Norma...or, as I would come to discover quickly, Not-Nice Norma.

Not-Nice Norma wasn't all that rude or nasty, unless she managed to get her hands on Tranxene. Tranxene was a B-list member of the benzodiazepine family, drugs like loraze-pam/Ativan and diazepam/Valium, commonly prescribed sedatives with addictive potential. The Tranxene itself wasn't the problem per se - Norma popped Tranxenes like most of us take Tic-Tacs. Once the drug started to wear off, though, she turned vicious, like Yoda with a bad hangover. Since Tranxene was the only chemical she ever had an affinity for, Norma had avoided the early demise so typical of alcoholics and heavy drug users. She was 77 with no mobility or cognitive problems, which meant she'd probably be able to avoid Phil's flirting. She was coming to the Geriatrics service to detox, for lack of a better word. Better to suffer through the unpleasantness among oblivious peers than young addicts, I guess.

Muriel and Merle were mingling down the hall when Dr. Eldercare and I met Norma for the first time. Dr. Eldercare wasn't much older than me, and knew her field inside and out. I've always admired geriatricians for fighting the proverbial good fight. They're few in number and sorrowfully underpaid as compared with other specialists. Considering their expertise is often the only thing standing between Grandma and a nursing home, the relative lack of remuneration and prestige made no sense.

"Hello Norma. I'm Dr. Eldercare, and this is Dr. Warsh, the resident looking after the floor. Do you know why you're here?"

Norma was visibly annoyed. "To get my memory tested, but it's fine!"

"No, Norma," said Dr. Eldercare, "that's not why you're here."

"That's what the other people are here for," said Norma, "except this one." She pointed to Myrtle. "She's an old woman, over a hundred years old! Is she just here waiting to die?"

"Norma, let's not worry about the other patients," said Dr. Eldercare. "We're here now to talk about you - especially about what happens when you take the capsules you've been getting from your family doctor."

"What, you mean my sleeping pills? Nothing happens when I take them, except I get a decent sleep."

"Norma, that is just not true. You turn into a very mean person on your sleeping pills. We're here to help you get off them."

"Get off them?!? My doctor almost never gives them to me! Was it his idea to put me here, to trick me into getting off my sleeping pills because he doesn't like to give them to me?!?"

"Norma," I asked, "when was the last time you took one of the capsules?"

"I had my last one yesterday after lunch," said Norma. "I was tired, and wanted a nap."

"You see?" said Dr. Eldercare. "You're only supposed to take them at bedtime. And yesterday you took one during the day."

"Well, my family doctor won't give me enough!"

Dr. Eldercare fought back a frustrated huff as the conversation looked to be heading in circles. I'm not nearly as disciplined, and barely avoided murmuring F-bombs. So much for sweet little old ladies that do nothing but bake and knit.

"Well, Norma," said Dr. Eldercare, "you're coming off those capsules for good, starting today. We're going to make you into the nice, friendly Norma I know you can be."

Norma grunted, signaling the end of the talk. Dr. Eldercare and I stepped out into the hallway, where Muriel and Merle were on morning rounds of their own.

"Good morning, ladies," I said. "It's cold out, but at least we've got a nice sunlight coming in."

"Too true!" shouted Muriel.

"Have you ladies met your new roommate Norma?" asked Dr. Eldercare.

Muriel and Merle shook their heads in unison. "Not yet," said Merle. She was wearing the same blouse as the pregnant Cardiology fellow I met the month prior.

"She wasn't very nice to us," said Dr. Eldercare, "but if she's rude to you we need to hear about it."

"Too true," said Muriel.

"Maybe you can ask her to join you for lunch? Or music?" I said.

"Six of one, half dozen of the other," said Muriel with a shrug.

"Amen," I said, carrying on with rounds.

AS YOU CATCH a glimpse of the finish line in residency, and the onerous demands on your body and your social life abate, it becomes easier to let go of the anger. I'm not sure if you reach the point of "taking the patients home with you" - I didn't - since the relationships are too transient, and as a resident you're preoccupied with not screwing up. But I do think there comes a point at which you're finally at ease being around misery, illness, and death. I wouldn't use the word *desensitized*, because it implies a measure of apathy, even nihilism. It's more an acceptance of the work you've been trained for, and a recognition that many days won't end well for the person coming to see you.

The one thing I never *quite* came to grips with, however, was the use of humor as a way to cope. As evidenced by the more tasteless stand-up comics out there, you can find humor in just about anything, even terrible, degenerative diseases. What's wrong with a wisecrack about an old lady whose speech is garbled and goofy due to Alzheimer's disease?

A lot.

But I do it anyway, and that's not good. More than most of my colleagues, I tend to cross that all-too-fine line between laughter *with* the patient and laughter *at* the patient. Sometimes I'm not sure if I'm being funny, unfunny, or demonstrating outright contempt towards the patient. If I ever had it, residency destroyed that part of my conscience, and to this day I don't realize when I've gone too far at a patient's expense.

In any event, residency ended with a whimper rather than a bang. The Big Scary Exam ended up neither scary nor overly big. When I finished it, all I could think was, *that's it*? Small wonder Family Medicine "don't get no respect", considering Kylea and her specialist peers would face the stress of their lives come exam time.

My in-city Family Medicine rotation wasn't terribly memorable either, although the doctors and nurses were terrific to work with. Apart from one woman with depression caused solely by her mush-mouthed husband - doctors should be able to prescribe divorce as an alternative to Prozac - I can't recall a single exciting patient from that time.

I did take part in a two-day crash course in the basics of managing a medical practice, which was like receiving the proverbial Key to the Executive Washroom. "You are weeks away from being done residency," a faculty member said to open the workshop. "It's okay to admit you didn't just go into medicine to help people."

Since I had switched programs, I was held back in residency for a few months before I could apply for full licensure. Not a big deal, really. It never hurts to have more experience under your belt, and my make-up time was a busy out-of-town Family Medicine rotation. I worked at everything I could without exhausting myself - deliveries, ER shifts, and house calls - since I was unsure what I would do right after residency. The plan was still a third year in Anesthesia, but neither the training nor a job were available on the east coast...longstanding doctor-turf issues, as I understood it. The added year would have to wait until Kylea and I were back in Ontario, once she finished her third year of Internal Medicine and entered subspecialty training.

Looming even larger was the fact that we would be back in Ontario with a child in tow, as Kylea was early into pregnancy with our first. We'd flown into my hometown for a wedding and broken the news to family and friends. This would be the first grandchild for either of our families, and everyone was euphoric at the prospect of us closer to home by the next summer.

For the time being I'd find work where I could for the eight or nine months before the move, paying down loans or saving for a down payment on a house. After all the gloom of residency, my career, my family, my financial plan...everything was falling into place.

"I WANT TO stay."

I was standing at a payphone in the atrium of the decorated-circa-1962 hospital in Fredericton, New Brunswick. I was nervous for my upcoming Advanced Trauma Life Support test, and this was *supposed* to have been a routine call to Kylea for good luck wishes. The ATLS course had been an intensive few days, but obtaining the certification would qualify me for higher-paying ER shifts. "I'm sorry, love, you...you what?"

"I want to stay, to do my Oncology here," said Kylea. "They're getting a Medical Oncology program up and running here. They want me as their first resident."

"This is sudden."

"Not really. The department's been talking about it for a long time."

"I've got the oral test in like, thirty minutes. Can we talk about this tonight?"

"We will. But this is what I want. Besides, there's news that even you will like."

I couldn't process this at all. "What's that?"

"They'll hire me on as staff after I'm done. I don't need a fellowship to work here. That means I get paid as staff at least a year earlier."

"Weren't we looking forward to moving closer to both my family and yours? To help with the baby and all that?"

"Frank, we were going to be here for five years anyway before you switched out of Anesthesia. This just takes us back to the original plan. Or maybe we're here longer. Wasn't the whole point to get away from our families?"

What's that Bugs Bunny line from *Rabbit Seasoning*? You've got me dead to rights, Doc. Do you want to shoot me now or wait 'til you get home? "You're right. We'll talk over the details when I get home. Maybe...maybe we can even start looking at houses."

Kylea wished me luck and we said goodbye. I sailed through the ATLS test. Not that I had any mastery of the material. I just managed to put on my best impersonation of Doc Vader and the examiners ate it up.

I drove home lost in thought. My family would be disappointed...shit, my mother would probably even try to blame herself. Kylea's parents weren't likely to be pleased either, but they're used to living at least one plane ride away from their kids.

But as usual Kylea was right. The plan was always to be out of Ontario for five years, give or take. Although I'd set up a locum right after residency - *locum tenens* is doctor-speak for covering someone else's practice - I'd need to find something long-term if we were to stay another three-plus years. That third year of residency was now out of the picture, but I could keep working ER shifts until I found the right fit.

And somewhere in all this I was going to be a father, which was awesome. It was time to forget about pleasing the parents, Dr. Warsh. Get on with your career and your family.

CHAPTER ELEVEN

The Greatest Story Ever Told

BEYOND A PRETTY straightforward locum - young families and healthy seniors - I cut my teeth as a doctor doing ER shifts in Bridgewater, a town one hour southwest of Halifax. That I felt comfortable flying solo in the ER was no small achievement. No way could I have pulled it off six months earlier, fresh off the Family Medicine exam. Though the hospital was small, it was the busiest of three regional emergency departments. Driving an hour from home to work could be a pain, in particular on the weekends, but I needed the experience and the cash until I found an office to settle in closer to home. Except for one or two ladies that were too burned-out and grouchy to converse with, the ER was staffed by a friendly and capable nursing team. It helped that I brought doughnuts, just like Marty taught me.

One of my first Sunday shifts was unusually busy. The patients were in for routine stuff - chest pain, dizziness, vomiting kids - and I was working full-tilt to clear the waiting room before I'd be relieved at four. Truth be told, I'd have rather been home, dozing off to a Bond marathon on TV, but I had payments to make on a bare-bones Mazda Protégé.

The more acute patients in the Observation beds were stable but in a holding pattern, waiting for blood tests to come back or a consultant to look them over. The nurses were already ahead of me, and filled the exam rooms so I could start clearing out the waiting room. The waiting room patients were also in for routine problems - bladder infections, sore throats, bad backs - increasing the odds that I wouldn't be leaving a mess at the end of the shift.

The chart for Exam 3 listed a Mr. Johnson in with a "foreskin problem" as his chief complaint. This should be quick, I thought. I knocked on the door and stroll in.

Johnson was a young guy, seated without any evidence of distress. "Hi, I'm Dr. Warsh. How can I help you?"

"Oh, thank you, Doctor," he said in the trademark south shore drawl. Funny thing about Nova Scotia...though it's a tiny piece of geography in the massive expanse of Canada, the local accent and dialect changes every fifty clicks. On the south shore, people speak in what could easily pass for an Alabama accent. It's apparently a fluke, because the locals share no ancestry with those from the American South. "I hope you can help me. You see, I was circumcised as a baby. Over the last few months, I've noticed that a layer of foreskin has grown back around the head of my penis. It almost looks like my penis is wearing a turtle-neck sweater."

"Umm...o-kay. Is it causing you any pain, or is it draining?"

"No, no, nothing like that. See, I didn't like the way this circle of tissue looked. So last week, I took a boxcutter and a bottle of peroxide, and--"

Sweet Jesus, he did not! "Why don't I get you to get on the table and I'll take a look?"

Johnson climbed on the exam table and dropped his drawers. There was no blood or pus, but...how to describe it? Ever open a can of soup with a loose old can opener? The lid doesn't come off neatly and the edges are all jagged? Well, that's a pretty close description of the guy's penis. Fucking pitiful, really.

"Weeeeell," I said, cringing, "there's no evidence of bleeding or infection, and it looks like the bruising is all gone. I think you'll be okay."

"Oh, no, Doctor, that's not why I'm here. As you could tell, I didn't do the best job on my own, and I'm really not happy with how my penis looks now. I was hoping, if it isn't too much trouble, that you could clean up my cuts, that are all crooked, and make everything neat and straight again."

"So...I'm sorry, you want me to straighten the scar on your penis?"

"Yes, Doctor, exactly!" He unfolded a piece of paper, with what I suppose was a schematic diagram of his ideal member. It was the outline of a penis all right, but with wavy undulations running along the sides of the shaft.

At the bottom of the page was written, 'Ribbed For Her Pleasure'.

"Uh...this isn't my usual area of expertise, but...hang on, I'm going to make quick phone call for you."

"Thank you so much!" said Johnson.

I shuffled back to the nursing station and pored through Johnson's old chart without uttering a word. Schizophrenia...no admission in years...stable on his medications for six months. I paged the on-call Psychiatrist, who, lucky for me, saw Johnson as an outpatient.

I related the story and the Psychiatrist thought for a minute. "Well," he said, "I suppose he's not really at risk to himself right now. He's clearly having some issues with impulse control." You think? "Maybe have him call my office first thing tomorrow? I'll get him squeezed in somewhere."

That solved the problem of Johnson's big head, but I still needed a plan for his little one. For a moment, I mused about sending him to the local family doc who does newborn circumcisions, just as a gag. But really, Johnson needed to discuss this with his own GP and a Urologist. I sent him on his merry way with an outline of the plan and carried on with closing out the shift.

I must have worn a disappointed look about me as I charted on the encounter. A perplexed nurse walked over to me. "Everything okay? What happened with that guy?" she asked.

"Oh, he's fine," I said. "He gave himself a second circumcision." The nurse stared at me, bemused. "Thankfully it's all healed. He wanted me to – no exaggeration - clean up the scar and remold his penis." I held up Johnson's stylized illustration. "No joke. I couldn't even make up a story like that while high. I'm just feeling a bit of a letdown."

"Why?"

"I've been in practice less than a month. After seeing *that* guy and getting *that* story, it can only go downhill from here."

NOTHING BEATS THE stories of the ER. If you're a doctor and budding raconteur, you owe it to yourself to work the ER as often as possible. One shift a week for a year gave me enough anecdotes to get through even the most interminable party without needing a drop of alcohol: a high school grad out for a hike in a streetwalker's skirt and stilettos, tumbling into a campfire thong-first; a guy distraught that the audio of his flatulence had changed from PLLLLP! to PFFFFT!; a middle-aged man who suffered severe chest pain every Saturday night like clockwork, just when his wife came onto him; and a menopausal woman complaining of labor pains, declaring her intent to give birth to Jesus Christ (it was only constipation). Sadly, I never did get that Holy Grail of ER stories, the Foreign Body up the Ass. *sniff*

Beyond the stories, though, the ER has its own grind found nowhere else in medicine. There's always someone cantankerous or belligerent, always someone malingering or drug-seeking, always someone needing a shower more than a doctor. Past a certain point, you can grow so jaded and cynical that you believe any patient not at death's door should be seeking care elsewhere. Doctors and nurses alike get burned out with the ER, some worse than others.

For me, I grew a little bored of the ER rather than burned out after a few years, but that wasn't the reason I ultimately gave it up. It was the long drive and evening shifts, more so once our son came along. It's very, very hard to leave a smiling baby behind to spend the night run off your feet, attending to the moans and groans of total strangers. By the time my practice filled up and Kylea was staring down the brutal prep for her Internal Medicine board exam, I couldn't justify the gig any longer.

But damn do I miss the stories.

"HERE'S ONE FOR you, Frank," said Nurse Sweetheart. I did not think it was possible for a veteran ER nurse to be this cheerful without a subtle sarcastic edge. "Mrs. Brit was sent here from her nursing home."

It wouldn't be a Friday night without somebody sent from a nursing home. "And Mrs. Brit is here for - wait, let me guess-weakness? Maybe dizziness? Weakness *and* dizziness?"

"Actually, neither. The chief complaint, according to the nursing home staff, is 'malaise'."

"She has a urinary infection," I said. The little old ladies always had urinary infections, even if they complained of something else. "I'll bet you a coffee that's all we'll find."

"I won't take that bet. But watch yourself with Mrs. Brit. She's a charmer."

I polished off my first coffee of the night and reviewed Mrs. Brit's old chart before heading to the exam room. She was physically spry considering her 80 years, but most of those years were spent in the company of gin. When I entered the exam room, Mrs. Brit was lying in bed in a ruffled white nightgown, looking more perturbed than unwell.

"Good evening, Mrs. Brit. I'm Dr. Warsh."

"Oh, what do you know?" Her voice was shrill, almost phony sounding, like an actress on a BBC sitcom or even an actor in drag. "Another Dutch."

"I beg your pardon?"

"So many of you doctors and nurses, all Dutch."

I chuckled while leaning in for the physical exam. "Ma'am, my family is of Polish descent."

"Oh! Quite the showing you made in the war."

Huh? "Ma'am, I wasn't born until the 1970s. In fact, neither of my parents was born until after the war."

"Oh, sure, that's your excuse, but..." Mrs. Brit went on and on and on, insulting every race, religion, and creed on Earth apart from her own. I should have been fighting back laughter, but instead I found the woman steadily creeping under my skin.

I finished the exam trying hard to ignore her, but lost my head and fell for the bait. "Well, everything seems to be okay, Mrs. Brit. We'll wait for your tests to come back before sending you home. Can I say, though...you seem to have a problem with many people around the world."

"Well, yes, of course! But the worst are those damned *Jews*...buying up all the land and all the best nursing homes..."

It was all a blur after that, as I couldn't keep it together any longer. I dashed out of the exam room and nearly peed my pants laughing. Jews are either horrified or endlessly amused by anti-Semitic cracks, and my family fell firmly on the side of amusement.

"Told you," said Nurse Sweetheart. "She's a charmer."

CHAPTER TWELVE

New Kid on the Block

"I'M SORRY, BUT you're too young to be my family doctor."

My first real go at Family Medicine was at a clinic in Lower Sackville, a blue-collar suburb of Halifax. Kylea and I were renting a house in Bedford, a fancier suburb that straddled the Halifax peninsula and its partner city of Dartmouth. The clinic office was in a strip mall on the artery road into Sackville, sharing real estate with a drug store and a deli. I had cold-called the clinic just weeks after two of the other doctors upped and left one day, in a hurry and without notice. I suppose I could have comparison-shopped job opportunities, or probed deeper into whatever the problem was with the other doctors, but the commute from Bedford was minutes. I felt no pressing desire to battle traffic each morning, especially with our first child due in late winter.

Joining a clinic close to home, however, was the first of *many* lapses in judgment in my early days of practice. It had nothing to do with my coworkers. I never had issues with Susan, my new associate, and in fact inherited a lot of her overflow patients. Likewise, I got along famously with Pam and Lorraine, the clinic receptionists, though I'm not sure they cared much for one another.

No, the problem was a lack of boundaries. For all the talk of doctor-patient confidentiality, the patients merrily broadcasted their entire catalogue of ailments - in graphic, florid detail - anywhere they happened to find me. And living close to work as I did, the patients found me pretty damn easily. Ever been accosted in a grocery store by someone preoccupied with his or her bowels?

"I'm telling you, Doc, you gotta do something about this for me. I'm on the toilet at least six times a day, and it's never solid.

I mean, first the cramps come, and then the liquid pours out of me like--"

Yeah, dude, that's charming. "Hey, listen, it's not a good idea to discuss this here. No privacy, no exam table, you know? Maybe you can call the office first thing and we'll see you in a day or two? Great, see you then." Now can I please buy my fucking eggs and go home?

Apart from the choices of where you work and whom you work with, the mistakes of early practice are unavoidable. It's rare to screw up something obvious, like missing a life-threatening diagnosis or prescribing an inappropriate medication. Though that happens, most of those kinks in your clinical skill set are hammered out during residency.

It's the subtle errors, from among the dozens of conscious and unconscious choices made in a day that get you. Which tone do I take to convince the patient to stop smoking? How long do I get the patient to wait before I examine that spot again? Am I being too cavalier in not ordering this test? Am I jumping the gun in switching medications this soon? Even more frustrating is that the answers change from patient to patient, sometimes for a single patient from visit to visit. That essential trust at the core of the doctor-patient relationship can be a fickle, even fragile thing.

I could have mitigated the stress by not delving too deep into each patient's agenda. I could have strived for constancy - deliver the same message, in the same manner, no matter who was sitting across from me - and I might have lasted longer in the job. Then again, I'd be going against the contemporary way medicine is practiced, eschewing doctor-knows-best paternalism for collaboration with the patient. I'd have missed those days my instincts were spot-on and the patients wound up better off. I'd also be bored out of my mind.

In my early days, I got taken, many times, for pills with serious street value and even more serious addictive risk. Sometimes the scammers used distance, driving hither and yon to score scripts in every postal code. Others were rather inventive, pricking their fingers to drip blood into urine samples.

"Doc, it's the kidney stones again." In fairness, this was a time when doctors were pushed hard to treat pain aggressively, going liberal on the narcotics if necessary. It wasn't just drug company advertising, either. This was the clinical zeitgeist of the day.

Then again, I didn't get into medical school by being a naive, bungling idiot. Sometimes a would-be drug dealer can forget that.

THE SUNLIGHT BEAMING into the waiting room didn't change the fact that it was brutally cold out. Whoever told me that Nova Scotia winters would be damp but livable was full of shit. For two months straight I'd seen storms dumping a foot of snow, followed by a deep freeze, foot of snow, deep freeze, with no end to the misery in sight. I was running out of space to put the damn snow when I shoveled it. The previous weekend our wingnut neighbor called the police on me for piling the stuff onto "his" snowbank. But I digress.

I was lucky that the bitter cold hadn't hurt my growing practice. I was up to 15 patients a day reliably, sometimes more, working two or more shifts a week in the Bridgewater ER if I could. I couldn't predict what would happen once Kylea delivered in another month or so, and wanted a financial cushion should I need more time off.

The patients in those early days were a mix of Susan's overflow and new families to the area. Lower Sackville saw a lot of young families come and go. Many families had one or both spouses working in the oil and gas industry, Newfoundlanders in particular, while others simply couldn't afford the price of a house in Halifax proper.

I said goodbye to a young mom and her toddler, and invited the next patient in for his first visit. The guy was in his late 20s, tall, thin, clad in a faded rock-music T-shirt, jeans, and a winter coat reeking of cigarettes. The intact Nike cross-trainers, lopsided moustache, and reasonably groomed mullet cemented my initial impression: he was neither homeless nor schizophrenic. Just plain old Urban White Trash.

"How can I help you, sir?" I don't know when I picked up the habit of addressing every male that walked through my office door as 'sir'. If the patient wasn't a working professional or ex-military, did he interpret the greeting as good manners or veiled sarcasm?

"Well, thank YOU for agreeing to see me, Dr. Warsh. I've seen a lot of doctors over the years, Dr. Warsh, and I find most of them have don't have compassion or a lot of knowledge. But you have a reputation! People say, 'if you're looking for a kind, caring doctor who really knows his stuff', you need to see Dr. Warsh!"

I'm not sure it's possible to do justice to this man's monologue in print. His tone was so abundant in transparently phony sincerity, the closest comparison I can draw is a one-shot Looney Tunes villain - a smug buffoon that Bugs Bunny chews up and spits out while winking at the audience. Or, if cartoons were never your thing, he was like a reject of *Welcome Back, Kotter's* Sweathogs. It had been a while since I'd had a laugh at work, so I decided to play along.

"Wow," I said, "I'm not sure what I did to earn that kind of reputation. Thank you ever so much, sir."

"Oh, no. Thank YOU, Dr. Warsh. And I really hope you can help me. You see, I've had this awful back pain for a long, looooong time. It started after I fell from a ladder while re-shingling a roof, and--"

"That's awful! Do you have your Workman's Comp claim number, then? I have to treat visits for work injuries differently than normal doctor's visits."

"Oh, no, uh...it wasn't work related. I fell when I was helping a friend do his roof."

"I see. Sorry to have interrupted. Please go on."

"Yes. So, I get this awful, awful pain in my back that's there all the time. They took an X-ray that said I had degenerating discs, that I'd be lucky to still be walking in a few--"

This was fun. "Who's 'they'? Is the X-ray in your old doctor's file? You can sign a form and we can get the report sent here."

"Uh, it was in a different town, in the ER of the hospital. I can't remember where it was."

"Where does your friend live? It would be in that town, wouldn't it?"

"Well, he's moved a bunch of times. I don't remember which town he was in when I fell."

"I see. So they said you might not walk again? You seem to have been very, very lucky."

"Oh, Dr. Warsh, if only that were true. You see, I've tried Tylenols, Advils. I went to a chiropractor. Nothing is making this pain go away. Except, and I know this will sound strange, when I take two Oxys - Percocets, I mean - I feel good enough to get on with my day, and then I take two at night and I sleep like a baby."

"So four Percocets a day and your pain goes away completely?"

"Absolutely, Dr. Warsh. Sometimes it can be as many as six, but yes. Absolutely."

"Wow. It's like a miracle drug."

"Mmm-hmmm. And everyone I talk to says, 'Dr. Warsh isn't afraid to treat pain. He's very caring and compassionate.'"

"Can I ask who's telling you all these wonderful things about me? I should be buying them coffee."

"Uh, unfortunately, I can't reveal who I heard it from."

"Oh. Well, was it one of my patients?"

"I really can't say. You know, doctor-patient confidentiality."

"Oh of course!" I couldn't stop a snicker from escaping. Playtime was over. "Well, sir, I'm very flattered by all your kind words, but you've apparently been misinformed. I'm actually focusing my practice on seniors and young families these days. I just don't feel confident in the way I manage chronic pain. So while I'm happy to continue to see you as a patient, I'm afraid I can't prescribe you Percocet."

"So...nothing?" I answered with a blank stare. "Well, Dr. Warsh, I thank you for your time, but I'm afraid I'm going to have to correct the people that said all those nice things about you."

"That's unfortunate, but I understand. And I hope you find the care you need for your pain, sir."

The guy left the clinic without incident, but I had a problem. Which of my patients was playing me for a sucker?

I NEVER DID figure out who was portraying me as a pill-doling naïf, but from that day I had to take a harder line with pain patients. I was still fooled, mind you. One married, middle-class woman, a mother no less, amassed a small fortune selling my prescriptions across the U.S. border. Another woman, who'd served prison time before coming under my care, landed me in court to testify about her prescriptions during a Child Protection hearing. One guy, who never even managed to weasel a script from me, was thrown against the waiting room wall by undercover drug enforcement cops. I missed the episode while on the toilet, getting the story second-hand from Pam. Suffice it to say I couldn't have been happier when Oxycontin started spawning negative headlines...it made turning down narcotic requests so much easier.

Notwithstanding the drug-seeking miscreants and ne'er-do-wells, it was a young and vibrant practice for the most part. It was convenient that my associate Susan's passion was delivering babies. She delivered the babies of many of my pregnant patients on top of her own. It pleased many of my patients, though I can't help wondering if it wore out the (pardon the pun) patience of hers. As dedicated as she was to delivering babies, she was almost never in the office. There were entire weeks she'd have to cancel to go in for deliveries. All the cancellations stressed the hell out of the receptionists, so much so that I felt guilty about those rare occasions I had to call in sick.

There were downsides to a practice full of young people, though. New families left town as often as they arrived, and it was a bummer having to say goodbye so often. That paled in comparison, though, to the most pronounced hazard of caring for the young: a natural expectation that they'd stay healthy.

CHAPTER THIRTEEN

Marianne

"THE ONLY REASON I made this appointment was to tell you why you are no longer my doctor!"

It was pure coincidence that Pam was running a fast errand and the waiting room was empty when Marianne delivered her message. I was stunned, and spent the next few seconds searching for anything other than hatred in her eyes. This was not a woman I would ever expect this from.

What in hell could I even say? I had no issue with her. None. "Uh...okay." I couldn't leave this hanging. "Look, I don't know what's happened, but please...I'd like to hear it from you."

She accepted my invitation and I followed her into the nearest exam room. It was one of Susan's rooms rather than mine, not that it mattered whose name was on the stack of business cards at that moment. I tiptoed past Marianne so she was closest to the door. We were as far apart as possible in the narrow room, both standing and staring in a brief silence.

Marianne was a lovely woman in her mid-30s. She was one of my earliest patients, having moved back to the Halifax area with her son after her marriage ended. She'd come in every so often for the normal stuff - aches and pains, minor infections - and we always had a friendly chat. I hadn't seen her in while, but that was hardly a cause for alarm. Unless a young woman needs birth control or some other script, there are few ways to herd her into the office for a checkup.

About two weeks prior, I'd received urgent requests for Marianne's medical history from an insurance company. It struck me as weird, but not unheard of. Given the number of insurance forms that crossed my desk in the span of a month, I didn't think too much on it. She was a single parent...maybe she was applying for life insurance? Or taking a trip?

"Marianne, I--go ahead."

"How many times have I come here, telling you I needed a checkup? And you! All you said, in that cocky way you talk to everyone was, 'Sure, anytime! No big deal!'. Well last month, I felt something just wasn't right, my neck was still bothering me, and I went to the walk-in clinic. Guess what? The doctor there found a lump on my chest." Oh, Jesus. "It was breast cancer! So now, with nobody to help me with my son, I have surgery, then chemotherapy, and God knows what else, all because you wouldn't lift a finger to check me over!"

No, no, wait. I flipped through her chart. "Marianne, I did a breast exam six months ago and didn't find anything." Why was I bothering? She didn't trust my opinion regardless. Was this just to try to get her to hate me less? Was I only making it worse?

Her eyes welled up. "After I was diagnosed, I spoke with a neighbor of mine, who's also a patient of yours. She told me that she brought her son in with a sore throat, and you said he didn't need antibiotics. He didn't get better, so she took him to the ER. It was strep throat!"

Fuck. I knew exactly who she was talking about. There wasn't anything I would have done differently with that kid. I used the guidelines I was supposed to, and he ended up being the 1 in 10 the guideline gets wrong. Whatever, it didn't matter. Don't start a fight, I told myself, it can only make things worse.

"Marianne, I'm sorry to hear you have cancer. I--it's awful." What the hell else could I say?

Everything became a blur at that point. I might have wished her the best, or might have just watched her storm out.

I had three or four more appointments that morning, and phoned in every one of them. One of the patients asked if I was okay. I made up something about my newborn son and lack of sleep. There was a stack of test results and other stuff I had to go through on my lunch break, but to hell with it. Thankfully it wasn't a Thursday, so I didn't have to sit through a drug rep's sales pitch. I snuck out the back to drive home for lunch.

My mind was all over the place in the car. I can't count how many women had given me shit over the years. For the most part I deserved it. So much tasteless, sexist, and racist crap had come out of my mouth it was a wonder I hadn't been beat up since I was a kid. This day was different, though. I'd never--

Get over yourself. You're not the one with cancer.

Would I have missed that a few months ago? My exam skills were never great, but isn't that sometimes the way the disease works? Should I have delved further into her neck pain? Taken a longer history? Referred early? How much of this is replaying the ninth versus making sure I'm being a good clinician? Should I--

Get over yourself. You're not the one with cancer.

Fuck. Just...fuck. Maybe it was my attitude, or communication style, or whatever. Maybe I was too hung up on seeing people quickly, on making a buck. What the hell would I do now? There was no switching programs, no--

Get over yourself. You're not the one with cancer.

She was one patient out of hundreds that were perfectly happy with me. Do I change the way I practice based on a single patient?

Get over yourself. You're not the one with cancer.

Kylea was in the kitchen, tidying up as I walked through the door.

"Well, hello!" she said. "I didn't expect to see you home for lunch."

I fell into my wife's embrace without uttering a word, sobbing.

THE ENCOUNTER WITH Marianne hit me hard. Not that I hadn't faced an angry woman before - patient or otherwise - but this left me...chastened, meek, frightened, more paranoid and more unsure of myself than ever. It's an experience I imagine every doctor goes through at some point, angry patient or not. It also renders all the evidence and guidelines in the world utterly useless, since statistics mean nothing to the person standing across from you.

This many years removed, that feeling of getting punched in the gut has faded, the wound scarred over but not forgotten. Whether Marianne had cause to lash out at me, or whether she just needed to lash out I'll never know. Some years back, roughly ten years after that day, I looked up Marianne on social media. It appeared she survived her diagnosis, but sometimes people create memorial pages on Facebook. I sent a message of well-wishes that wasn't returned, but I had no expectation of hearing back either way.

Despite the bumps and bruises of the early days, my first year in practice brought about my greatest joy to date. Benjamin Avery - Ben - entered the world in the middle of March 2003. He was an absolute runt, barely six pounds as a newborn, with an intractable colic that all the midnight drives and gripe water in the world could not cure. **Nothing** - not textbooks, not teaching sessions, not videos - prepared Kylea and me for parenthood. But he was the Center of Our Universe for now, a tonic to the everyday headaches of practicing medicine.

CHAPTER FOURTEEN

The Everyday Headaches of Practicing Medicine

ONCE UPON A TIME, someone said that a doctor's practice eventually comes to reflect his or her personality. If that's true, I need way more psychotropic medication than has been suggested to me over the years. And possibly gender reassignment surgery, based on the proportion of my patients that were women. And drugs. Lots and lots of drugs.

In all seriousness, there's a kernel of truth to the aphorism, but it's not as important as you might think. Unless you take over an established practice, your early patients are going to be whoever walks through the door. Newcomers to the neighborhood, people without access to transportation, young people that didn't need a doctor before - pregnancy being the most obvious reason - these are the bulk of the patients you can look forward to meeting.

The next category of patients is pejoratively labeled "doctor shoppers". This is probably where the notion of the practice reflecting your personality comes from. Many, many people don't like their doctor, or fear for their doctor's impeding retirement, and jump at the chance to meet the new guy or gal in town. It doesn't mean that they'll be problem patients or drug seekers, or that their old doctor is a poor communicator or poor clinician. There just happens to be a mismatch between what the patient expects and what the doctor delivers. You might expect this would be less and less common as family doctors are guided, bribed, or forced into various models of care, team practices, alternate payment structures, and so on. Nope.

The final category of patients is really a subset of the other two, and these folks are the source of all the headaches...well, apart from bureaucrats, lawyers, and insurance companies, but I digress. *Every* doctor that cares for live humans beyond infancy has their headache patients. Allow me to elaborate.

No matter where I've worked, half of the patients have always been a joy to see. Young, old, sweet, sassy, spry, moribund...it doesn't matter. These are the folks that allow me to drop the stiffness of my professional persona and be myself within reason. Another 30% of the patients I am neutral towards. In some instances, the person has a developmental delay or mental illness that precludes a warm doctor-patient relationship. At other times, the patients just aren't big on chitchat.

10-15% of the patients are nuisances. They might show up in the office too often for their own good, whine a lot, or generate reams of paperwork. The catch is that although they suck up a lot of my time and energy, I'm not typically unhappy to see them.

Seeing the name of a headache patient on my list of appointments was enough to make me dread coming to work. They were the bane of my professional life, and the strain of trying to care for them ate away at me personally time and again. Just to be clear, I'm not talking about people with advanced cancer or parents dealing with the death of a child. Those patients suffer terribly and you can't help but take it home with you. That kind of emotional stress, and the teary breakdown that might follow, is cathartic in the true Classical Greek sense of the word. You grieve for and alongside these patients, and the emotional release is healthy. It can make you a more caring doctor, and a more caring person as well.

Headache patients generate a more insidious kind of strain. To begin with, they complain. *A lot.* They'll have symptoms that are nebulous, but serious enough to warrant exhaustive investigation. Without a clear diagnosis, their symptoms don't respond to standard treatments, and even the addictive pills - narcotics, tranquilizers, stimulants - barely make a dent. Almost all of them have a Personality Disorder of one form or another, patterns of thought and behavior that result in wildly dysfunctional relationships. Without getting into too much textbook psychiatry, the bottom line is that the core communication skill of medicine

- empathy - is of little practical use with these people. Sometimes trying to be empathic just makes things worse, in fact. Without empathy, the doctor's bag of tricks is rather light. You're left trying everything from reverse psychology to Jedi mind-tricks.

As each test comes back non-diagnostic, each consultation unhelpful, each medication trial unsuccessful, you're still left with a patient that complains. *A lot.* What's left to do? Express pity? What use is that? Annoyance sets in. If you aren't prepared to deal with the patient - and nothing but experience can prepare you - or if you can't find a way to diffuse the frustration of spinning your wheels, sooner or later it spills over into your psyche. It leaves you emotionally drained at the end of a day, without the energy or patience for the people that matter in your life. It's then a tug-of-war between your patient and your personal life, and none of the possible outcomes is pretty.

OH, JOY. LIMPING Lisa. I should count my lucky stars it was only the second time I'd seen her that week. Then again, her visits *did* cover a big chunk of my car payment. Maybe I shouldn't be so ungrateful.

"Hi Lisa, come on in."

Lisa leaned on her cane to get up from the waiting room chair, neglecting the safer and sturdier armrests. She adjusted her sunglasses and ambled towards the exam room. Sunglasses were a rare sight on people these days, as this was day nine of a miserable springtime cloud system. Damn Atlantic weather. Lisa was surely in for a migraine.

I get migraine headaches myself. I used to have mild ones as a kid, but as an adult they came on with a vengeance. Thankfully they were almost always due to caffeine withdrawal, so I could head them off at the pass with a hit of espresso.

Lisa's migraines defied all the textbook triggers. She had them whether it was sunny and dry or dingy and damp. Her diet never changed, and was bland and innocuous by her description. Her father was an alcoholic, so she didn't touch booze. Caffeine ignited her heart palpitations, so she avoided it much as she did alcohol. She had a hysterectomy not long after her second child, so menses were out as a possible cause. She hadn't worked in years, and denied using a computer that might strain her eyes. Her migraines were as resistant to treatment as they were to prediction. Advil, Tylenol, caffeine pills...that stuff all stopped working years before. Preventive medications? She didn't tolerate them. Even narcotic painkillers didn't help, and she came to me on plenty of them for her fibromyalgia. Fibromyalgia is otherwise known as the doctor's "F word". It's a syndrome comprising chronic pain, poor sleep and various other symptoms. Many consider it a "diagnosis of exclusion", a catch-all label doctors give to unexplained symptoms that aren't life-threatening nor easily treated. These people consume a lot of health care, but it's the endless complaining that drives doctors crazy.

I wasn't sure how Lisa had become such a mess. She had a terrible childhood, enduring abuse that, while documented, she never discussed. Still, she had an unremarkable adolescence and normal first decade of marriage. Things seemed to start downhill after her second child, but you'd need a spreadsheet to piece the story together from there. She started contracting one undiagnosable symptom after another, seeing a bevy of specialists to no avail.

She settled as gingerly into the exam chair as a senior recovering from major surgery. I couldn't believe this woman was only forty-five.

"What can I do for you, Lisa?"

"Uuuuuuuuuuuuuuh." Great. Moaning right off the bat.

"Is it another one of your migraines?"

"No. The left leg has started again. It gives out. I've been falling. Yesterday I tripped and smacked my head into the door."

"What part of your head?"

"Uuuuuuuuuuuuh. The front." She raised a weary, tremulous finger to her forehead. Not even a faint bruise to be seen.

"It looks okay, Lisa." I ran my hands along the spot she pointed to. "Not even a goose egg."

"But the pain...it won't go away this time."

"It will, Lisa. It might take a few days."

"Uuuuuuuuuuuuh. Shouldn't I get a CT?"

"No."

"But the pain--"

"Lisa, you do not need a CT. That's the hardest part of your head you're pointing to, and it doesn't even have a bruise on it."

"But the pain...and I've been throwing up--"

"Lisa, we've been through this. You don't need a CT every time you fall or hit your head. The neurologist that you saw last year ordered one, and it came back normal."

"You keep interrupting me. You don't listen."

Oh, for the love of..."Lisa, you're in here at least once a week. Whatever test you didn't have done before becoming my patient, you've had done since. I don't know what's going on with your leg. Based on what you described, there is no reason to suspect you have bleeding in your brain, which would be the only reason to do a CT."

"You haven't even examined me--"

"ENOUGH! I'm done with this! You either trust my opinion or you don't. If you do, then nothing more needs to be said. If you don't, I'm sure there are other doctors accepting patients. I'll even send them your chart for free. As for today, this visit is over." I opened the door without uttering another word.

Lisa sauntered out at a brisker pace than she entered with. Some days she would collapse to the floor upon leaving the exam room, necessitating her husband moseying in from the car to help her up. This day she remained upright on the way out. I related the outcome of the visit to Pam, who was subject to twice as much of Lisa's grunting on the phone as I was in the exam room.

Pam was sharper than her quiet demeanor let on. She was busier than she let on as well, handling the administrative end of her husband's plumbing business on top of her job at the clinic. Pam had once come close to quitting after a verbal altercation with Lorraine. Lorraine was a senior who'd been with Susan for years, and was growing a little too set in her ways. Susan, who handled the business end of things at the clinic with her husband - I just cut them a cheque each payday for my share of the expenses - somehow diffused the crisis. I never did find out what lowered the temperature, though Pam and I often confided in one another. "What do you think Lisa will do?" asked Pam.

"No idea," I said. "Hopefully she's fed up with not getting what she wants and will find someone else. Or go back to her old doctor. Or bother the walk-in clinic. I really don't care." I took five minutes in the back office to decompress and get on with my day.

Three hours later, Pam pulled me aside between patients. "You won't believe this. Lisa asked me to pass on a message."

My eyes widened. "She's leaving? I'm done with her?"

"She said, 'Tell Dr. Warsh I love him for what he said to me. He's absolutely right and I trust him more than any doctor I've ever had.'"

Goddamn it. She was mine forever.

CHAPTER FIFTEEN

Room to Breathe

FAMILY MEDICINE WAS not all that hard, at least not considering the intellectual prowess that's expected of med school applicants. Sure, you need the experience saving (and ending) lives that comes with residency, but the real challenge is being able to handle difficult interpersonal situations with people that are basically strangers. Even if they've been your patients for *years*, you only see them for fifteen-to-twenty-minute bites of time. And those visits are in your office, not in the patient's home or out socially. It's all too easy to lose sight of how little you know about the people under your care, especially when you're instructing them on how to live their lives. I don't mean the no-brainers - quit smoking, use a condom - but telling people how and what to eat? How and when to sleep? How and when to confront their spouse? Yes, the advice is solicited, but to what extent? I've had more than a few (ex-) patients deserve an apology for what I can only call my own arrogance.

It begs the question, then: with so much of the job about communication - empathy, clarity, authority - rather than retention of scientific knowledge, why is med school full of science majors? Most doctors have little interest in research, and the minority that do rarely end up running a lab. Would it not be wiser to find prospective doctors from people that thrive with people, and teach them the science of medicine? Rather than training chemists and biology majors into "people persons"?

Then again, most doctors can handle most patients on most days without a problem. On those other days...well, some days it won't matter how good you are.

"I DON'T LIKE Dr. Warsh!"

I adored the little blond girl, who greeted me with the same harrumph each visit. Her mom was recovering from a molar pregnancy - a rare but normally benign tumor of the uterus - and was in to review her blood test results. Mom's hormone level had dropped into the non-detectable range, which put her in the clear after months of misery and medical appointments.

I crouched down to the girl's eye level. "Mommy's all better, sweetheart. Can I get a high five?"

She wrapped around Mom's left leg. "I don't like Dr. Warsh!"

Maybe next time.

It was only mid-morning, but the waiting room was already full of pregnant women and young kids. Susan was in and over-booked, so it would be that crazy most of the day. Hopefully I wouldn't fall behind and see the waiting room turn into musical chairs. It wouldn't be easy, since my next patient was Otto von Oxygen.

Otto von Oxygen was a burly German fellow in his mid-60s. He had terrible lungs from decades of smoking, and was too stubborn to quit after his last hospital admission. He surrendered his home oxygen equipment, seemingly to spite his internist, and was reluctant to reapply for it. Now he reached the point of being unable to complete a sentence or walk ten feet without getting winded.

Otto had nobody to look after him. He lived in a filthy apartment that the public Home Care service refused to enter, and his closest contact was a probation officer. A few months after taking him on as a patient, I learned that Otto was a convicted former pedophile. I saw all kinds in my early days.

Like many husky old men, Otto wore clothes that hadn't been in style, nor fit all that well, since the 1980s. His belly peeked out through gaps in his Hawaiian shirt, between buttons he clearly struggled to do up. As he took his seat in my exam room, the scar on his knee pointed to too-short shorts, and what those too-short shorts should have rightfully been hiding. I didn't need to see that. "What can I do for you, Otto?"

"I think I need a new puffer, doctor. AH-bbbooo! AH-bbbooo!" People with bad emphysema inhale by gasping, then purse their lips to exhale slowly. Otto was no different, except his breath came out as a guttural bellow, what I imagine a tuba might sound like in the hands of a novice.

"Otto, I just renewed that prescription last week, with lots of repeats. How often are you using it?"

Otto pulled the inhaler from his left breast pocket. The right breast pocket held his pack of smokes. I inspected it and gave it a shake. It was expired, and clearly empty. "Otto, this puffer isn't the one I renewed. It must be at least a year old. Where is your new one?"

"I lost it in my couch. AH-bbbooo! AH-bbbooo!"

Christ, he still hadn't called a maid service. I spoke with his probation officer about the situation a month prior. Otto had a little money put away, so it was more likely he forgot to call a maid each time his blood oxygen level dropped. You'd think living among overstuffed trash bins and dirty dishes would have changed his mind. Then again, I recall a house call on woman whose trailer smelled like a giant-sized cat box. Perhaps Otto hadn't quite reached his breaking point.

I spent a few minutes showing Otto how to use his puffer properly, and called the pharmacy to send him a replacement. I escorted him back towards the waiting room and brought in my next patient.

The next patient was a simple follow-up, so when I finished I invaded the receptionists' area to sneak a peek at the day's lab reports. Through the window, I saw that Otto had settled back into a waiting room chair.

"What's Otto still doing here?" I asked Pam.

"I'm not sure," said Pam. "He usually hails a cab or goes down the block for a coffee."

The waiting room was still packed with women and kids. Otto was watching a preschooler fiddle with Tinkertoys. "What are you making? AH-bbbooo! Is this a flower? AH-bbbooo! AH-bbbooo!"

Otto's outfit left *nothing* to the imagination. Fuck, this was a disaster in the making. "Pam, we need to get him out of here." I slid the window open. "Otto, what are you still doing here? Do you need us to call you a taxi?"

"I'm waiting for a friend to go for coffee. AH-bbbooo!"

I marched out into the waiting room. "Otto," I said, "maybe it would be better if you went to the coffee shop right now. We'll tell your friend where to find you." I rifled through my pockets for some coins. "Here, Otto, I've got some change. Your first coffee is on me."

"No, doctor, it's okay. My friend will come soon. AH-bbbooo! AH-bbbooo!" He sat back, oblivious to a room suffused with maternal anxiety. Even if the women avoided catching sight of his crotch, they could all sense he was a creep.

"Otto, you need to leave! NOW!" Otto looked perplexed but complied. It took a moment before the silence lifted in the waiting room. Sometime later I'd instruct Pam and Lorraine to restrict Otto's appointments to times that Susan wasn't normally scheduled, barring an emergency. I planned to give the probation officer a heads-up as well.

The episode bothered me all evening. Whatever his past, I humiliated the guy. Was there anything else I could have done? Any better way I might handle him in the future? Otto was a sick guy that needed to see me every few weeks.

I gave him a call at home the next morning, during a break when I was confident he'd be awake. "Hello Otto, it's Dr. Warsh."

"Yes?"

"Otto, I want to apologize for what happened yesterday."

"What? I don't understand. AH-bbbooo!"

"When I made you leave the office in a hurry. That was rude, and I'm very, very sorry."

"I don't remember this, Doctor. Did I get the new puffer? AH-bbbooo!"

"I'll call the pharmacy to find out for you. Take care, Otto." That man was not long for this world.

CHAPTER SIXTEEN

Home for the Holidays

BEING A DOCTOR has its advantages. I don't mean rich-asshole kind of perks, like access to senior bank managers or invitations to luxury-car launches. No, I mean the sheer convenience of not needing a doctor's appointment or walk-in clinic to deal with sick family members. Kids are *always* getting sick, especially if they're around other kids in the run of a day. I doubt that the world's seediest brothel could match a daycare for spreading infections (granted, by very different germs). There's a lot to be said for cutting out the middleman in the procurement of antibiotics or rash cream.

The drawback to being *able* to tend to your family's medical needs, however, is being *expected* to tend to your family's medical needs. If living close to the office can lead to doctor-patient boundary issues, that's nothing compared with the boundary issues that arise when would-be patients have your address, home number, cell number, Facebook page, and wedding picture in their possession.

I don't have a problem with good-natured teasing from friends or family. I give as good as I get, so go ahead and quack when I enter a room, or make me sit through the corniest proctology joke ever told. Likewise, go ahead and show me whatever it is you're worried about that popped up on your nether regions, so long as you understand that a) I might have no clue what it is, and b) you're giving me license to turn what you've asked of me into a story. I don't even get that upset by family or friends seeking a second opinion about something their own doctor prescribed. I've learned how to answer questions without actively interfering in someone's medical care, and I don't interfere if the stakes aren't high.

What irks me the most are those moments around family or friends that feel like I'm still at work. I don't need to read any

more x-ray reports or blood test results so long as I live. I don't
need to hear about what a specialist said or did, unless there was
a story worth sharing - you were mistreated, you were treated
like royalty, something funny happened - because I've seen it
and heard it before. And I have **zero** interest in your diet. My
own patients never followed the dietary advice I dished out, and
God knows I've never been a paragon of nutrition.

So how do I handle being a doctor around family, apart from
liberal ingestion of alcohol (that admittedly works best)? The
most successful tactic I've found is to avoid acting like a doctor,
and more importantly, preventing family members from acting
like doctors as well. It's an approach that makes family gatherings demanding I stay sober far more tolerable. More notably, it
also provides an underappreciated glimpse into what patients
might do once they leave the exam room.

WHOEVER WROTE BALLADS about Christmas in the snow
clearly didn't spend much time near Lake Superior. It's a white
Christmas this year in Thunder Bay, Ontario, but my toes went
numb just staring at it through the frosty living room window.
Southern Ontario was rarely this cold growing up, but back then
I was young enough to put up with it. Now I'm a complete pansy
when it comes to the weather, so much so that I can't figure out
what the hell the French and English were thinking, fighting
over Canada for all those years.

We were in Thunder Bay to spend Christmas with Kylea's
family. My in-laws Ann and Emil had put in a lot of time with us
after Ben was born, helping us acclimate to the challenges of
parenthood. My Mom chipped in as well, and ended up being
the only one who could successfully get Ben to take a bottle.
Emil returned to Nova Scotia for an extended stay in the summer, when Kylea's parental leave reached its end but Ben wasn't
quite old enough to attend the local day care. That much time
around parents and in-laws led to some predictably testy moments, many of them my fault. Though I was willing to take
responsibility and apologize, the relationships were never quite
as close again.

That winter Amy was a newlywed living in Boston, and Mom was invited to Thunder Bay so she didn't have to spend the holidays alone. It was a lot of bodies packed into a humble bi-level house, but Kylea and I were sequestered in the basement come bedtime.

It was mid-morning on the 24th, the first breakfast we were eating together. Ann had been awake and cooking like a machine for a while. A social worker for the disabled, she was away from the office but remained on call for her clients. Emil had been busy with chores and errands for hours. He was well into his 60s but a dynamo, cycling and swimming for hours each week, regardless of the season. He stayed on his toes as a caregiver for his older, infirmed siblings. Mom was late getting to the table, still in pajamas and a housecoat. She hadn't slept well, but then again she never did.

It took time to get the seating arrangement figured out, because Ben's high chair ate up a good amount of floor space in the snug dining room. Still the lone grandchild, Ben simply reveled in the nonstop holiday attention, and looked stoked to get his tooth-free gums on some grown-up comfort food.

Once seated to savor the first bites, Mom broke out her morning medications from a housecoat pocket. "Mmmm! This is too good for the Jews," she said, munching on a strip of bacon while futzing with a pill bottle. I had no idea what medication she was on. She'd been with the same doctor since before I was born, so thankfully never looked to me for a second opinion.

Ann darted to and from the kitchen for her own meds and let out a raucous laugh. "Ruth, you kill me."

"You're young and healthy, Ann," shouted Mom. "What medication do you have to take?"

"Oh, they're for my heart. I inherited something from my father, and the cardiologist says I need to take them."

Emil reached behind himself to the bottom drawer of the buffet. One by one, he retrieved bottle after bottle of vitamins and minerals. Insofar as I can tell, he had both the Roman and Greek alphabets covered. "Ann, are these omega-3 capsules yours?"

Kylea and I fired a resigned glance at one another, as the dining room table started to resemble the setup of a chess board. So much for getting away from work. "No," said Ann. "I don't take that. My doctor says my cholesterol is fine."

"Well whose are they?" said Emil. "I take the cod liver oil, so I didn't buy them."

"Maybe your nephew forgot them here last month," said Ann, "and I put them there thinking they were yours."

"Cod liver oil?!?" said Mom. She was either truly aghast or pretending to be. "My mother always took that when I was a kid. Doesn't it make your breath stink?"

"It used to," said Emil. "I remember having spoonfuls of it shoved in my mouth all the time growing up. But the capsules these days aren't bad for that. At least I don't think they are. Ann, does my breath stink?"

"What are you taking, Ruth?" said Ann.

"In the morning," said Mom, "pills for blood pressure and estrogen. If I have a headache, I might take a Tylenol. Speaking of which, do you guys have any?"

"Nope," said Emil. "Upsets my stomach, even with the antacids."

"Ma, you just woke up," I said. "Why not start with a coffee?"

"Ruth, you're taking estrogen? Like for hot flashes? You still get those?" said Ann.

"My doctor wants me on them, so I take them," said Mom. "But no, I haven't had hot flashes in years."

"My hot flashes are terrible," said Ann. "I've been using this Evening Primrose Oil, but it doesn't help. And my doctor won't give me estrogen. He says it's too risky for me."

"My doctor gives me whatever I ask," said Emil. "Even if his secretary gives me attitude about getting a refill, I don't take no for an answer."

"Did you want to try one of my estrogen tablets?" said Mom.

"Ma!" I said in horror. "Those are yours. Prescribed to you, not anyone else. Do not share them." Surely she wasn't serious, offering pills like a bowl of M&Ms. "I'll rat you out to your doctor."

"It's all right, Ruth," said Ann. "It might interact with my water pills anyway."

"Oh!" said Mom. "A water pill...I'll try one of those! I get swelling in my ankles!"

Ann shrugged and reached once more into her bottle.

"Oh my God! Mom!" Kylea and I shouted in unison at our respective mothers. Is this what really happened when I wrote a script? "What are you thinking?!?"

No exaggeration, I was aghast at this display. Notwithstanding my mother's occasional histrionics, there was nothing to make me think that either set of parents were out of the ordinary when it came to their health care. Their respective friends and family spoke as openly about their ailments and medications as they did, which was no surprise, but horse-trading pills? And not the fun pills, like tranquilizers and pain killers - it's no secret how that stuff makes its way into the streets - but diuretics and estrogen?!? It might have been something I ate, but I felt an ominously familiar twinge in my belly that moment.

Emil patted at the air to dampen the anxiety in the room. "Relax, Frank and Kylea," he said. "Relax. It's all good. It's Christmas, and we're family!"

CHAPTER SEVENTEEN

Shauna

DESPITE OUR IMPRESSIVE educational pedigree, Kylea and I sometimes lacked for common sense. Amidst Kylea's return to work, and the preparatory work for her genuinely Big and Scary Exam, we decided to buy a house and move right in time for winter. There's a reason most people move in the spring and summer, because a **brutal** fucking winter it was. The highlight was "White-Juan", an ungodly blizzard that hit the Atlantic coast five months after 2003's Hurricane Juan. White-Juan dumped four feet of snow on Nova Scotia in an eight-hour stretch, paralyzing the province for two straight days while everyone dug themselves out. Since the new house had a much larger driveway on a steep pitch, Kylea and I were stuck alternating between the shovel and our stir-crazy toddler from dawn to dinner time, until neighbors with snow blowers and plows came around to help.

At the time, I'd been pushing myself hard at *three* jobs: the family practice, the ER in Bridgewater, and an ER/urgent care centre in Lower Sackville. The urgent care centre, while billing itself as a full-service ER, wasn't much more than a glorified walk-in clinic. The only shifts open to me were in the late afternoon-to-evening, after I'd already put in time at the practice, and the work was as boring as watching bread rise. Any patient with a remotely serious problem was punted to the ER proper in Halifax, leaving a waiting room full of minor infections and low-acuity aches. The money just wasn't worth the tedium of mindless walk-in medicine. I respect docs that enjoy that kind of work, but I just saw it as a waste of my time and credentials.

I'd already put in my notice at the urgent care, and was pushing through the grind of my next-to-last shift. Nothing too dramatic early on, but a full waiting room nonetheless. I turned to the nursing staff about by next patient. "This young woman in Bed 3, with the complaint of anxiety...anything I need to know?"

I could never remember the nurses' names at this place. "It sounded like she might be in withdrawal," one of the nurses shouted back. "She was pretty frantic, talking a mile a minute. Another addict."

I closed the curtain behind me at the exam bed. "Hi, you're...Shauna, is it?"

The woman was hysterical, hyperventilating and crying uncontrollably. "Yes, that's me! Please...help! I've been taking these pills. They were my dad's, and he's dead. I stopped them, and I feel like shit, but I don't want them anymore! I don't want them anymore!" She buried her face in her hands again, spraying more tears.

"What pills did you take, Shauna? I'm just trying to figure out what help you might need."

"I used to take crack. It's not crack. It was his hydromorphs...the pain pills. Dad had cancer. I took the pills, but I don't want them! I don't want them!"

"Is it okay if I examine you?"

"Whatever you need to do! Just make it stop! Make it stop!"

Shauna's exam was unremarkable, and her basic blood and urine tests came back normal. The urgent care didn't have spot urine testing for toxicology, but there were no signs she'd overdosed. Withdrawal from narcotics fit the story she'd blurted out. "Shauna, I have to ask. Are you thinking about hurting yourself, or ending your own life?"

"No! No! No! I have a son! He was taken away! I need him back! I need him back!" Shauna needed to calm down, but more importantly needed support to get through what was evidently the worst crisis of her life. She was my age but looked a few years older, having lived a life clearly much harder than mine. She also had no family doctor listed on her chart. Shit.

"Shauna, it looks like the pills you took have worn off. Whatever else is going on in your personal life, you're in withdrawal. That probably explains why you're hyperventilating and can't stop yourself from crying." I spent a few minutes asking Shauna about what kind of supports she had, and whether she had a place to sleep and someone to look out for her. She was staying at her parents' house, where her mother had locked away her late father's supply of addictive painkillers. "I'm going to pre-scribe you just a few Valium tablets. They'll hopefully stop the panic attacks and help you get sleep."

I sighed and fetched a business card from my wallet. "This is my card. I have a family practice just two minutes up the road from here, right next to the Shopper's pharmacy. I have some open appointments tomorrow around 11 in the morning. The slot is yours if you want it. I'll let my secretary know that you're coming, if you're interested." She nodded and thanked me. "Okay, I'll see you tomorrow."

The rest of the shift passed uneventfully, and I spent a good chunk of the evening after Ben went to sleep wondering what I would do, what I would say when Shauna showed up the next morning. I corrected myself - not when, *if* Shauna showed up. She'd confessed to past drug problems, and left urgent care with a script for tranquilizers, after all. Odds on her showing up were pretty low, come to think of it. What in hell was I thinking, giv-ing her my card and a next-day appointment? Didn't I have enough troublemakers in my practice?

Ownership, I reminded myself.

Ironically, the most important lesson I learned as a resident came from surgeons - what it meant to take ownership of the patient. For a surgeon, it was akin to the "Pottery Barn rule": you cut it, you own it. If a patient you'd operated on had a complica-tion, it was on you to deal with it, no matter which surgeon in the group happened to be on call. I had a mountain of admira-tion for that approach to patient care.

As a family doctor, serious complications were obviously much less common. A patient could just stop a medication they reacted badly to. Still, I took the idea of ownership to heart, and that meant doing what I could for people otherwise accustomed to being shown the door.

The following morning was a quiet one. I had some routine follow-ups to start the day, with much of the 10 o'clock hour tied up with a wonderful elderly couple getting ready to say good-bye. The husband was an insanely tall man of Austrian descent in his mid-80s. He had the usual problems of a man his age - aching joints from carrying a tall and lanky frame, an oversized prostate - and he was a doting caregiver to his wife. His wife, still in her 70s, had a history of recalcitrant asthma. By itself the asthma was managed, but she had a slew of complications after years of high dose steroids - cortisone that suppresses the immune system, not the stuff athletes take to bloat their muscles - diabetes, collapsed vertebrae, and more. They'd been an absolute delight to look after, while their daughter in British Columbia had been busy arranging care for her mom. They'd be moving out west come the spring, but only if the wife's breathing and other symptoms were stable.

The 11 o'clock hour came and went, with no sign of Shauna. I was unusually disappointed for a no-show, something that happened several times a week in a practice full of young patients.

"Dr. Warsh", said Lorraine, "it's 11:30. I don't think that girl is coming. Shall I lock the door and put the answering machine on?" Lorraine was probably headed to her son's place around the corner, for lunch and playtime with her granddaughter. She was Lorraine's only grandchild, the apple of her proverbial eye. If there was no work to do, I wasn't one to force a secretary to stick around just to sit by the phone. I'd zipped home many times for lunch with Kylea and Ben in the past.

I sat down in Lorraine's seat to go through the contents of my mailbox when a rap came on the clinic door. Well I'll be damned.

I unlocked the door to let a frantic Shauna in. "I'm sorry, I'm sorry, I'm sorry! I missed the earlier bus, but I so didn't want to screw this up, and--"

"It's okay. Come on in. Nobody else is on the schedule so I'm going to lock the door behind you. Do you have anyone with you?"

"No, no, no." She opened her backpack and thrust a shoebox into my hands. "These are the pills! Please take them. I don't want them. Get them away from me!"

I brought Shauna into the exam room and had a lengthy chat with her, stretching into my lunch hour. Like so many other

young people, she'd left school too early and fallen in and out
with the wrong crowd. She would put herself together and find a
good job now and then, only to let a boyfriend into the picture
and watch her life come apart. She had a son, a preschooler, in
Child Protection custody, and crack use stripped her of visitation rights. She'd been clean from crack for a while, but moving
home with her dad in palliative care brought her into contact
with narcotic painkillers. She hadn't taken many before the episode of withdrawal that brought her to the ER the night before.

To her credit, Shauna had connected with the local Addiction
Services team, making arrangements to get counseling and move
beyond her blotted past. The long-term goal was regaining custody of her son, but that was a long way off. As for connecting
with me, she wanted bread-and-butter primary care: testing for
sexually transmitted diseases, Pap tests, help to quit smoking,
and so on. Nothing outside my comfort zone.

SHAUNA PUT HERSELF together much faster than I predicted.
The first few visits were dicey, as she fought back panic attacks
and urges to use crack. She never caved, though, and some six
months later she was poised, confident, and clean. I lost touch
with Shauna soon thereafter, as she moved elsewhere in the
province with her new fiancé, pregnant as well if I heard right.

There were others like Shauna, too many to combat my
deepening cynicism about problems society showed little interest in solving - addiction, poverty, and the violent depravity of
men. I struggled to stay objective with more than a few of my
patients, even after Otto von Oxygen died.

As I'd settled into a groove in practice, though, I had new but
festering questions about my work. What *was* this job called
Family Medicine? It wasn't about making a clever diagnosis,
picking up clues in the manner of Sherlock Holmes. The vast
majority of diagnoses were made instantaneously or after basic
tests...not much more than simple pattern recognition, really.
And curing disease? Minor infections were about the only things
I "cured", though I use that term loosely. I wasn't a surgeon that

could cut out the cancer or abscess, and it was the antibiotics that did the actual curing.

I was something between a social worker and psychiatrist, defusing young women's panic attacks and trying to stave off their unplanned pregnancies. The other stuff - chronic diseases, preventive care - was mind-numbingly simple most of the time.

It wasn't what I signed up for, that's for sure, but I didn't mind it at the time. It also turned out I was good at it, which surprised me more than anyone. If I didn't know better, I was *meant* to be where I was, doing what I was, as if - dare I say it - this was all part of somebody's plan?

CHAPTER EIGHTEEN

When Your Time is Up

RELIGION AND MEDICINE make for strange bedfellows. With undergraduate science as the main road into medical school, I was surprised to see so many devout believers among my peers and colleagues. It wasn't just active practice of the rites and traditions, either, but deep, sincere devotion to the respective faith. More surprising to me was how many of them *stayed* devout, even after residency. With all the blood, all the pain, all the *death* - in children no less - how do you reconcile that with belief in an omnipotent, benevolent spirit?

Yes, I'm an atheist. Scratch that. I'm worse than an atheist, because on top of my atheism I'm a terrible, terrible Jew. I don't keep track of the holidays, have never tried keeping the diet, and don't bother with the rites outside of a funeral. And - full confession here – I've even been known to use the word 'Jew' as a verb. That's as bad as it gets short of an actual criminal offence.

Over the years I've asked some of my peers how they held onto their faith, how they could reconcile it against the tragedy that's part and parcel of the job. Some embraced a post-Enlightenment idea of God, dismissing the notion that a divine being meddles in the mundane here on Earth. Others found comfort, healing, and solace in the message of their faith, which I understood implicitly if not entirely. Still others didn't seem to process the question, evidently seeing no need. I'm almost envious of them.

I faced the opposite problem, seeing my *lack* of faith tested every so often. Not just my career ending up in a different place than I'd envisioned. Sometimes things just happened that defied my understanding of the world.

I WAS CRANKY. It was my last two months of ER shifts in Bridgewater, and it was time I moved on. The excitement was long gone, and my tank was starting to run dry. I could muddle through the hours binging on coffee or Diet Coke, but my eye would start twitching again and my bladder would go spastic. That was not a good recipe for a decent post-shift sleep, a sleep typically broken anyway by a noisy, incontinent toddler.

More importantly, I just couldn't summon the wherewithal to deal with the less-acute patients anymore. I was getting indifferent, even sloppy at times - a liability to the patients and the department. I hadn't even been at it two years. How did doctors and nurses keep working the ER for decades?

My next patient - call him Rob Doe - was in for back pain and leg weakness. He was a husky middle-aged guy with a thick, and I mean **thick** maritime accent - probably a fisherman - and I could hardly make heads or tails of what he mumbled. The sparse triage note meant the nurses experienced likewise. Time for veterinary-style medicine.

"Veterinary medicine" is by no means a derogatory term. When the patient can't provide a history - kids, seniors with dementia, new immigrants - all you're left with is test results, the physical exam (that's spectacularly unreliable), and your gut sense of whether or not the patient is genuinely ill.

Rob Doe had come to the department on his own, and he was unmarried. By his chart he was no frequent flier, only visiting the ER for lacerations and the odd hardware-related injury. He wasn't a known drug seeker, making him eligible for "treat and street" - doctor-slang for shuffling the patient home quickly with a doggie bag of painkillers.

He had nothing to find on physical exam, really. His chest and heart sounded normal. Though fat, his abdominal exam was normal as well. The range of motion in his low back was good. He had no signs of a herniated disc. His reflexes were normal. He was slow to get out of his chair, though, and he struggled to take even a few steps.

It was probably nothing. Maybe not outright malingering, but he was a whiner all the same. Treat-and-street.

But it wasn't like he was in the ER all the time. Whiners and malingerers are always frequent fliers. It was a weekend...would the guy want to be in the ER if he didn't feel the need? He had no drug or extended health benefits, so I can't imagine he'd have disability coverage if he couldn't work. Then again, his vitals were fine and his ECG looked normal.

Call it Qi, call it ESP, call it "Spidey-sense", whatever. I don't know why, but I decided to order the basic blood tests. They'd all come back normal and I'd be free to treat-and-street.

The lab gave me the heads-up an hour later. The blood was diluted five times, and Rob Doe's CK still read over 10,000. CK, or creatine kinase, is an enzyme released into the blood by damaged muscle tissue. A normal CK level is between 100 and 400. What in hell, I asked myself. He's got rhabdo?!?

Rhabdomyolysis, or massive acute breakdown of muscle tissue. It's rare, typically caused by crush injuries or severe hyperthermia. It's one of those conditions med students get palpitations over, because it sounds so ominous. Left untreated, rhabdo can lead to acute kidney failure, ending either in dialysis or death. The dire prognosis only feeds into the mystique.

I alerted the nurses to get a proper observation bed ready for Mr. Doe. It might be hours before the on-call Internist could assess and admit the poor guy. I returned to the exam room to break the news.

"Sir, your blood tests show you are having major damage to your muscles. I need to ask our specialist to have a look at you. You will probably need to be admitted, so the nurses are going to move you to a different part of the ER. Can I ask you some questions? You can answer them with a yes or no. Have you been sick lately? Had a fever or felt nauseous?"

"No."

"Have you been doing any work outdoors, something harder than what you normally do?"

"No."

"Did you take any medications? Even something that wasn't prescribed?"

"No."

Weird, weird, weird. He'd need admission to have his kidneys flushed with fluids for a few days. Maybe the internists could figure out the cause...they're the ones that are supposed to know everything. I wrote up some orders and carried on with the shift.

Two weeks later I arrived a bit early into Bridgewater, and took a few minutes to chat with the same specialist who consulted on Mr. Doe. "Hey, whatever happened to that guy with the rhabdo?"

"Him?" said the Internist. "We never did figure out the cause. He was doing well after four days of steady fluids. His CK came down and his kidney function stayed normal. I wanted to keep him in for another two days, but he signed himself out against medical advice. Then just this Wednesday, he ended up back here. Massive coronary at home, dead on arrival."

I was flummoxed. "You're kidding. After all that - the fluke bloodwork, the admission, the fluids - dead just like that?"

"I know. Bizarre."

The shift was a busy one, if unremarkable. I was on my feet all evening, save a quick break for supper, and didn't have time to contemplate Mr. Doe's fate. As I cranked the radio for the lengthy drive home, my mind finally had time to reflect.

How to explain this one? I catch the man's rare health catastrophe, all from a hunch out of the blue. He's admitted, treated, and seemingly on the mend. He leaves hospital early, but not too early, then ups and drops dead anyway.

They say when your time is up your time is up, but this was ridiculous. It's as if Rob Doe was *supposed* to die. My dumb luck doctor's intuition arrived in the nick of time, seemingly to save the day, but whatever Higher Power wanted him dead *really* wanted him dead. "Fine, I tried to make his death interesting - something wacky for a change - but *you*, Dr. Warsh, you had to go and screw it up. Now I'll just have to kill him the old-fashioned way."

Is THIS what divine intervention looked like? And is this what they mean by a religious experience?

I NEVER DID have a "come to religion" moment, even after that head-scratcher. It's just as well, since it's not like I had any track record of reliably adhering to faith. But I did leave the ER and never looked back, even years after the fact. The experience was invaluable and the stories won't ever be forgotten.

Nevertheless, 2004 proved a stressful spring and summer, as Kylea's Internal Medicine Board exam pushed our family to the brink. I don't understand why the professional establishment considers this nerve-wracking, demoralizing crucible of Board exams at all necessary, nor how it possibly makes someone a more caring and passionate doctor. Kylea and her peers spent **months**, over and above full time work, poring over textbooks and journals and articles and practice tests...note-taking, memorizing, reciting, re-reciting. I was more or less a single parent to Ben all this time, with a busy practice that had finally filled.

Thankfully, Kylea passed the exam on the first attempt, saving her the humiliation and the agony that followed the many who needed to repeat the ordeal. As Kylea cried in my arms upon reading her results, releasing the pent up the stress and torment, all I could think was, *residency's pound of flesh wasn't enough of a 'rite of passage', you arrogant, Ivory Tower cocksuckers?* If there was a justification to it, beyond the self-satisfaction of Kylea's predecessors who'd gone through it themselves, I didn't see it. To this day I don't see it, and I doubt I ever will.

As Kylea and I ushered in 2005, things were back on the upswing. We were settled in a terrific neighborhood, around the corner from a park on the water, where Ben could climb on the monkey bars or laugh endlessly at ducks battling over scraps of bread. Kylea was training full-time in her chosen field, dipping her toes in research and building her reputation. We were both done with weekend shifts and sleepless nights for good, and even found time to socialize. Ben was shifting gears from tantrums to talking, becoming the easiest kid in the world to parent. I chipped away at the balance on my med school loans, and rediscovered the simple joy of television. Nothing could derail things for us.

"YOU WON'T BELIEVE this," said Kylea, stomping into the kitchen one January afternoon, looking mighty peeved.

"What's going on?" Please don't let it be me. Please don't let it be me.

"Well, my division head came up to me today. Apparently, the negotiations between the province and the hospital doctors have broken down. The funding for the job I was promised was tied up in the collective agreement. I asked what that meant. He said for now, I can't be offered a contract. He did say if I was interested, I could job-share a practice with one of the staff docs and there would be money for me to do a fellowship."

"What did you tell him?" To piss off, I hoped.

"I said I would want my Master's degree funded, and that I'd have to talk to you and think it over."

"Kylea, tell him he can kiss my ass. That amounts to a two-thirds pay cut for the same work, with no guarantee of a job down the line. Not to mention it's the main reason we stayed here."

"But we're happy here now. Aren't we?"

"Yes we are, but..." Fuck. "Did he know anything more about the status of the negotiations?"

"The negotiators took off for a holiday in Cuba."

And just like that, the first half of 2005 became a clusterfuck. Kylea gave a deadline to be offered the position she was promised, with the understanding that beyond that date all bets were off. The deadline came and went, as we knew it would, and shortly thereafter the e-mails from other centres started rolling in. By the time a new job offer was on the table, things between Nova Scotia and the doctors had grown toxic. Kylea's mentors advised her to get out while the getting was good.

Some of my patients were heartbroken to hear that we were moving, others understandably infuriated. One fellow raised holy hell over it, calling any politician or member of the press that would take his call. It led to my first brush with low-level celebrity, a televised interview on the evening news, that won me the title of Media Whore from my family and friends.

I had moments of genuine sadness as well. The little blond girl cried her eyes out when I broke the news to her mom. "No! Now I like Dr. Warsh, but he's leaving and I won't see him again!" I would sorely miss the seniors and young families I'd come to adore, some I'd shared laughs with, others I'd helped navigate through rough waters. And I'd miss the life we were building. We'd made the dearest of friends with our next-door neighbors, put work and a fresh coat of paint on the house...

But fate had a plan for Kylea and me all along. Five years on the east coast, no more and no less. And like they say, when your time is up your time is up.

Now we were heading back to Ontario, almost certainly for good. Family would be closer, Kylea's job would be secure. The only question was what I would do. After all, Ontario is the most populated part of Canada. Surely there's a family doctor's office on every street corner. Where the hell was I going to find work?

CHAPTER NINETEEN

The Right Thing to Do

"SO, DR. WARSH, can you tell us what caused such a critical shortage of family doctors?"

Who asks a question like that to someone that just moved from another part of the country? Not that I hesitated to answer, because a) the question came from a reporter and I was a Media Whore, and b) I was confident that I knew what caused the doctor shortage.

(As an aside, I would later discover that what I answered was complete bullshit, but bullshit peddled as fact for years by pundits and doctors' groups all the same.)

Apparently, I was wildly off base thinking it would be hard to find work. This region of Ontario was desperate for family doctors, and by a dumb fluke I was the first one recruited to Rutherford City, Ontario in eons. Phone calls from the Mayor, news interview requests, invitations to city functions, cash incentives...it was surreal. The day my practice was announced, a month before we'd even left Nova Scotia, the local paper reported a lineup to register with me stretched around the block. My entire first month of appointments filled up in an hour...not as fast as tickets to Bruce Springsteen might go, but still hard to believe.

And HOLY SHIT did the star treatment go to my head. I carried a swagger about me I hadn't had in years, if ever. I'd always been cocky, but I honestly walked around like the city owed me something.

Setting aside my ego trip and the euphoria of low-level stardom, it was evident that the area *was* badly in need of doctors. Advanced heart disease, insulin-dependent diabetes, depression...folks were getting treatment for these at walk-in clinics, which was not only inappropriate but dangerous. I mulled over what made the most sense ethically, the mistakes I'd made in practice out east, what kind of patients I enjoyed seeing, and which ones drove me crazy.

Ultimately, I triaged prospective patients as best I could. It meant a heavier burden of illness than I'd been used to, in particular among seniors, but I was just hitting my stride as a clinician. I owed it to the city, and it was the right thing to do.

Not that I should be accused of sainthood. While I actively took on the gravely ill, the pregnant, and the frail elderly, I avoided otherwise-healthy chronic pain patients like the plague. This was not long after the pendulum swung fast and hard away from treating non-cancer pain with narcotics, a reaction to the epidemic of deaths attributed to Oxycontin. If a patient's application listed pain as their only medical problem, and Oxycontin or Morphine or Percocet as their only medication, to the bottom of the pile it went.

By a year or so into practice, however, whatever I had tried to engineer was no longer relevant. The pregnant women delivered their babies, the gravely ill died, and the frail seniors found their way into long-term care. People still had chronic pain, still generated paperwork, and still periodically drove me up the wall. I did see a more diverse ethnic mix of patients, as the office was in a neighborhood full of new immigrants, many ex-refugees in fact. Apart from being hopelessly deficient in conversational Spanish, Polish, Arabic, Serbian, Portuguese, Kurdish, and Urdu (to name but a few), my family practice was still a family practice. It was still, at its root, about the very human interaction between doctor and patient.

YIKES. IT HAD been three weeks, and I still wasn't through with the highest-priority group. I thanked my lucky stars there were so many young, able-bodied applicants in that crazy first-day lineup. Then again, I'd seen some interesting stuff - Addison's disease, motor neuron disorders, congenital heart defects - so I could look forward to being kept on my toes. Seeing nothing but people with hypertension or high cholesterol would be drudgery in no time.

My next patient was Corinne. She was a gorgeous young woman, married with a preschooler son, but came to the appointment on her own. She was cheerful and outgoing, despite the head scarf as a hallmark of recent chemotherapy. We exchanged greetings and I opened her file.

"Okay, let's have a look at your registration form. Sorry about making you go through this, but it was the only way I could make sure the most urgent--"

"It was nothing," said Corinne. "I'm so glad you guys called. Thank you so much. I'm not really here for myself, though."

"Okay," I said, somewhat confused. I glanced at her registration form. Breast cancer, which is why she was triaged to the high priority group. She was stage 4 - metastatic to other parts of her body. Jesus, she was younger than Kylea.

"Your eyes just widened," she said. "I take it you just read my diagnosis and staging."

"Yes. I'll confess, I saw the diagnosis and automatically put you in the urgent pile. I didn't even look at your age." Stage 4 and under 30...really, really awful. "What...what can I do for you? Do you need pain medication? Anti-nausea drugs?"

"I've got all that stuff, but thanks. I'm here for my husband and son. They don't have a family doctor, but they'll need one after I'm gone. My son, especially, is two and I worry about him."

"I understand." No I didn't. What would I say to Ben if his mother were going through something like this? "I mean...I can't possibly understand, but I get it. Look, if one member of the family is my patient, everyone in the family is my patient. Of course I'll look after your husband and son. Write down their names and I'll make sure they're added to the roster."

"That's amazing. I am so, so grateful! Thank you."

"It's honestly nothing. It's my honor."

CORINNE LIVED ANOTHER year, though I'd only end up seeing her at home as her disease progressed. Once cancer patients develop metastases, specialists tend to take over as the primary doctors, with family doctors reentering the picture for Palliative Care visits at the end. Apart from the overarching sadness of your patient facing a fatal diagnosis, there's a bittersweet feeling to seeing another doctor assume your patient's care. You grow attached to your patients whether you intend to or not, and it's always hard to let go.

Corinne's widower eventually moved out of town for work, but emerged from his grief in one piece. After a period of acting out, her son ended up a happy, active kid. Despite moving away, I invited them to stay in my practice so long as they wished. It was a promise to a dying woman that was easy to keep, and it was the right thing to do.

CHAPTER TWENTY

The Noblest Profession

MY RUTHERFORD CITY office was in a sparkling new medical building owned by a pair of pharmacists plus or minus some partner investors. It was in the north end of the city, worlds away from the downtown core, with almost no medical offices around to speak of.

It was a great setup, built for one-stop shopping. X-ray, pharmacy, urgent care, and a lab were on the ground floor, with the upstairs all laid out for family docs. The clinic had all the fixings and help I could ask for - secure indoor parking! - though staffing proved to be a challenge.

Since I was constantly rotating through different hospitals and departments in med school and residency, I'd never noticed just how much staff turnover there is in health care. The front desk of the new office was a merry-go-round, with people shuffling in and out almost constantly. One receptionist lasted little more than a week, spending 90% of her time on the phone with an abusive boyfriend. You can imagine how that pleased the patients. Another was well and truly crazy, spouting off accusations about other folks in the office that were clearly fantasies. She wasn't manic or psychotic or otherwise mentally ill...just plain old bat-shit nuts. And this was on top of the normal turnover from maternity leave, back to school, health issues, and so on.

The nurses didn't stick around either. One took a hospital-based position, perhaps out of frustration from working with me. Another stormed out in anger one morning for reasons that will forever remain unknown. A rather diminutive nurse - I nicknamed her Frodo - left around the same time as her daughter, one of the many girls that worked the front desk for a time.

But the doctors were fixtures, right? Family doctors, soldiers on the front lines of primary care, worker bees of modern medicine, quarterbacks of the health care team, gatekeepers to the broader health system, and whatever other trite metaphor I've left out...they stuck around, right?

Nope.

I was convinced that our office, built to house four doctors, had some sort of curse hanging over it. In my six years there, the office enjoyed a full complement for scarcely a few months. Otherwise it was one recruit in, another out the door. One doc practiced for barely a month before vanishing to the U.S. for more training. Another decided he hated the work after six months, and rededicated himself to urgent care. The urgent care was in the same building, mind you, which both confused and infuriated his ex-patients. Another lasted a year, then found a new love interest and moved out of town. And the fate of one doctor is a story in and of itself, so stay tuned.

My first associate was Claudette, a funny and amiable woman with ten years' experience on me. She moved to the building with her practice essentially full, avoiding the free-for-all lineups and media spotlight. After all the comings and goings, we were joined by Peter, a workhorse of a doc originally from Kazakhstan. Peter had the misfortune of being recruited shortly after *Borat* ran in theatres, but he seemed unperturbed (if unimpressed) by the spoof of his native country. Last was Tom, who worked as a PhD before entering medicine. Tom loved a good laugh, a good whiskey, and a good insult directed at government.

And that was the office. It was a ten-minute commute from home, possibly shorter than my commute to Lower Sackville, but I rarely ran into patients while out and about running errands. Good setup, good support staff, good colleagues...no better place to spend my prime years as a doctor. A doctor...expert clinician, caregiver to the sick, mentor to learners, pillar of the community...

MY EYES ROLLED as I surveyed the nurse's note. Paula was in once more to address her bowels. The stool softeners and fibre drinks I gave her two weeks earlier apparently cured her constipation, but now she had gas and cramping. And she felt something "down there". Happy Monday to me.

"Good morning, Paula! The nurse tells me you've got some bowel issues again."

"Always," she sighed in resignation. "What you gave me worked, but I think I feel something down there." Paula was on disability for chronic depression and post-traumatic stress disorder. She was stable on medication but that was about it, probably beyond the point of feeling willing or able to deal with her past.

As a consequence, Paula wasn't terribly interested in the mind-body connection that governed her preposterously irritable bowels, so micromanaging her colon became Paula's *de facto* full-time job. As the old Yiddish saying goes: when you have nothing to do, shitting is also work.

"You feel something," I said, "like a hard bowel movement that won't come out?"

"No, more like a bump. And it feels like it's on the inside."

I asked Paula all the questions that would point to a serious problem. As she was in my office every other week without evidence of deteriorating health, the answers remained no. Flipping through her notes, I noticed that I'd only ever done a manual rectal exam.

"Well, Paula, if you feel something I should probably have a look. I'll use a plastic anoscope. It's uncomfortable, but it'll tell us for sure if you have something minor like a hemorrhoid or something more serious." I fetched a paper drape, and guided her onto the exam table into the fetal position.

Much like the atomic bomb, the plastic anoscope is a contraption I wish we could un-invent. It's a fancy name for a cheap transparent tube, with a removable torpedo-shaped rod running down its center as a guide. The scope is lubricated and inserted into the patient's back passage. Finally, the guide is removed and you do your best to keep it in place. Some sort of portable light or headlamp is flicked on and voila...three to four inches of anus is visible, give or take. Hemorrhoids, polyps, skin tags, anal warts...just like a Cracker Jack box, you never know what the prize is inside.

I got everything ready including my ultra-modern headlamp. Forget those old-school flashlight/mirrors on a headband - this looked like something a Special Forces trooper dons for night missions. Paula exposed her considerable rear end. I lubed up the anoscope and pushed it in without too much discomfort on her part. Out came the guiding rod...

...and out came shit. Nasty, oozing, unformed shit. FUCK ME. I extracted the anoscope and scrambled to tidy up the evidence. The room would need a serious cleanup and hit of air freshener, but I could mouth-breathe through the rest of the appointment if I made it quick. I gave Paula a blood requisition and planned to bring her back sooner than usual. That should make a somewhat truncated appointment more palatable to her. The hardest part would be holding my composure, while my inside voice screamed bloody murder.

Shit on the exam table. A metaphor for my career choice if ever there was one. *Stay in school, they said. Study medicine, they said. Pinnacle of the professional world, they said. No nobler career, they said...*

CHAPTER TWENTY-ONE

For Adults Only

I KNOCKED ON the exam room door to make sure everyone was all set. Linda, the nurse with me, had already set up the tray, so it was just a matter of the patient having time to get changed. The first visit of a pregnancy is always a long, involved appointment, even when it's the woman's first and there's minimal history to go over. There's a lot to get done - referrals, test requisitions, counseling - with a Pap test and vaginal exam as the main event.

Linda came to the clinic as part of a package deal with Claudette and Nancy, the only secretary who stayed during the whole of my time in the building. Linda was a stellar nurse, and her knowledge of who and where to refer my patients to locally was invaluable during my first year of practice in Rutherford City. She and I would butt heads from time to time, particularly over how best to solve our staffing headaches, but that's par for the course in health care.

The patient, Frau Freundlich, was a German woman who could not speak a word of English. Lucky for me, her husband did, and fluently no less. It would have been a painful appointment otherwise, since my German vocabulary was limited to the exclamations of villains in *Captain America* comics. Had I a lick of common sense, I would have recalled hearing Claudette speak German with her family members, and asked her either to translate or take Frau Freundlich's history in my stead.

Herr Freundlich was a senior manager in the auto industry. Whatever fires broke out when Daimler bought Chrysler, he'd been sent overseas to put out. Gotta keep *die autos* coming off the line.

Linda and I strolled into the room and, oh my, Frau was naked. Like, buck naked. And just standing there. Buck naked.

I looked away instantly while Linda scrambled to drape a sheet over Frau Fruendlich and guide her onto the exam table. Frau was confused by the kerfuffle, and shot her husband a thoroughly perplexed look. "*Was ist los?*"

"Oh, that's right, we're in North America," said Herr. He explained our embarrassment to his wife. "In Germany if the doctor tells you to undress, you undress. Here you're all so uptight."

I DON'T KNOW if I've convinced you yet that I was ill suited for medicine from the get-go. There's more to tell from the point of view of the job, but it's time I disclosed some less-than-glorious details about myself. That is, beyond the cockiness, crankiness, cynicism, and potty-mouth you might have already picked up on.

I had two part-time jobs before being accepted to McMaster, both of which better reflected where my aptitudes lay. The first was keeping the books for my father's business. The second was scripting cartoons for a ~~porn~~ adult-content website.

Yeah, I left that one off the med school application.

I had a fascination with sex as a youth that went beyond, and in some ways at odds with, the typical slavery-to-hormones preoccupation of my peers. I wasn't obsessed with porn, nor did I indulge in any fetishes or paraphilia (though I might have, given the chance). I did, however, make doodles of anthropomorphic genital superheroes well into high school. I interrogated my friends, guys and gals alike, about their sexual exploits. I celebrated books by Howard Stern as though they were Gospels.

I didn't date much.

In fact, the closest I came to pussy in high school was reading *Garfield* in the Sunday paper.

That said, I found no pleasure whatsoever in the countless physical exams I've had to perform on women. A doctor's exam room is just about the least arousing place you could imagine, except perhaps for a coroner's table. A gynecologic exam is probably as awkward for the doctor as it is for the patient, though only my female colleagues can verify or refute that claim.

There's also an upper limit to the number of those exams you can perform in a day and maintain your grip on reality. For me that number is five. I can't explain *why* examining six sets of genitalia is any different than examining five, but it is. Maybe it's because I can only ad-lib so much distracting banter in a day, maybe it's unresolved guilt over my aforementioned line of work. Who knows? I do, however, know that I'm not alone in this. Many of the nurses, residents, and nurse practitioners I've worked with over the years feel the same, male and female alike. Five sets of sex organs, and your psyche is done for the day.

I suspect it's natural to have apprehensions about all this. If I didn't, I might be justifiably labeled a creep. The human body is indeed beautiful, but I don't believe it was designed to be inspected with latex gloves under fluorescent lights. Like it or not, though, sex and nudity are part of the job.

YOUNG MR. SEXTON, all of 23 years, slumped in the chair, exhausted and downtrodden. It had been three months since his meet-and-greet, and the guy was spry as a hummingbird then.

"Geez, man, you look awful. What's going on?" I asked. I was casual around young patients, probably more so than I should have been. I find formality to be alienating, even counterproductive, with teens and twenty-somethings, so I set it aside more often than not.

"I'm feeling okay Doc," he said, "but I wonder if I can get some help from you with my girlfriend. I think I need a prescription for some Viagra or Cialis pills."

"Seriously? You're having trouble keeping an erection?"

"No, no, it's not that. See, my girlfriend and I live kind of a 'swinging' lifestyle. Most days I have no problem, but if I've had a hard day in the factory, and she just wants to go, go, go, I can't do it. The last time we went to a party, this guy gave me one of those pills, and just like that, I was fine and ready to go."

"How often are you having this...problem?" And boy was I using that term loosely.

"I don't know, maybe once a week. My girlfriend loves sex, but sometimes I just can't do it as often as she wants."

"Well, how often are you guys having sex?"

"We try to go three times a day. I just don't have it in me to do that every day of the week, you know?" Oh, sure I do. Sure I do.

Viagra and its brothers are for men suffering from serious problems with blood flow to their tallywhackers. Some men I'd prescribed it to hadn't had sex three times in the preceding *decade*. This guy needed a nap more than he did a penis pill. How could I have some fun here? Ask every conceivable detail of his sex life and pretend it was relevant? Nah, he was a swinger - high risk of him answering every question with enthusiasm. Go all 'Church Lady' on him, and quasi-preach about sexually transmitted diseases? Eh, he would have heard it all before, and the public health unit gave out free condoms anyway.

Terrorizing was the clear winner.

"So, someone gave you a Viagra tablet, and you took it?" I said.

"Yeah," he said. "And it totally worked great."

"Did you have any problems? Any side effects?"

"No. All good."

"You're very, very lucky."

"I am?"

"Those pills are normally for people with diabetes or badly clogged arteries. They increase the blood flow to the penis. If a young, healthy guy such as yourself takes it, there's a serious risk of a condition called priapism. That's an erection that won't go away, sometimes for hours."

"Is that a problem?"

I opened the cupboard and fetched the mammoth syringe we use to flush out earwax. "See this? This, attached to a large-bore needle, is what they use to drain the blood from your penis when an erection won't go away."

"Seriously?!?"

"Either that or surgery. Otherwise the penis can get disfigured, even die."

"No!"

"Yes. I'd avoid those pills if a buddy offers them to you again."

"What can I do about my girlfriend then? She kinda pushed me to come here to get help."

Tell her to find a hobby?

THE DISTINGUISHED GENTLEMAN settled his mother in the wheelchair to escort her back to the waiting room. "Doctor, do you have a minute? I have a problem of my own if you aren't too busy, and it's not something I can discuss in front of my mother."

Managing time is probably the #1 challenge for a doctor, in particular if you've got young children in school or day care. The Family Member Squeeze-in is a risky proposition to agree to, although not as bad as the Hand-on-the-Doorknob Question. Squeezing in a child almost never takes much time, but an adult? It depends on how well you know the patient, and whether you're caught up.

The Distinguished Gentleman wasn't a frequent flier and my day was moving at a good clip. "Sure," I said. "If you want to get your mother to the waiting room, just come right back."

"Thank you so much, Doctor."

"No problem, sir. What can I do for you?"

"This is very unusual, and I admit that I'm a bit embarrassed. In the past few months, anytime I have oral sex with my girlfriend, I get terrible diarrhea the next day."

Huh? My brain was depleted of coffee, so the gears were a little slow to process that one. "Is this happening when you *perform* oral sex or *receive* it?"

"Perform."

"Any blood in the stool? Any fever or vomiting?"

"No to all of those. No stomach pain, even."

He wasn't exactly high-risk for an STD, and I'd never heard of one causing that symptom anyway. "Does your girlfriend use any unusual cosmetic products or soaps down there? Douche, exotic bath salts, perfumes?"

"Not that I know of."

"Well, I don't know of any disease that would cause those things to go together, so it might just be a coincidence and you have something going in with your bowels." Or you need to stop going down on your girlfriend STAT. "Why don't we do some basic blood tests, make sure you don't have obvious evidence of inflammation in your intestines? I'll see you two weeks after you get the bloodwork done."

Later in the day I was at my desk, following my stream of thought. The answer to The Gentleman's problem hit me, and I started chuckling uncontrollably.

Claudette, at her own desk swamped with paperwork, gave me a strange look. She was the easiest doctor I'd ever worked with, and never seemed annoyed by the everyday ups and downs of practice. I was moody as hell by comparison. "What's the matter with you?" she asked, chuckling herself.

"I've never had this before - a patient encounter with a built-in punch line." I related The Gentleman's story.

"That's weird, but what's so funny?"

"The diagnosis just hit me. Montezuma's revenge...profuse diarrhea when you eat south of the border."

CHAPTER TWENTY-TWO

Chewing the Fat

I TRIED MY best to keep a straight face as I politely declined the pamphlet from the Jehovah's Witness, who was in for a routine blood pressure check. I never shied away from asking about my patients' faith, despite my own misgivings about religion. In the case of Jehovah's Witnesses, it's essential to be aware of their faith for the provision of care: no blood transfusions, no blood products, got it. Still, when an ordinary doctor-patient exchange ends with the unfurling of a Bible genealogy poster - "you see, it's a straight line from Adam to Jesus" - I know I've let things go too far. I renewed the man's medication and said my goodbyes.

Charlie - Chunky Charlie - was up next. So much for my chipper mood.

Charlie was roughly my age and fat. Really, *really* fat. He was on disability with a diagnosed Bipolar Disorder and a bad back, though I couldn't fathom him ever exerting the energy to go manic nor injure himself. People were diagnosed with bipolar illness with a shocking frequency in Rutherford City, especially young people. If I didn't know any better, I'd have sworn Bipolar Disorder was a new strain of flu.

"Good morning Charlie." I rifled through his chart. "I don't see that you got the bloodwork done I asked for on your last visit."

"I couldn't do it."

I tried not to sound annoyed, but failed. "What was the issue? We have the lab here, and there are others all over town."

"You said I had to be fasting to get the blood tests done."

"Only for twelve hours, Charlie. In fact, you can usually cheat and just fast for ten."

"I can't fast for ten hours either."

Was he serious? "Charlie, you couldn't fast for ten hours? For one night? This is to find out if you have diabetes. That's a life-long disease with all kinds of severe complications."

"I know. But I'm bipolar. I struggle with depression, and when I get really depressed, I eat. Ten hours would be too long for me to go without food."

Oh, for the love of... "Charlie, why did you make this appointment?"

"What do you mean? You told me to follow up with you."

"Yeah, after you got the tests done. You complained about being tired, about having no energy. I said to get the blood tests done so I can get some idea of what's going on in your body. You're telling me you can't wait to eat for a few hours after you wake up in the morning? It's too much to get basic questions answered, and to rule out diabetes?"

"What am I supposed to do? You won't listen to me. You don't think there's anything wrong with me. But I have a diagnosis, and I am disabled from it!"

"Then what do you expect me to do for you? I can't treat without a diagnosis, and I can't make a diagnosis without having test results. There is nothing I can do for you until you do something to help yourself."

Fat fuck.

IT'S A TOUGH call as to who gets the bum's rush more in the medical system, people on narcotic pain killers or fat people. Based on what you've read thus far, you might think it's the chronic pain patients. I'm not so sure. You can be pleasant with a patient on Percocet, and opt not to renew their prescription. It's the pills, not the people, that are the problem. Fat people, on the other hand, are truly modern medicine's second-class citizens.

When I say fat, mind you, I don't mean overweight like 60% of the population or whatever the statistic is up to. I don't even mean obese by the clinical definition of a body mass index (BMI) over 30. No, I mean the grotesque fat slobs, regardless of BMI, especially the men. For all the talk nowadays about not prejudging someone, or being mindful of not blaming the victim, doctors have few such qualms about the "morbidly" obese.

A heavy smoker with angina is a "vasculopath", someone with badly clogged arteries. The same guy plus 100 pounds is a "time bomb". A carpet layer's knees get "wear and tear". The same guy plus 100 pounds has knees that "won't support his weight anymore". A man with stomach pains and a negative physical has an abdominal exam that's "unremarkable". The same guy plus 100 pounds has an abdominal exam that's "non-contributory" - he's too damn fat for the doctor to bother.

It only gets worse from there. Need to weigh an obese patient to dose a medication? Break out the hospital's freight scale. Need to repair a hernia on someone obese? Call in three or four extra helpers to keep the patient propped up on the operating table. And while you're at it, please ask a nurse to spread some anti-fungal powder under the breasts and rolls of belly fat...you know, to counteract the "fat-person odor".

It's far from just a hospital problem. Fat patients get abused in the community as well. Sometimes a doctor will just tell it like it is, advising the patient "you're too fat", as though the patient was unaware of their weight problem. The most unique method I've heard of came from a consultant who rated patients in accordance with what he titled the *Uqhuq* rating scale, where *uqhuq* is an Aboriginal word for blubber. As you can see, I'm just as guilty as anyone else, though I shouldn't be. I remember being the fat kid at one point in my life. It sucked. Even though we can't all be selfless, globetrotting angels, shouldn't doctors at least aim to be better than the schoolyard bully?

Doctors aren't even that nice to each other when it comes to weight problems. One staff doctor I had the honor of working under as a resident happened to be clinically obese. He was also the smartest and kindest doctor I've ever met, an exemplary clinician-teacher, and an avid researcher. I'm no mind reader, but I would not be shocked if his professional overachievement was partly a way of heading off sneers from coworkers about his size.

I can't count the number of times I've heard tell of, or directly witnessed a patient being commanded to lose 50+ pounds before they'd be eligible to receive some form of care or another. There's no small irony in making such demands, since it's not like we have anything to offer apart from "eat better and exercise more". The pills we used to dole out are long since pulled from the market due to serious side effects. The billions upon billions pissed away each year on gym memberships, exercise equipment, meal replacements, and snake oil would suggest that there is no magic fix out there. Bariatric surgery - stomach stapling and similar procedures - *can* work, but even then, a substantial number of people regain at least part of the weight.

In the decade and a half since I received my medical degree, I've seen one patient successfully take charge of his diet and exercise to such an extent that he could lose 100-odd pounds, sustain the loss, and get off medications for heart problems and diabetes. **One.** The rest lose then regain, lose only a modest amount, or don't lose at all. I would hope that newer evidence can prove me wrong, but that's beside the point.

I wish I knew where the hatred aimed at obese patients comes from. By my eyes it goes beyond society's general dislike of fat people, mutating into a contempt seen nowhere else in health care. Sure, the obese use up scarce(ish) health care resources, but who doesn't? And if the treatment for diabetes won't control the sugars, or the surgery doesn't keep the hernia at bay, is it any reflection of poor skills on the part of the doctor?

Yeah, this from the guy who thought of his patient as a "fat fuck". Those who live in glass houses...

CHAPTER TWENTY-THREE

Cheese Puffs

BY 2006, THINGS were settled in Rutherford City. Kylea was establishing herself as both a clinician, administrator, and teacher. We took our first real holiday since the honeymoon - no more pissing away vacation time to see family - and started planning for a second child.

Work was steady and busy for me. Much to my chagrin, I was through the relative grace period of the first six months of practice when paperwork was at a minimum. Now I was back to devoting my lunchtimes and Friday afternoons to writing referrals and filling out forms. Oh well, the fresh start was fun while it lasted.

Actually, work was more than just steady and no longer fun, it was becoming something of a pain. The two doctors that came and went in relatively short order left a whole lot of people high and dry for medical care. With Claudette's practice full from the start, the responsibility for patients with high-priority needs - pregnant women, frail seniors - fell to me. It was the only ethical thing to do - I couldn't just let these people languish until the building owners could recruit another doctor. But it stretched me thinner than I'd anticipated, and tested the limits of my temper with patients I wasn't crazy about.

NANCY POPPED HER head into the doctors' work area. She'd caught me at a good time, between patients on a rare bit of a breather. Nancy was a sweetheart and deeply loyal to Claudette and me, but she was slow in her work for a busy clinic with a diverse patient base. She had her own stressors to deal with, including a husband with poor health and a troubled teenaged granddaughter. The chaos that ensued with doctors coming and going didn't help matters, but eventually she settled into her role.

"Frank," said Nancy, "pharmacy from downstairs is on the inside line. It's about Annie...something to do with her prescriptions."

Grumble. "Achy" Annie snuck onto my roster before I started triaging the patients by urgency. She was a scrawny, scraggly thing from a trailer park on the outskirts of town. Her chronological age was somewhere in the 40s, but she was haggard. I would have pegged her at 55 or older on looks alone. She'd spent the previous ten years on morphine for...well, I really didn't know. Seriously, I had no idea why she took it, except for some nebulous pain in the neck, the shoulders, here, there, and everywhere. I didn't have her old records, nor know her well enough to decide whether she even needed a narcotic as strong as morphine. But she was on it, so I'd keep renewing it until I had the entire picture and could think up a better plan.

I guessed right on the right phone line. For a smart guy, the office phones confused the hell out of me. "Hi, it's Dr. Warsh."

"Hi Doctor, it's pharmacy from downstairs. We have Annie looking for a renewal on her morphine."

"I just saw her last week. How could she be out?"

"She said you never gave her the prescription, or she might have lost it. She had a week's worth of pills left at home that she's been taking to get by."

"Does she only use your pharmacy?"

"Hang on," said the pharmacist. What was Annie up to? "She usually comes to us, but the last prescription date fell on the Sunday of the long weekend, so she took it to Wal-Mart."

"Last prescription? I thought she said she lost it."

"Hang on." Annie didn't strike me as a player. Plus, she signed a contract with me, so she knew the rules. "Now she says the one before that one went to Wal-Mart."

"What was the last script she filled downstairs?"

"She brought it in three months ago, one month with two renewals."

Hmmm. "This doesn't add up. Send her upstairs and I'll see her." For the last time, unless she had a damn good explanation for this.

I saw my next two patients and brought Annie into the exam room. I was more annoyed than irate, so I took a deep breath and resolved to keep Bad Cop locked up, at least at the outset.

"Good morning Annie. Do you know why I asked you to come in?"

"Well, I need my prescription," she said. "I didn't get it last week. Or I lost it. Either way, I'm out of pills."

"Annie, losing your prescription is one thing. But I wrote a three-month prescription of morphine you took downstairs. It should just be running out now."

"And it did!"

"So what's this about you going to Wal-Mart a few months ago? Was that one of my prescriptions?"

"Wal-Mart? That was months ago! Has nothing to do with this prescription!"

"So where did you get the extra pills you've been taking this past week? Was that from downstairs or Wal-Mart?"

"I don't know! Pills are pills. I don't remember."

"Have you been taking them as I prescribed them?"

"Yes! I might have missed a few doses, but--"

"You missed enough to get you through an entire week? That's more than twenty doses."

"I don't know. I guess."

And there's what I was fishing for. She wasn't taking them as prescribed. I would not be taken the way I was down east. Zero tolerance for bullshit. "I'm sorry, Annie, but I see too many inconsistencies between what you're telling me and what you're telling the pharmacist. I'm not convinced you're taking the medication as prescribed, and for all I know you're misusing--"

"Never! I've never abused my pills! I've been on them for years!"

"Regardless, you've violated the terms of the contract you signed for narcotic medications. I honestly don't feel that I can trust you, I'm afraid you'll--"

"--need to find another doctor."

As Annie completed my sentence, the reality of the situation slapped me in the face. *This is not the first time she's heard this from a doctor.* There was a beat or two of silence, then Annie collected her things and left without a word.

What had I done?

WHEN BEN WAS just a year old, he discovered cheese puffs. They're a ubiquitous item at birthday parties for toddlers. Perhaps it's because they dissolve in the mouth and don't pose much of a choking hazard, or perhaps it's because they're a dirt-cheap way to keep kids away from the adult snacks. In any event, cheese puffs were a form of crack to the kid. He'd snatch a bunch of them at a time, saving space in his palm by having them stick out between his fingers. He'd wolf them down until his face glowed neon orange. What do you know...we had found the perfect "special treat"!

One day, we invited some friends over for an afternoon visit, our company bringing their own kids in tow. Besides the big bucket of Thomas the Tank Engine toys, we put out a bowl of cheese puffs for the kids to snack on. Ben grew wide-eyed and dived at his orange, salty beloved treat. When it became clear to Kylea and me that he would empty the bowl, spoil his appetite for supper, and likely constipate himself in the process, we took the snacks away. He threw a fit. I plunked him in the corner for a time out until he smartened up and behaved himself, never mind who put the snacks out in the first place. That was the end of the cheese puffs for our family.

Ladies and Gentlemen, I submit to you modern medicine's approach to chronic pain medication: children and cheese puffs.

Pity the man or woman of modest means in chronic pain. If he or she has no coverage to pay for massages, chiropractic, and braces for various body parts, all that's left is pills. Sedating, constipating, and highly addictive pills.

It takes months to find a pill that works for the patient, and even more months to get to the effective dose. But there's a catch: sometimes the patient will *never* get to an effective dose, because the prescriber simply won't go above whatever they're comfortable with. And here I'm talking about patients with *verifiable, objective* conditions that warrant the use of long-term pain medication - backbone fractures, inoperable degenerative disc disease, diabetic nerve damage. Forget the people whose pain is ill-defined, who are well and truly screwed.

But wait! The patient will be expected to sign a contract before receiving a prescription for strong painkillers. The conditions of said contract will include any or all of the following: random urine drug tests; restriction to one prescriber and one pharmacy; safe storage of medication, possibly under lock and key; and an understanding that **any** transgression will lead to tapering and/or immediate discontinuation of the drug. Oh, and possible termination of the doctor-patient relationship.

There's still more! Should the pain worsen acutely for whatever reason - weather, heavy housework, a bad night of sleep - the ER will treat the patient's pain only so many times before assigning the patient the label of "drug seeker". This is a *de facto* blacklist from getting the benefit of the doubt from overworked ER staff.

And finally: should the patient actually consent to all this - and what choice does he or she have? - but *still* screw up in the eyes of the prescriber, the only alternative offered is referral to an addiction centre. There, the patient is guaranteed to be in the company of, and treated as, an addict - a street urchin, the lowest of the low.

This outrageous approach to patients with pain was many years in the making, and nobody has the right answers. Painkiller abuse has become so widespread that managing patients with pain is now inextricably tied to fighting drug addiction. That's fine for society as a whole, but fails miserably at the level of individual doctors and patients. Should I not take the patient at face value for their complaints, if they aren't at high risk for abusing their prescriptions? Am I responsible as a doctor for what the patient does with his or her pills? People don't even take antibiotics properly. And unless I work in Public Health, is it my job to prevent drug diversion, reduce addiction in the community, and fight crime?

So we muddle on, treating people with pain like dirt or turning them away outright. Easier to avoid the headache altogether. Mind you, Percocet works wonders on a headache...

I SLUMPED IN my desk chair, ruminating on the visit with Annie. I'd fired patients before, but this time I was out of line. I baited Annie, hunted for a pretext to be done with her because...why? Because she reeked of cigarettes? Couldn't keep her story straight? But the deed was done and the bridge was burned, my lesson learned at the expense of the patient.

I related the story to Claudette over lunch. Wow was it easy to paint the picture as I pleased, to play up Annie's inconsistencies and play down my own high-handedness.

"Do you think she was trying to pull a fast one?" said Claudette.

"I don't know, to be honest," I said. "I mean...she's obviously not taking all of her pills. Now is that because she's getting them somewhere else, or is she on too high a dose and is too stoned to remember every pill?"

"I don't think you did anything wrong. Whether she's a drug seeker or not, it sounds like she causes problems for her doctors and her pharmacists. You sure do pick some winners!"

"Yeah, that's me...hero to the downtrodden." Who found little difficulty treating a patient like dirt. Not one of my banner days.

CHAPTER TWENTY-FOUR

Poop Doodles

"SO WHAT DID my bloodwork show, Doctor?" asked Liz. Liz was friendly and polite, but a textbook example of the Worried Well...healthy but neurotic patients I didn't need to see as often as I did.

"Nothing, my dear," I said. "Thyroid is fine, blood count is fine. Even the x-ray we took of your chest was fine."

"So why I am I getting sweaty so much?"

I chuckled. "You're fine. It's just the change of life."

"You mean the mentalpause?"

"*Menopause.* You had a hysterectomy years ago, so you wouldn't have noticed that you don't get your period anymore." The 'mentalpause' is what happened to **me** every fucking morning when I came into work.

I was hungry. An apple at 10:30 just wasn't cutting it anymore. I hoped Liz was my last patient of the morning. It was Thursday, and I had the hankering for a drug lunch.

I gave Liz the two-minute spiel about estrogen replacement for her menopause treatment. The evidence and recommendations seemed to be changing each month, which made it hard to keep my sales pitch straight. It causes cancer! It doesn't cause cancer! Use it only for symptoms! Try this other crap first!

Liz opted to wait. Good, because the Thai aromas were wafting into the exam room. I saw Liz back to the waiting room, checked my mailbox for anything urgent, and zipped back to the lunchroom.

I loved it when the drug reps took the lunch order beforehand. There are only so many times you can feign interest in the same old lines about high blood pressure while eating the same old sandwich wraps. But Asian takeout? Not only is it a tasty treat, but if I zone out during the presentation I can just blame it on the food. This talk was about Zelnorm, a new pill for Irritable

Bowel Syndrome (IBS). Yum! What better way to spend a lunch hour than listening to a talk on irksome bowel symptoms? While my colleagues and I stuffed ourselves, the drug rep presented the data and prescribing information. Exciting stuff. Well, at least she was eye candy. The drug reps almost always are, women and men alike. After the meal, the rep handed us some "clinical information material" the company felt we might find useful.

"We have a variety of tools you can use in assessing your patients," she said. "The one we get the most positive feedback is the Stool Chart." Each of the doctors received a copy of the Stool Chart, a laminated pictographic rating scale for bowel movements. "Especially for your patients that are hard of hearing, or, as I know in this area, don't speak English well. You can get them to point to the picture that matches their stool pattern."

As with diabetes, medicine had now figured out how to subdivide a patient's bowel movements into subtypes - seven in all - from "separate hard lumps" to "watery, with no solid pieces". Each was associated with a (supposedly) standardized diagram of the different ways stool can appear.

"We're supposed to use this with our patients?" I asked.

"Yes," said the rep. "You can also use it to monitor their response to treatment, whether they've gone from a watery stool to a soft but lumpy stool, for example."

"These are pictures of poop," I said.

The rep smiled. "I think the clinical term is 'stool'."

"Right." I hemmed and hawed over what direction I wanted the conversation to go. Do I let the lunch end and get my paperwork done, or point out that this "clinical information material" resembles the doodles I used to pass to my pals in grade 7 for a cheap laugh? Eh, it's the company's marketing gurus that put out this shit, pardon the pun. Let the poor rep finish her talk in peace.

I stared a long moment at the poop doodles. Somebody earned a graduate degree, a fat research grant, and/or truckloads of cash in royalties for poop doodles. And I'd been offered - no, *encouraged* - to use them in my job, a job I could only take after how many years of post-secondary education?

Poop doodles.

I tried to focus on my paperwork, but couldn't, and ended up e-mailing a stream-of-consciousness diatribe to my close friends and old med school chums. It was a stop-the-world-I-want-to-get-off moment for me. Either the practice of medicine was becoming something most adults would justifiably ridicule and nobody else saw it, or the poop doodles were Perfectly Acceptable Medical Progress, and I was losing my fucking mind.

On top of that I was swamped. And more than a little bored.

The truth is that after a few years in practice, there isn't much new to see in family medicine. Even when you do see a genuinely exotic condition, and feel the exhilaration of diagnosing a real head-scratcher, at the end of the day it's just a person with a rash or funny-sounding heart murmur. The job is more about managing the patient's reaction to the condition or treatment than any "a-ha!" of solving the puzzle. The same size cancer, in the same body part, and at the same stage, will send one patient scurrying from treatment in denial, another complaining about the inconvenience, and a third emotionally unable to cope.

They say confession is good for the soul, or at least they said it in the first *Superman* movie. I liked most of my patients, even adored some of them. I found it refreshing that people from all corners of the earth - Columbian doctors, Palestinian filmmakers, Sudanese shepherds - had the same everyday problems and neuroses that ordinary North Americans did. But managing patient emotions was neither the thrust of my training nor my greatest strength. I was often drained at the end of the day, without an intellectual challenge to offset the frustration.

I also didn't anticipate just how much paperwork I would face by the end of each week. Ontario's bureaucracy bowled me over with its boundless capacity to spawn forms and letters that needed completion before I could get *anything* done for my patients. I began spending Friday nights and statutory holidays in the office just to catch up on the pile. Okay, sometimes it was an excuse to escape my visiting mother, but I again digress.

Once more I felt lost...annoyed, frustrated, unhappy with what I was doing. But Kylea was pregnant and I had no interest in quitting. This would pass. I hoped.

CHAPTER TWENTY-FIVE

What I'm Here For

"DIRTY" DEB AND "Dingy" Don. I couldn't stand this couple. I suppose I felt sorry for their adoptive son, whose biological parents drank heavily, but the two of them made my skin crawl. I could dislike them for their hygiene alone, or lack thereof, but it wasn't that. No, it was that every appointment was a demand for something - not a request, but a *demand*. He needed a note for missing a shift, she needed a form to get taxi coverage, he needed a letter so the phone would be covered by welfare, she needed a letter so welfare would finance their move to a bigger apartment.

I shouldn't have had such a problem with them. If anything, I should have looked forward to seeing them. Neither adult had a major illness, and I could bill the government for the forms...easy money, really. But I could not get past the sense of entitlement, the matter-of-fact way they'd take anything from the welfare system without a moment's hesitation, as if every benefit were a God-given right. They were the two in a hundred that gave welfare recipients a bad name, that made it all too easy to have contempt for the poor.

And, yes, their hygiene sucked. Would a shower before seeing me have killed them?

I checked the nurse's note for why they were in. Yup, forms.

"Good day, folks," I said. "What can I do for you?"

"I need to try applying for disability again," said Deb.

"Her last doctor didn't do the forms properly," said Don, "so they turned her down."

"What do you mean?" I said. "You've been my patient for over a year, so this must have been a while back. Didn't you appeal?"

"The doctor didn't put enough down," said Deb. "The lawyer said I had no grounds to appeal."

"Well, Deb, I'm not sure I have much to put down, either," I said.

"Well," said Deb, "I've still got the heartburn, even after the surgery and with the pills. I have to get those scopes done every year. Plus my hemorrhoids...I get problems sitting. And those two things make it too uncomfortable to have sex."

I did not need that visual. Eww. "Deb, hemorrhoids and heartburn do not constitute a disability. The government doesn't care if you can't have sex."

"Our worker said to do this and the federal application as well," said Deb.

This was the most pointless, idiotic thing I'd been asked to do since I was instructed to order a patient a banana as a med student.

"No," I said.

"No what?"

"No, I am not filling these out. It's a waste of time."

"You have to," said Deb.

"And you get paid for them," said Don.

I was Officially Annoyed. "Whether I get paid doesn't matter. You don't have a disease that's causing a significant disability. You will not qualify for the pension. It's a waste of my time to fill it out, it's a waste of time for whoever is going to read it, and it's a waste of the lawyer's time if you decide to appeal."

Deb and Don looked at each other, flummoxed. "We'll talk with our worker, I guess," she said. "But I don't think you can refuse to do this." They left the exam room without another word passing between us.

IT WAS MID-MORNING on Friday. Some weeks Friday morning felt like a sprint, other weeks like a crawl to the finish. Friday afternoon was ordinarily paperwork time, but this week's pile wasn't bad - mostly requisitions and referrals. I started fantasizing about an hour to myself to peruse the bookstore before picking Ben up from the daycare.

I stared at my appointment list. No real sick people left to arrive, and no troublemakers. Could I even have time for a test drive? I welcomed the distraction with kid #2 cooking in Kylea's belly.

Bonnie and Connie were up next. They were mother and daughter, but Bonnie delivered Connie at a shockingly immature age. They easily passed for sisters most days.

One of the few oversights in the design of the building was a lack of dedicated desks in the clinic room. I ended up using the foot of the exam table as a makeshift workspace to take notes or write scripts. That wouldn't happen this day, because every square foot of the table was occupied by a form - Medical Update, Provincial Disability, Special Diet Allowance, Transportation Allowance, Federal Disability Pension, Tax Credit - to the point where the exam room looked like a Dim Sum buffet for paperwork.

"What's all this?" I asked, nonplussed.

"Updated forms, plus some things from our worker," said Bonnie.

"--and that tax thing the accountant gave us," said Connie.

Some of this shit would keep. If I could find an hour to myself, I was taking it. "Look, I'll get them done, but it will take some time."

"It's a two-hour drive from where we're staying now," said Bonnie, "and we need to get a lift with our neighbor. I was hoping you could do them now."

"Now? You're kidding, right?"

"Well, by the end of the day," said Bonnie. "We can pick them up later before we drive back. How late are you open?"

"Bonnie," I said, "some of these forms take me hours. I need to review your chart, pick out what I need, make copies...there's no way they'll be done today."

"Well that doesn't help us," said Connie. "You're our doctor. This is what you're here for."

An awkward silence fell on the room, and I was **pissed**. I couldn't decide whether to throw them out, right then and there, or let it go.

Sigh. They didn't create the forms, and it was Friday. I was close to blowing my stack, but was not in the mood for a fight. "Bonnie, I will get them done when I can. I might have them done in a week, maybe longer. If you book a ride for two or three weeks from now, I can make sure they're ready for pickup."

Bonnie and Connie left without protest. I took a breather in the back office to try and calm down.

You're our doctor. This is what you're here for.

This was what I signed up for? "This is what you're here for"?!? There was no medicine, no science, no answer to any kind of sacred calling. This was whining and paperwork, or whining *about* paperwork, day in and day out.

I was at the end of my rope. What could I do, though? Kylea was settled, I was settled, and another baby was on the way. I had a ton of old and sick patients that needed care, and the city had already seen two family docs come and go inside of a year. But I could not see myself putting up with this shit for another three years, let alone thirty.

I needed a change, but I needed to be smart about it.

KYLEA MAKES FUN of me nowadays, because she knows that every three or four years I snap and make a drastic change in my career. While I can't disagree with the evidence, I think each career change came about for its own reasons.

At that point I didn't actively dislike my work. But the combination of the banality - colds and flus, blood pressure, diabetes - with the daily grind and the paperwork left me constantly cranky. Our second baby, the feisty and irresistible Chloe, who had the same sleepless colic as her brother, didn't help my stress level either.

But I had responsibilities - to my family, to my practice - and I couldn't just do as I pleased in the way that I switched programs as an intern. I needed to be patient, to be methodical, and to make sure whichever direction I went down was the correct one.

I connected with a vocational counselor that specialized in mid-career professionals. It was a unique experience, I'll say. First came the personality test, the Myers-Briggs or one of its imitators, that sorts all human beings into one of a dozen or so groups. Apparently I had a rare personality type: a reclusive, sinister mastermind, better suited to making my fortune as a Bond villain than a doctor. Who knew? Next was a consultation with family and friends as to what they felt I might be good at. Some said I should write, some said consulting, others advised "anything but working with people".

My own interests lay in public policy, not so much for the politics as for the chance to use an entirely different part of my brain. After exploring who and what was out there, I came around to Public Health as a complementary field to find work in. As luck would have it, there was an open position in a not-far-off county, and the province offered different paths I could pursue to upgrade my qualifications: I could go back into residency for three years, earning the full specialist designation; or I could work part-time and complete a Master's degree on the side. My opportunities would be fewer if I went the second route, but I'd be able to stay in practice, at least part-time. I didn't envision myself as any kind of "major player" in Public Health, and I had no interest in taking a provincial position that would require a move back to Toronto. Ten years removed from living in the megacity, I had no interest in a return to the hustle and bustle. More importantly, the second option satisfied my duties and conscience. The choice was an easy one.

In hindsight, the entire exercise was selfish and boneheaded. If a practice chock full of high-needs patients was starting to burn me out, what could I expect from doing that *plus* one day a week in public health *plus* completing a Master's degree on evenings and weekends? With a preschooler and infant at home? I had just laid the groundwork for the worst crisis of my life, all in the name of alleviating boredom.

But disaster was still a few years away. For now, it's time to get acquainted with an enduring professional nemesis of mine: The College of Physicians and Surgeons.

CHAPTER TWENTY-SIX

The Old College Try

TODD WAS MUCH closer to the typical image of a family doctor than me. He was tall, thin, and soft-spoken, with a decade's worth of experience beyond mine. He was recruited to the office not long after the in-and-out doctors left. He brought along some patients from his old practice, but opened the door for newcomers as well. While he administered Botox injections to earn extra cash, his core clinical focus was addiction and mental illness. You need the patience of Job to handle that patient population. As an ordained Minister as well as an MD, Todd set a better Biblical example than the rest of us.

Within a few months of joining us, things started to turn sour for Todd. He started taking phone calls from his wife that went on for long stretches of time, eating into his schedule. He'd cancel half-days at a moment's notice, frustrating his secretary and making her an undue recipient of flak from boss and patients alike.

It soon became clear that it wasn't marital conflict, but rather his wife suffering a serious health problem. That the illness was proving a challenge to diagnose only made matters worse. Todd had been her family doctor years prior, and now he was spending big chunks of his day pulling strings to get her booked for the right tests and into the right specialists. Then someone called the College on him.

TODD WAS SITTING at his workstation when I strolled into the doctors' back office. He was just staring at nothing, a morose look on his face.

"Is everything okay? Something to do with your wife?" I asked.

"No," he said, "not her health, anyway. I've been dealing with a complaint to the College, and it looks like I'm finished."

"Finished? What, like your license is revoked?" He nodded. "Holy shit! What happened? A complaint from one of the patients?"

"No, my ex-wife."

"Are you serious? Over what?"

"Sexual assault. I fell in love with a former patient. To the College, that's sexual assault."

"That's bullshit. She's your wife, for God's sake! Isn't her word good for anything?"

"Not according to the College or my lawyer." He sighed. "According to the investigation, I never formally ended the doctor-patient relationship. With all the calls and referrals I've been making on her behalf, that's evidence that I'm still her doctor as far as the College is concerned. They have a zero-tolerance policy for sex between doctor and patient. It's abuse by their definition."

"So your ex-wife calls the complaint, but the word of your wife means nothing? That's ridiculous."

"The law is an ass. There's absolutely nothing I can do. I lose my license, and the reason will be on the public register...forever."

"What are you going to do? I mean for work, if you can't practice?"

"I've got a few leads - medical writing, other industry stuff. The jobs are in the States, but close enough to the border that I can commute home on weekends. I'll see how it goes before I commit to relocating."

"This is all so absurd. I'm so sorry."

The news spread that Todd lost his license, and his practice had to close at once. I picked up what few patients that I could, but the ones with serious personality disorders and substance issues flipped out, hollering at the front desk and clinic owners. One of the patients called the local paper in a fit of rage. The paper reported the story about Todd being barred from practice permanently for sexually abusing a patient, information presumably lifted from the online College registry.

The story disgusted me. It was bad enough the guy lost his license because of an ex-wife's vindictiveness, but now the paper was trashing his reputation? I obviously had no influence on the College, but I wrote a scathing rebuttal to the local paper. I've never known a letter to the editor to amount to anything, but Todd's in-laws, some of whom were coincidentally my patients, were touched and thanked me sincerely. Who knows? Maybe the paper would think twice next time before ruining someone's reputation without all the facts. After all, it could have easily been me getting caught letting my mouth run too loosely one day, putting my ass in line for a public shaming.

ON PAPER, THE College of Physicians and Surgeons is responsible for the "self-regulation" of the medical profession, including the issuance of licenses and investigation of possible malpractice. In reality, it's a self-righteous, metastasizing bureaucracy that does little more than bully doctors into cowering before its demands.

However sex-obsessed I might have been growing up, I have **nothing** on the College of Physicians. I don't know what proportion of College council meetings is devoted to sex. Judging by the deluge of sex-related edicts routinely issued by the College, however, this supposedly sober institution is on par with a frat house.

This is no exaggeration. Every other month, the College sends out its members' magazine. The back of each issue gives the lowdown on recent disciplinary investigations and actions. Almost all of them are stories of sexual transgressions on the part of doctors, showcased in lewd and lurid detail. Some are real cases of abuse, so no argument from me. But the College keeps broadening its definition of sexual abuse, to the point that almost any contact without four layers of clothing between doctor and patient can end in a license being revoked. The way the College carries on, you'd think the profession of medicine was overflowing with rapists – six-foot animated penises, rampaging through hospitals sporting a stethoscope and keys to a BMW.

I can only hope that sexual abuse of patients becomes less and less frequent as more women enter the profession. As I'd be reminded again and again by my most vulnerable patients, there are few forms of life lower than sex criminals. But to put on "zero-tolerance" blinders in every case, regardless of the details? When the complaint comes not from a doctor's coworker, patient, or patient advocate, but an ex-wife? If a surgeon removes a mole on his mistress, is he committing sexual assault? Is the College acting in the interests of justice, or just absolving its disciplinary panels from needing to think?

For a time, the College of Physicians acted as a Mafioso-like enforcer for the provincial government, auditing doctors' billings to the tune of thousands upon thousands of dollars a head. Normally a function of the government's own armies of bureaucrats, this "public service" was conspicuously absent from the College's Mission Statement. It put a fear into doctors unmatched by anything short of an Ebola outbreak. It took a doctor's suicide in the wake of an audit to finally put a stop to things, but the College marches on, inventing new ways to make life miserable for its members.

My own encounters with the College had nothing to do with sex or billings, but it was one pain in the ass after another since the day Kylea accepted the job in Rutherford City. Naturally, the College decided it needed to sign off on my venture into public health, months after I'd already been in the job without incident. It started with a 10-page application and exhaustive review of my Master's program. Then they decided I'd need a supervisor – that met their approval - issuing quarterly reports until I was finished the degree some three or four years down the road.

That I wouldn't have executive authority over the health unit didn't matter. That the Ministry subsidized my degree as a recruitment incentive didn't matter. That the province's chief public health doctor *invited* me to go this route didn't matter. The rules were changed in the middle of the game, whether I liked it or not.

Come to heel at the yank of the leash or walk away and find some other way to cope with the tedium. I was so far into things, it seemed silly to change course at the time. I had more pressing things on my plate anyway, like a funny little pain in my hip that refused to disappear.

CHAPTER TWENTY-SEVEN

Private Matters

"SORRY TO INTERRUPT, Frank," said Nancy, "but there's a police officer on the phone, calling about Lynette."

"No problem, Nancy," I said. "I'm just sitting a minute. Put it through to the inside line." I kneaded my left thigh muscles, wondering when the physio was supposed to make the discomfort go away. I'd had the discomfort for well over a year, though it was only since I started the stretching that things began heading downhill.

A few seconds later my phone rang. "Hello, it's Dr. Warsh."

"Hello Doctor, thanks for taking my call. It's Officer Colin Copps, hoping you can be of help to me with regards to your patient Lynette Lonesome."

"I can try."

"Thank you. So, Ms. Lonesome was found deceased in her home yesterday--"

"Oh no. That's awful! She wasn't that old...please say it wasn't foul play or an overdose."

"Most likely it was natural causes, but the Coroner won't make a final determination until the autopsy results come back. In fact, I'm surprised you haven't been called yet for her medical history."

"We're not the easiest office to get through to on the phone. Technical thing. Anyway, Officer, how can I help you?"

"Unfortunately, we found nothing in Ms. Lonesome's basement apartment that named a next of kin or attorney that might have a copy of a will. Her landlord wasn't of much help either. I called the hospital to see if there's a next of kin on her file, but they refused to release any information."

"Did you want me to try?"

"That would be great, thank you. I've left my contact information with your secretary, since I imagine you're quite busy to be looking after this."

It was another half hour before I could sit down to try the hospital's Health Records department. As usual, the hospital operator needed three tries to get the right person on the line, giving me time to nurse my injury yet again.

Shortly after the move to Rutherford City, I was looking for a better way to stay in shape than a gym membership. The nearby place had a pool, which would be a great place to take the kids for a swim in the winter, but I was a typical one-month-steady, one-month-slacking, six-months-off client of the gym. I preferred to piss away money on home equipment over the gym, so at least I'd have something to hang my pants on.

It turned out there was a martial arts club a few blocks from the house, offering classes in aikido, the martial art Steven Seagal used to beat up bad guys in his early movies. I'd always wanted to take up a martial art - it was more than a "bucket list" interest, but less than a driving passion - so the neighborhood club was a good fit. It was also a way to meet a good group of guys outside of work, since most all the adult members were of my approximate age.

Aikido practice entails a lot of deep, static body positions, many of them exceedingly unnatural. I did no sports as a kid after my parents split up, and had exercised only in fits and spurts through my teen and young adult years. Stretching for flexibility and injury prevention was alien to me, and the range of motion in my joints was pathetic.

Once I'd earned my brown belt, I began to experience a funny pain in my left knee and thigh. It wasn't constant at first, and only showed up during certain movements, or if I overdid it on a bike ride. I decided to live with the discomfort for a while, holding off on getting it treated if possible, until after my black belt test in summer 2009.

I earned my black belt and consulted a doctor and physiotherapist as I'd promised myself. Neither were certain what was going on, but I was given a series of exercises and stretches to loosen and strengthen the muscles that seemed most likely to cause the problem. I did the prescribed stretches religiously, wanting to be back at 100% as soon as possible.

As sometimes happens, the diagnosis was off, and the treatment along with it.

"Yes, hello, it's the Manager of Health Records." She spoke with the measured inflection of a bureaucrat. This conversation would be as fun as an abscessed tooth. "How can I help you, Doctor?"

"I have a patient who unfortunately died suddenly a day or two ago. She was estranged from her family, but I'm wondering if there's a name or number of a next of kin or friend on her chart. As it stands, there's nobody to even arrange her funeral."

"Oh dear. What's the patient name and date of birth?" I rhymed off Lynette's details. "Oh, I'm sorry, Doctor, that file's been flagged because the police contacted us. We can't release any information without a request going through the hospital's designated Privacy Officer."

"That's not you? You're the Manager of the records department."

"The Privacy Officer deals with all external requests for patient information, including auditing of the digital--"

"Look, all I need is a name or phone number."

"I'm sorry, Doctor, that would be in violation of the hospital's privacy policy."

"But the patient is dead. What's the problem?"

"According to the record, this file was flagged when the police tried to obtain access to her information. The hospital's privacy policy--"

"The woman is *dead*. I don't think she's likely to file a complaint about her privacy rights. I'm also pretty sure the law allows for information to be released at the discretion--"

"I'm sorry, Doctor, I can't help you any further. I'll have to ask you to call the Operator again to be put through to the Privacy Officer's extension. Goodbye."

Was I losing my fucking mind? I had to be losing my fucking mind.

THE PRESCRIBED EXERCISES only aggravated the pain, damaging the cartilage inside my left hip socket. It sounds wholly innocuous - the sort of injury pro athletes deal with all the time - but it proved to be anything but.

Within a month of exercising as prescribed, I had to stop training in aikido. Not long thereafter, I gave up just about everything else that could be labeled as exercise. Through all of it, I was desperately trying to juggle my practice, part-time work in public health, Master's degree studies, and keep up with my share of the housework and child care.

By the time 2011 rolled around, I was in pain every waking hour of the day. Not a crippling-doubled-over, I-need-narcotics-pain...but a deep, constant, grinding discomfort that never seemed to let up. I'd do the simple chore of buying groceries, and be relegated to resting on the couch for next four hours. This wasn't the vague stomachaches I had in med school that were glorified panic attacks, or a buggered back from moving a couch. Something was very, very wrong with my hip, and I pressed the experts to figure it out.

GOD, THE WAITING room was freezing. And it was an MRI of my hip, not my chest. Why could I not wear a sweater?

A nurse in standard-issue hospital wear - scrubs and an OR gown to keep warm - stopped by to ask questions and take my vital signs. There were other people around, each in his or her own alcove of the waiting area, but I couldn't make out any of them. The frames of my glasses were metal, a no-no for an MRI machine.

"Now, Mr. Warsh, are you on any medications that we need to know about?" She's wasn't exactly discreet in projecting her voice.

"No ma'am."

"And we're going the MRI of your left hip, is that correct?"

"So far as I know."

"Okay, I'm just going to check your blood pressure and pulse here..."

As she connected me to the BP machine, I heard a familiar voice from another nook of the waiting area. "Doctor Warsh!"

I squinted around the room, finding the outline of a hand waving at me. "David?" David happened to be my patient, as were his wife and mother. They were a terrific family to care for, though his mother, like so many, had a preoccupation with her bowels. "Fancy meeting you here," I said. "What's that line from *Casablanca*? 'Of all the gin joints, in all the towns...' What are you in for?"

"You should know," he chided. "You sent me! What, you don't remember every test you order on every patient?" We both snickered.

"Mr. Warsh," the nurse interjected, "or I guess Dr. Warsh is it? Your blood pressure is up today. Have you ever been worked up for high blood pressure?"

Right in front of my patient. Nice. At least I wasn't there for an MRI of my scrotum. "No, I haven't," I said, rather peeved.

The nurse directed me to a wheelchair into the MRI suite. Without my glasses, I couldn't tell if the hospital's privacy policy was posted for public scrutiny. What's worse when it comes to hospitals and privacy, the lunacy or the hypocrisy?

And since when did I have blood pressure problems?

Going Down

IT WASN'T LONG before I was spiraling down and in complete denial of it, or at least blind to it. Despite getting no exercise and eating no less, my weight was dropping, and I was down to a size I hadn't been since high school. The pain no longer restricted itself to waking hours either, and both my sleep and intimate life broke down.

The pain did more than disable me physically. It left me hollow, both personally and professionally. I had nothing to look forward to - no social life, no activities. I was short with Kylea and the kids, barking and cursing at the slightest annoyance. I was bereft of empathy towards my patients, all semblance of caring little more than an act. It was as insincere as the Lowly Intern shtick I pulled as a resident, but the only way I could get through the day. And just about any minor frustration would set me off.

FUCK. IT WAS "Test-me" Trent again. How many times would I have to tell this loser there was fuck-all wrong with him? His *father* had health issues. His *mother* had health issues, albeit caused solely by his father. But Trent? Nope. This was just another fucking visit for him to ask for another fucking test. You would think he'd have more important things to do at age 22, like, oh, finding a job or getting laid. Nope. Back to the doctor - me. Fuck.

I took a minute to compose myself before stepping in the exam room. "Hello Trent," I said. "How are you?"

"Doctor," he said, "I still have that headache and funny dizziness."

"I can't explain your symptoms. Whatever it is, it's nothing serious."

"How do you know? I get this almost every day. You tell me it might be my eyes. I get them checked, it's not my eyes. You tell me it might be my teeth. I see the dentist, it's not my teeth. You tell me--"

"Trent, there is nothing wrong. You've had bloodwork, you've had CT scans, you've seen the specialist. You have symptoms, and they are harmless. You don't need to come back here. Try to--"

"But maybe you didn't send me to the right specialist. I saw the Neurology doctor, but maybe I need--"

"ENOUGH! I'm done with you!" I threw the door open. "Get the FUCK out of my office, and go whine to someone else. Leave NOW!!" I stormed into the back office to try and calm down, all to no avail.

The hip was burning, and I still had weeks to go before the consult with the surgeon. And I had to finish my part of that fucking group project for the Master's. Fuck. Being back in school was fine, but the group assignments were painful. I'd just as soon have written the 10,000-word paper myself.

I stared into space, hoping Kylea remembered to get something for dinner. Or did I say I would?

Fuck, I wanted the day over with.

LIKE COUNTLESS OTHERS, I've had bouts of depression, both as a youth and an adult. They'd persist for weeks, even months. But every time, there was always that day, that one day, when the clouds parted and I woke up feeling like a million bucks. Sometimes it took medication to get there, but that's what it's for, right?

This was a different set of feelings entirely, if you can call them feelings. There was no sadness, or despondence, or anxiety. I felt...less than human. I was a zombie, an automaton. Morning routine. Work. Dinner if it was my day, laundry if it wasn't. Bath- and bedtime for one or both kids. Study and write papers. Lather, rinse, repeat.

I was confused, paranoid, losing my grip on reality. How could a tiny fucking piece of torn cartilage render me a cripple in the prime of my life? Was I destined to be the next Achyspine or Sadsack, just a poor slob begging and blubbering for an operation that the surgeon didn't think was worth the trouble? Was I going to be *that* guy?

Maybe I could have lived with it - the practice that bored me, the studies, even the pain - if it weren't for the nonstop anger. Anger at myself, for being arrogant to take on two jobs and school while needing to parent young children. Anger at the patients, for the ceaseless whining and reams of paperwork. Anger at the College, for dumping roadblock after roadblock in front of me. And anger at my family, for...well, for no identifiable reason.

I was a creature - a bitter, vicious animal - deserving of a cage more than my family.

I tried to keep my sense of humor about me. Some days it wasn't hard, what with many of the patients "hygiene-impaired", so to speak, and I confess to making more than a few jokes at their expense. Other days, it was getting harder and harder to even *act* like I gave a shit. My patients were booked every ten to twenty minutes, but at least three of every ten minutes were squandered as I paced in pain, trying to put on a game face. The patients never said anything. Neither did my coworkers, except those days I mused about faking my own death. Maybe I was a better actor than I give myself credit for.

Then came the morning I felt flushed.

AM I COMING down with the flu?

BLEEP-beep.

Oh no. Not them. Anyone but them.

BLEEP-beep.

I take off around the corner from the exam rooms to hide in the staff kitchen. I do not want to see those two. Yeah they've got their problems, but they've turned their home into a makeshift ICU. They check each other's blood pressure almost hourly, blood sugars just as often. Every little symptom, every drop of urine, every morsel of food measured, recorded, researched. All for me, so I can pore over every detail as though I were reading an ex-girlfriend's diary, as though I'm expected to care.

They're getting closer. I can hear that electric wheelchair. *BLEEP-beep.* Every time it pivots, rolls forward, or brakes. *BLEEP-beep.* They're in for the same thing. He's broken, she's broken. Fix us, doctor. When her sugar goes up, her blood pressure goes up. When his blood pressure goes up, he can't sleep. The Cardiologist says X. The Cardiac Surgeon says Y. I tell them to stop checking. They don't listen. Their kids agreed with me until they didn't.

They just keep talking and talking and talking, complaining and complaining and complaining. I can't process it. I feel like...like I'm drowning. Like I've been desperately treading water and I'm finally out of strength. Like there's nothing I can do but let them say their piece and leave in peace.

Words leave my mouth, but they're not the words I hear in my head. I hate this. I hate this. I hate this.

I say some shit that seems to placate them. I write some shit in the chart. I say good-bye but they'll be back. Fuck.

BLEEP-beep. It's getting fainter. I can relax now, they're gone. The flushed feeling isn't.

There's a drug lunch today but I don't feel up to it. Keep your wraps or chicken balls or casserole. I'm not hungry. Or I'll eat the leftovers.

What the hell is going on with me?

I wander into my exam room unseen and hook myself to the blood pressure cuff. 180/114. Must be that I just walked. Wait five minutes.

186/103. Try the other arm.

179/107. Lie down for a bit.

183/102. Oh God...what do I do?

CHAPTER TWENTY-NINE

The Great Crash

KYLEA WAS OFF to another conference out of town. As if it mattered. It's not like there was any delight in being around me. She tucked the kids into bed and packed the last of what she needed for the trip.

I watched her in the kitchen, scurrying back and forth to get her bag into the car. "Okay, I'll call from the airport hotel. See ya," she said.

"Is this it?" I asked. "'See ya'?"

"What do you want, Frank? It's been a long week, and I have a plane to catch in the morning."

"I don't know, some affection? A sense that I actually matter?"

"You're right, Frank. I'm in the wrong, again. I'm always the one in the wrong."

"The sarcasm isn't needed."

"What do you want, Frank? Seriously, **what...do...you...want**? I'm sorry I have this meeting out of town. I'm sorry to leave you alone with the kids, again. Do you think I like being away from you and the kids?"

"No, of course not, and--"

"So what will make you happy? You want me to stay home and be the good housewife? We can't afford that, and I don't want that. You want me to give up tennis? It's the one thing I have for myself, that makes me feel like a real person, other than a mother and a wife and a doctor.

"**You** went looking for a new job when we had a newborn baby. **You** went back to school, to start this Master's that ate up all your free time. I stood by and supported you because I thought it would make you happy. But it's brought you no joy. All it's done is stress you out and make you more miserable! And I get that you're in pain, and I can't wait until you have your surgery and you finally have relief. But once that's done, will you have your '*joie de vivre*'? Or will it be more of the same? Bitching about your patients, bitching about your paperwork, bitching about your studies...when does it stop?

"Frank, you're a terrific husband. You're an amazing father. And yes, I do love you, more than anything. And I will not give up on our marriage or our family, because I refuse to let our children go through that...that misery, just for my sake."

A minute passed in silence.

"Look, I need to go," said Kylea. We hugged tightly.

"Call when you're at the hotel," I said.

"I will."

I WAS A WRECK. A burned-out shell of myself, a cripple. I didn't want to lose my family. Even if I medicated the shit out of my blood pressure, had the surgery...would it change anything? Would it fix what I'd become?

I sat back on the family room couch in silence, a relentless torrent of voices in my head.

The patients love you to pieces, Frank. It's an act. It's always been an act.

You always listen to me. No I don't. I just fake it.

You're the warmest, most caring doctor I've ever known. No, I'm not! It's bullshit, all bullshit! Lines, speeches I've picked up from mentors or textbooks or...fuck, even movies!

You're not leaving like the other doctors, are you? And do what? Go where?

My husband and son...they'll need a family doctor once I'm gone.

BLEEP-beep.

God, I can't do this anymore.

I CAN'T COUNT the number of articles, blog posts, and forum threads I've seen on physician burnout. There's an entire cottage industry around it - books, seminars, meditation retreats. It even has its very own vocabulary. Sometimes it's called "compassion fatigue", sometimes "work-life imbalance", sometimes "inadequate self-care". Whatever. It's all in the abstract until you experience it yourself. Bottom line, it sucks.

I've had several episodes through my life that I could label as nervous breakdowns, not that the term has any clinical meaning. This didn't feel like one of those spells. Then again, my memory's a little fuzzy from those days. I was in a dark, bleak place, possibly on the brink of psychosis, though I can't be sure. Psychiatry isn't a do-it-yourself field of medicine.

I walked into the clinic the following Monday morning and closed my practice. I could have called it temporary or indefinite, but I knew better than to dangle false hope at the patients. Whether or not my health turned around - and I was confident it would - I'd been unhappy as a doctor for a long, long time.

What's striking is how insidiously it all unfolded. Whether by circumstance or choice, little by little my life fell apart. I was the frog in the pot of water brought to a boil, cooking to the core without a clue to jump free.

My immediate need was rest, and that's what I did. I discovered some tasteless television, and rediscovered some old friends and past interests. It would be months before I'd be free from physical pain, but day-by-day I reclaimed my humanity.

At the time, friends and family asked if I was relieved, or even joyful to be out of family practice. To this day, the answer remains an emphatic no. I felt nothing but sadness and lament. Not for myself, but for the patients. I took on some of the most frail and debilitated members of the community, but ended up just walking away, and not on my own terms. One more time a washout.

From time to time, I've bumped into a former patient at a store or public event. Even years later, I'm invariably greeted with a smile and best wishes. It's both heartening and humbling to receive, a salve for the scars from the lowest point in my life.

Work didn't stop entirely during my crisis and recovery time. I did what I could to bridge the gap for my patients while they sought out new doctors, renewing prescriptions and completing their forms. I still had coursework to complete for the Master's degree, which proved much less a pain when I could tackle it in the daytime. And I still had a part-time gig with Public Health to pay my share of the bills.

But it was my turn to play the part of the patient, and holy shit did that ever give me perspective.

CHAPTER THIRTY

Domo Arigato

I NEVER DID find out precisely what my MRI showed. I tried to get a copy of the report, and was slapped once again with the Almighty Privacy Policy. While the thought crossed my mind, I didn't dare ask Kylea to look up the result. She'd get reprimanded with a dreaded Incident Report for sneaking a peek at the chart of someone that wasn't her patient. No big deal. I finally had my appointment with the surgeon. Now I just had to make sure he'd take me seriously, not laugh me out of the clinic like all those miserable slobs I encountered in residency. Sometimes being another doctor creates immediate rapport, other times you're presumed to be diagnosing yourself.

It was over an hour past my allotted time slot before I was put in an exam room. Not like I couldn't see that coming. I don't know how people ever stuck it out in doctors' waiting rooms before phones had gigabytes of video games on them. Old golf magazines and issues of *Reader's Digest* hardly make the time pass quickly.

I was to see a clinical fellow before meeting the consultant surgeon. It was a Dr. Shogun from Japan, a family doctor training an extra year in Sports Medicine. How much Japanese did I remember from aikido class?

"Hello, Mr. Warsh," he said.

"*Konnichiwa*," I answered.

"You speak Japanese?"

"A few words," I said with a laugh. "I trained in aikido before I got hurt."

"So you're here for your hip?" he asked. Not much for chit-chat I guess.

Shogun did a cursory physical exam as I pointed out the pattern of my lingering pain. He then plunked down in front of the digital radiology station and pulled up my MRI. Without uttering a word, he ate up the next three minutes playing with the mouse, zooming the image in and out, futzing with the contrast, and jumping back and forth from one view to the next. The silence crossed a line between awkward and rude, and I wondered whether Shogun was scrutinizing the MRI or just playing mindlessly with a high-tech toy.

He finally rose from his digital meandering. "I don't think surgery will be of much help to you."

"Excuse me?"

"Surgery...I'm not sure an arthroscopy will help your hip."

"Thank you, but I think I'll wait to speak to the surgeon. You are aware that I'm a doctor, right?"

"I didn't know that. You're too busy to take time, I think, from work."

"Why don't you let me worry about that, after I talk to the doctor I'm actually here to see?" I had almost ten years of experience on this punk, and he had the gall to try and put words in my mouth? So much for Japanese people showing deference to their seniors.

"I will go get the surgeon, then."

"*Domo arigato.*" Prick.

When Shogun came back with his supervisor, I refrained from saying anything. Not that I was afraid to speak my mind, but I didn't trust myself to keep my temper in check. If I blew a gasket, the consultant might get ticked off, walk out the door, and I'd be screwed. Fuck, is the patient ever powerless.

The surgeon turned out to be much less presumptuous than Shogun, but explained that he needed to be sure the hip was the problem before booking the operation. He suggested an injection of local anesthetic directly into the joint. If numbing the joint relieved my symptoms, he'd go ahead with the surgery. It was a reasonable proposition, and I was still at home resting most days. The injection, which needed to be done under x-ray, was scheduled for a few weeks down the road.

The injection was done late on a Friday morning. It hurt like hell going in, but the freezing kicked in on the ride home from the hospital. For three fleeting hours on an unseasonably mild day, I remembered what it was like to feel normal.

CHAPTER THIRTY-ONE

Now That's a Pisser

I WOKE UP from the surgery in dire need of a toilet. I presume that the entire contents of the empty IV bag had made its way through my bloodstream, because the urge to pee was intense. I was also groggy as hell from the anesthetic, which made it impossible to puzzle-solve my way out of the tangled IV tubing and into the washroom. Thank goodness for nurses.

As I returned to the gurney, my hip, stained orange-brown with iodine, tingled along the incision. I didn't worry about it – it felt no worse than a bad cut - but the burning in my hip was gone. I was...free. The undoing of all my happiness, my intimate life, and to a large extent my career, was gone. My eye began to well up with a tear...

...when Kylea and my nurse instantly shoved two Percocet at my mouth. "Take these," said Kylea. "I do not want you in any pain. You are going to have a pain-free recovery, and I'm going to make sure of it."

"I haven't taken anything stronger than an Advil since I had my wisdom teeth out," I said. "That was twenty years ago. Won't this like, put me out?"

"Frank, I'm not giving you an overdose," said Kylea. "You've just had surgery. You need to take it."

My nurse shot a *don't-argue-with-your-wife* glare at me. "Your surgeon prescribed a bottle of sixty tablets," she said. "If you need more, you'll need to see your family doctor."

How long would sixty last me? Let's see...two tablets every four hours, minus eight hours sleep, divided into twenty-four hours, minus the two I just had, times...fuck it, math is a no-go. I closed my eyes and slept off the rest of the anesthetic, and Kylea drove me home to recuperate.

Kylea booked off the day of the surgery, but with or without Percocet I'd be useless around the house for at least a few days.

Though it was July and the kids - now 8 and 4 - were out of school, they'd still need lunch, dinner, and laundry taken care of. My Mom took the week off work to stay with us and cover some of the kid-care chores.

I was still woozy late in the day when Kylea force-fed me another two Percocets. "I'm not that bad, Kylea, really," I said in protest.

"Enough," said Kylea. "You're not bad because you're taking the pain medication like you're supposed to. I don't want you having to chase your pain, because then it will take an hour for the meds to kick in." Strike two.

"Oh," said Mom, "it's time for the *Y & R*. Can you put it on for me?"

"Huh?" I said. "Oh, right, *The Young and the Restless* comes on now." I fiddled with the myriad remotes to find the right channel on the TV. Mom and Amy had watched the *Y & R* for eons, while my soap opera of choice since childhood was World Wrestling Entertainment. I was sucked into the *Y & R* between undergrad and medical school, then again when I was bowled over by the pandemic Swine Flu. In the fifteen years that I missed, little had apparently changed with the show, apart from cast members' hairlines receding further, and an obvious increase in the use of Botox.

It wasn't long before the Percocet kicked in again, though I'm fairly certain the previous dose had yet to wear off. I tried to focus on the television - thankfully *Y & R* wasn't terribly taxing to my powers of concentration - until the horizon line of my sight started to float up and down. I started to giggle. *Whoa, I thought digital TVs didn't have a vertical hold.*

Mom gazed over at me, as the giggling refused to stop. "What's the matter with you?

"Abso-fucking-lutely nothing," I said. "As in, I can't feel a thing, including, it would seem, the effects of gravity."

"Just from the Percocet? Your grandmother could take that and it wouldn't touch her arthritis."

"Nana always was tougher than most." Jesus, even that night I spent in the hotbox couldn't compare with this. "I gotta say, now

I understand why this stuff goes for a buck a milligram on the street. This is good shit!"

"I'm glad all those years of schooling have made you so articulate." Mom gives as good as she gets, and I was way too high to come up with a retort.

Though I hadn't had much of anything to eat or drink - the surgery wasn't nauseating but the Percocet was - once again Nature's Call beckoned. It was quite the task getting to the washroom safely, hobbling on crutches and stoned out of my gourd as I was. But I made it unharmed, and sat down to pee. And sat. And strained. And sat. And strained.

At one point, I even poked at my lower belly, as I recalled the kids trying in their early days of potty training.

Not a drop.

Not good.

I stumbled back to the family room, a deflated and anxious look about me.

"Did you need me to dig it out?" asked Mom, referencing an oft-cited story from my preschool days.

"It's not that kind of problem. And no jokes this time, I need a ride to the Emergency Room. Apparently I'm not able to pee on my own anymore."

We made it to the ER where I was ushered in almost immediately. Though not an imminent threat to life, urinary retention is not uncommon after anesthesia and potent medications. It's also treatable within seconds. That's right...I'd be getting a fucking catheter bag.

I lay back on the gurney, resigned to my fate while a nurse gathered the implements. The Percocet fog was lifting, and I was treated to the bustle and sounds of the ER.

"Sir, can you point to where it hurts?" said a voice behind the curtain on my left. "CAN YOU POINT TO WHERE IT HURTS?" Ah, the patient must be foreign. You can always tell, because the standard response to patients that can't speak English is to shout at them in English.

"So there's blood from the vagina?" said a voice behind the curtain on my right. "Are you certain it was your vagina and not your rear end?" *Your privacy is important to us.* "And you're not having a fever, right? No vomiting, right? You've been through menopause over a year, right?" *Open-ended questions*, they said. *Dig to uncover the patient's needs and agenda*, they said.

A large brute of a nurse emerged through the curtain of my gurney. "Good evening...Doctor, is it?" he said.

"Yes," I said, "but not at the moment. It's my turn to be on the receiving end, it would seem."

"I guess I don't need to go into detail, then. We'll empty your bladder first, then I'll get the tubing and bag all connected. I'll send you home with a spare, just in case there are problems."

"Any idea how long I'll need this for? Will I need a consult or something?" You'd think I would know some of this. Nope. "I'm immobile for the next two days, but I'd rather not have it in for my post-op physio."

"Best thing is to keep it in for at least a day, then see where you're at. Once all the drugs wear off you should be fine." No more Percocet for me, got it.

The catheter insertion - yes, it's a tube right up the dick - wasn't pleasant, but it was over quickly. The nurse remarked how impressed he was with the volume of urine I had retained. There was probably a good punch line to that comment, but I was too relieved to care, and awestruck by the indignity of the entire episode. As they say in the comics, *whatta revoltin' development.*

OKAY, I ENDED up taking a few more of the damn Percocet, but Kylea accepted my disinterest in taking it regularly. Besides, I felt better. The incisional pain was no big deal, ice was helping the hip, and I'd be progressing from crutches to cane ahead of schedule.

I sailed through the first night with the catheter, but after 24 hours or so it started to irritate like hell. It wasn't as bad as my bout with prostatitis a few years' prior - too much information? - but it also struck me as too soon for an infection.

Kylea watched me squirm in discomfort under a blanket on the family room couch. "What's the matter with you?" she said.

I made sure nobody else was in earshot. "It's the catheter," I said. "It is really starting to annoy the shit out of me."

"Is your pee going into it? Could it be blocked?"

I lifted the blanket to do a quick check of the tubing. "There's piss in the bag, but not much. Kind of hard to see anything with the light in here."

"Check in the washroom. You can always change it for the spare."

Kylea helped me to the nearby washroom. I flicked on the light to do a closer inspection, inch by inch along the tubing, and--

"Oh, fuck ME!!" I hollered.

"What is it?" said Kylea through the door.

"I'm taking it out. It's blocked - the flow in the tube is blocked."

"Blocked with what? You've only had it in for a day. It's not clotted blood, is it?"

"No, it's not blood. It's fucking semen. My catheter is clogged with globs of come. That 'irritation' I felt was the tube giving me a fucking handjob from the inside."

Kylea snorted a laugh. "Eww."

"It's not funny! Fuck!" I emptied the bag and removed the catheter in disgust.

"How did that even happen? Is there a hole in the tube or something?" said Kylea.

"Who cares? But I'm not putting the other one in!" I sat down on the toilet seat and strained. And sat. And strained. And sat. And strained. And peed. Ahhh.

THE SWELLING IN the hip settled by the weekend, and my mobility returned with a cane. Though still off work, I could start pulling my weight around the house once more, driving the kids from point A to point B as needed. After two weeks of inactivity, I was ready to get back to Public Health, and start exploring options for employment outside a traditional family practice. I'd end up working some hours at a Community Health Centre, joining a team that looked after some of the area's poorest and most disadvantaged people, but all that in due time.

O Public Health, that singular point of intersection between medicine, bureaucracy, and politics. Ever seen those movies about public health catastrophes? The ones where some lethal, heretofore unknown infestation sweeps across the planet, and the brilliant, tireless public health professionals risk life, limb, and reputation to contain it? Or parachute in as 'The Man' to seize control of said disaster, preventing a plague from triggering society's collapse into anarchy?

Absolute, unabashed nonsense.

CHAPTER THIRTY-TWO

The Boiling Point

NOT FIFTEEN MINUTES from a major city, and not twenty minutes from Ontario's arterial highway, Adelaide County – don't bother with a map, it's another made-up name - is somehow underserviced for doctors. On the surface, anywhere in the region would make an excellent place for a medical practice: idyllic rural scenery, bountiful farm-fresh food, terrific golf courses, and a walkable tourist spot right on a picturesque lake. You're a short commute to the amenities of a big city, and there are never traffic tie-ups in that part of the province. On the surface, it's almost too good to be true.

On the surface.

But like French onion soup and a cadaver, it's what's beneath the surface that counts. Adelaide County has problems. Its central city, Fort Sussex, is a factory town that was badly hollowed out by the financial crisis and downsizing of the automakers. The rural areas are home to an orthodox religious population that is both rapidly growing and poor. And that spot on the lake? Between the water toxicity and seasonal mosquito problem, it's not a great spot to take your toddler for a dip.

Still, Adelaide was my gateway into the world of Public Health, and after a year of forms, interviews, and more aptitude-personality tests, I was named as the region's Acting Medical Officer of Health (MOH). I would've been properly anointed as MOH - without the "acting" qualifier - once I earned the Master's degree, but as you'll discover I didn't stick around for that day to arrive.

I tried my damnedest to develop a workable novel about Public Health, one that reflected reality instead of what's found in cheesy medical thrillers or plague-disaster movies. I had a workable outline of a story, and a rogue's gallery of politicians, doctors, and bureaucrats to draw on for major characters. Unfortunately, it's impossible to paint a realistic portrait of Public Health without accounting for the endless hours of meetings, teleconferences, webinars, consultations, and accreditations you're subjected to in the run of a week. It was every form of tedium imaginable, on a spectrum from mundane to inane. Unless bureaucrats reading complete sentences off PowerPoint slides gets your adrenaline pumping - and if it does, seek help - or you find yourself enthralled by managers wrangling over budgets, some days in Public Health are as dull as watching a bicycle rust. Stephen King couldn't make that into a page-turner.

But what about the outbreaks? Some badass germ rips through an unsuspecting community, leaving anguish and death in its wake...that must provide some thrills, right? I suppose, though the "unsuspecting community" is most often the crowd at a church picnic, with cramps and diarrhea replacing "anguish and death". But the point is taken. Public Health does have its moments that can approach a degree of something that sort of seems like it might be described as resembling a little excitement.

"FRANK, IS THERE any way you can come in tonight?" asked Stavros. He was the CEO of the Health Unit, but not a doctor himself. It's atypical but not unheard of for a health unit to be led by an administrator, particularly in rural areas where recruiting doctors is a challenge. Still, a doctor is needed to exercise authority under the public health law, like ordering someone under quarantine or declaring a town's water unsafe for drinking.

I swallowed my forkful of dinner. "I guess," I said. I'd hoped to enjoy a dip in the pool, but them's the breaks. "What's going on now?"

"National news wants an interview about the Boiled Water Advisory," said Stavros.

"Didn't I field that call earlier today?" I said. "I even heard my sound bite on the drive home."

"That was radio. This is TV."

"National TV? For a boiled-water alert?"

"It's the biggest one since Walkerton."

Earlier in the day, Fort Sussex's water system had tested positive for the *E. coli* bacteria, and by law we had to put the city on a boiled water advisory. The 0157:H7 strain of *E. coli* can cause vicious intestinal symptoms, destruction of blood cells, and even death, so positive *E. coli* tests are never taken lightly. Boiled water advisories are declared all the time in rural areas, but it was bizarre to see it in a city system that adds chlorine - which kills the bacteria - to the water at its source. Stranger still, the Fort Sussex system showed normal chlorine levels throughout, which should have made a positive test for *E. coli* all but impossible.

In 2000, the water system of Walkerton, Ontario was contaminated by farm runoff. *E. coli* in the effluent caused a health crisis in the community that culminated in several deaths. Though the water system operator in Walkerton was found negligent, the incident made national news and sparked a major overhaul of the laws and standards around drinking water. Anything raising the spectre of Walkerton was bound to make headline news.

I threw on a shirt and tie and zipped down the road to the health unit. My afternoon had been derailed by the Advisory, as I was bombarded by phone calls from key people and interviews with local radio and newspapers. The risk to city residents was almost negligible, and it was vital to get that across to the public. I met with Stavros and the rest of the team briefly to get the details straight. We were in a holding pattern overnight, until the follow-up lab tests would come back the next day.

The TV crew pulled into the parking lot and everyone was introduced. I couldn't pronounce the journalist's last name, but she was spunky and up-front.

"We're going to do a walk-out establishing shot, Doctor," said Newsie Spice (for lack of a better name). "I'm sure you've seen this on the news before. I'm going to be talking to you without the mic as we walk to the parking, but you need to keep your eyes on me." She exchanged signals with the cameraman. "Ready, Doctor?"

"I think so," I said.

We strolled through the sliding front doors into the dark of night. "Just look at me," said Newsie. "Keep looking at me. You're just walking and looking at me."

There was a light as bright as the sun off to my left. *Jesus, what is that?* I thought I might be struck by a car like a deer in the headlights. I turned to make sure and...oh. It was the camera.

"Um, I looked at the camera," I said. "Sorry."

Newsie huffed, annoyed. "Damn it. Tom, he looked at the camera," she shouted to her cameraman. "Can we edit that out? Yes? Do we need to try again? Good." She composed herself, this time with the microphone. "So Doctor Warsh, can you tell us how high the *E. coli* count in the Fort Sussex water is?"

"The level is low, although when we use numbers we're talking about thousands of individual bacteria in each teaspoon of water, so the absolute count isn't really important. Right now, the chlorine levels are steady, which is a good sign that the risk is low."

"Well, at what level are you worried? I mean, how much *E. coli* needs to be there before we risk another Walkerton?"

How many licks does it take to get to the Tootsie Roll center of a Tootsie Pop? "As I said, the absolute level isn't that important. For now, things look okay. The boiled-water advisory is a precaution for now."

A few more questions brought the interview to a close. I offered a second apology for looking at the camera, getting rolled eyes in return. Should have let that sleeping dog lie.

The next day I was summoned once more to Fort Sussex, this time for an afternoon Q&A alongside the municipal leadership. I wasn't taking center stage for this one, though I was handed some unsolicited talking points: this was cooperation between health unit and municipal partners at its finest, proof that the new precautions work, blah, blah, blah.

Most of the heat seemed to center around who knew what and when. This Alderwoman defended a tweet about the boiled water alert before the City issued the news release, that Mayor bemoaned the slow social media response, the local gossip columnist had his knickers in a knot about health unit salaries...

The entire spectacle mystified me, given the trivial risk to people's health. I zoned in and out during the Q&A, which was evidently more about political posturing than public safety. That's what you get with a political kerfuffle on a Friday in summer. Just as I was on the brink of nodding off, the event drew to a close. I accompanied a member of the health unit's Board into the Fort Sussex Mayor's office for a final debrief.

"Thank you for coming again, Doctor," said the Mayor. I was stunned to discover the man was so animated upon meeting him. I had dying patients less weathered and gaunt in appearance.

"It's my pleasure, Your Worship," I said. Obsequiousness was a necessary evil when dealing with politicians, at least until I could get them drunk.

"The press got a bit obnoxious there with all the accusations around lack of communication and waste. The City is actually very appreciative of the time and effort put in by health unit staff."

"In all honesty, Your Worship, I'm only concerned with public health. I leave the budget and political concerns to the Board." The press? That twit from the local paper is now 'the press'?

"Unfortunately, I have political enemies trying to make hay of this incident."

"Another reminder of why I don't belong in politics, Mr. Mayor." Enemies? In a town of 20,000? Was he serious? "And with that, Your Worship, I will excuse myself to enjoy what's left of a lovely Friday afternoon."

Two hours later, I got a call from one of the Managers at the Health Unit. "Hi Doc, you won't believe this."

"Why? What's going on?"

"The lab called. The positive *E. coli* culture? It was the wrong sample."

"You're shitting me. All that over a lab error?"

"It's crazy, I know. What do you want us to do?"

"Call everyone to give them the heads up. We get the repeat test back in an hour, so let's wait for that definitive result before we rescind the advisory. No sense having egg on our face twice over a lab screw-up."

What's that line by Shakespeare? *A tale told by an idiot, full of sound and fury...*

CHAPTER THIRTY-THREE

For Adults Only, Part II

DESPITE THE TESTY nature of their relationships, doctors and nurses share a real camaraderie when it comes to unglamorous, in-the-trenches work. I saw it most often in the ER, where the crowding, chaos, and cursing might indeed be reminiscent of a battlefield. Ironically, the other place I found it was in Public Health. True, much Public Health work is as remote from the front lines as it gets - meetings with politicians, anti-smoking campaigns, and so on - but it's unavoidable in the Sexual Health department. Genital herpes, fetishes, counseling for sex workers...there are no secrets and no shame in Sexual Health.

"I'm ready to puke," I announced behind the closed door of the nurses' workroom. "That guy might be the most revolting patient I've ever dealt with." At some point, I agreed to work the sexual health clinic as part of my duties in the Public Health job. No two ways about it, the decision was a mistake. If I was looking to escape maddening patient contact, sexual health offered no refuge whatsoever.

"Dr. Warsh!" said Andrea in mock horror. Andrea was a veteran sexual health nurse, and something of a kindred spirit in her cynicism. But she never failed to put the patients' needs first, something I admired greatly. She'd also forged relationships with some of the patients as close as any I'd seen in family practice. "I take it he still has the genital warts?"

"The guy doesn't have genital warts," I said. "His entire crotch is more wart than normal skin." No exaggeration. The man's penis looked not like a sexual organ, but rather a deep-fried pickle breaded in chopped cauliflower. "How in the hell does a man let himself get that bad? He'll be having his dick burned with acid every few weeks for *years* before that all clears up."

"We'll be right here with you to hear all about it," said Marla. Marla, the other sexual health nurse, was an odd fit for the service. A ringer for Snow White, her background was in mother/newborn nursing. Breastfeeding moms and newborn weigh-ins are as alien as it gets to the down-and-dirty world of sexual health. It was hard to hear Marla discuss anal sex and venereal disease while keeping a straight face.

"No way," I said. "I'm close to the end of my rope with these infested dicks."

"Well cheer up," said Marla, "your good friend is all undressed and ready for you!"

"Cinnamon's back again?" I said. "Didn't I just see her last week?"

"It's been *two* weeks, Dr. Warsh," said Marla. "She's a busy lady. We should applaud her for being so careful of her health."

I knocked as both Marla and I stepped into the exam room. Cinnamon was already lying on the table, feet in the stirrups. "We need to stop meeting like this, my dear," I said.

Cinnamon erupted in giggles. She was a pure joy to chat with, always bubbly and giddy, if only because she smoked weed in advance of her appointments. "I know," she said, "but I just need to make sure everything's okay down there. I have big weekend plans."

Cinnamon – that was her online avatar name - worked as an escort, and made a ton of money at it. I learned more from her about the economics and logistics of prostitution than I ever thought possible. It was fascinating, really. For example, her biggest expense? Exorbitant tips to hotel maids, both for repeat cleanings and hush money. Made complete sense, but who knew?

"Big plans? Or big *work* plans?"

More giggles. "I have ten clients booked. I need the cash for clothes, and I have expensive tastes, you know? I had to quit that factory job, too. It sucked and the pay was lousy."

"Have you spotted anything you're concerned about?"

"No." Cinnamon inspected her nether regions obsessively. "But I did have a mishap two weeks ago. I was on the road to meet a client, and got my period all of a sudden. I didn't have a tampon, and had to use a makeup sponge instead."

"Oh my. Did you--"

"Don't worry, I cleaned up afterwards with apple cider vinegar - I heard that works - and didn't see any other clients that week."

"Any *other* clients? Tell me you didn't--"

"There are ways to make it work."

I left it at that and performed the exam. As was always the case with her, everything was fine. "Well, Cinnamon, I'm probably at the point where I could pick your vagina out of a lineup. It's spotless as usual today. Marla will get your urine sample, and I'm sure we'll be seeing you soon."

"Of course you will," said Cinnamon with a flirtatious wave.

I headed back into the nurse's room, shaking my head.

"How was Cinnamon today?" asked Andrea.

"She and her vagina were a delight as always," I said. "Who have you got?"

"Some counseling around a possible sexually transmitted infection scare," said Andrea. "She's married, and is panicky about talking to her husband."

"Did the husband know about the affair? Or is she an IV drug user?"

"It's a little more complicated than that. She's...she's part of a fluid bonding circle."

"A what?"

"A fluid bonding circle. It's a group of people that commit to each other, and have open, unprotected sex."

"So they're like swingers?"

"She called it *polyamory*. With swingers, it's just sex. This is real, committed love with multiple partners. So long as they get regular testing and stay faithful to the circle, they stay in the circle."

"And somebody broke the circle?"

"Don't know all the details. The one who tested positive apparently lives in Chicago."

"Wait, they travel for this? So the patient is an everyday citizen, not like our usual crowd here?"

"She works at the library the next town over."

I fired a quick text to Kylea. **I'll be late getting home. Last patient will take a while. Story must be told in person.** "Okay, you can do the talking, Andrea. I don't know if I can keep a straight face."

We greeted the patient and I was struck by how normal she looked. No wild tattoos, no zany piercings, no rainbow hairdo. This was nobody who would be hanging out with a Cinnamon or a Mr. Cock-warts School of Wizardry that I'd seen earlier. She was just an ordinary civic employee with an extraordinary sex life, it would seem.

Andrea walked through the woman's story, making sure we had all the details straight. We took turns answering her questions. The patient hadn't tested positive to date. Assuming she wasn't already infected, it would be some time before she could put the scare behind her, given the latency period of the disease. After the nuts-and-bolts discussion, the woman fell into a fit of crying.

"What's wrong?" asked Andrea.

"It just...it just feels like my life is ruined," said the patient. "I love these men so much. Not just my husband."

"You can still love them," said Andrea. "You just have to take precautions, use protection, until you know for sure that you haven't contracted the virus."

"You...you can't understand. So much of who I am, so much of my life is centered around my sexuality, my vagina. The thought that I won't be able to do it anymore...it's awful!"

A life centered around her vagina...

Andrea adopted the extra-comforting tone we're all trained to use when breaking bad news. "You still have your vagina. And you'll be able to use that vagina in the same way, with those men that you love. You just need to be careful until you know it's safe to have sex without protection."

After the patient left, Andrea stayed surprisingly calm. I was mystified, given that she had just uttered the most absurd patient instructions I'd ever heard. We had a good chuckle about the episode.

"Can I go home now?" I asked.

"Yes! You are done," said Andrea.

"Awesome." I had my own 'fluid' to bond with...a nice stiff shot of tequila.

The Milk of Human Kindness

I WAS DEEP in hostile territory. I scanned the area in a desperate attempt to find a familiar face, a pair of eyes that wouldn't glare at me with suspicion, with venom. Nothing. Whatever horrors I was set to confront, I would be forced to confront them alone.

"Welcome, everyone, to the National Breastfeeding Coalition's annual Baby-Friendly Expo!"

The emcee waited for the applause to settle. "I have a quick housekeeping issue before we get started. Restrooms are located just across the exhibitor's hallway. With apologies to the one...no, two gentlemen attending, we are appropriating the men's restroom as well. The gentlemen are asked to please use the restroom in the Starbucks downstairs."

Fuck me. How in hell did I let myself get talked into this?

The province was forcing every health unit to get certified as "Baby Friendly", which was code for pushing breastfeeding as the default way to feed an infant. Maternity hospitals all over the country latched onto this (pardon the pun) "Good-Breastfeeding-Seal-of-Approval", but it was an unorthodox move for the government to mandate it. The Baby Friendly people weren't a recognized medical or nurses' association, nor were they a cadre of scientists.

I had a problem with it from the word go. I didn't disagree with the science behind the "breast is best" mantra, and I get that North America's love-hate relationship with the tit makes a lot of women uncomfortable nursing in public. But the Baby-Friendly program struck me as prescriptive and strict, even draconian. It treated bottle-feeding as the product of a Nefarious Corporate Conspiracy, which was at odds with everything I learned in medical school and residency. I'd heard the odd woman express shame around the decision to bottle-feed, suggesting the pendulum might have swung too far.

My concerns were "duly noted" but summarily dismissed by the Ministry of Health. You can't fight City Hall, as they say. I was at this conference to get some insight from health units that had been through the Baby-Friendly process, and put my misgivings to rest. Just go with an open mind, Frank. It can't be as bad as you think.

The keynote speaker was introduced. He was a Scandinavian breastfeeding guru, a globetrotting speaker with several books, books that, not coincidentally, we were invited to buy after his lecture. His talk opened with slides of a kangaroo and its joey, then an African mother nursing at work in the field. This...Swedish Chef was positively effusive about babies and breastfeeding, proclaiming that nothing could make a baby truly thrive, "except in the warmth of a mother's embrace."

He presented the many facets of evidence around nursing a baby: animal experiments, observational studies of tribal families, global breastfeeding statistics, and so on. Some of it applied to Public Health in North America, much of it didn't. Swedish Chef was a good speaker, but there was nothing in my eyes to cement the notion that babies were doomed, "except in the warmth of a mother's embrace."

Babies didn't need the trappings of modern medicine. They didn't need incubators or monitors. They needed nothing "except in the warmth of a mother's embrace."

It wasn't long before Swedish Chef had the crowd *enraptured*, joining him in hypnotic repetition, "except in the warmth of a mother's embrace."

I was in dismay. Hundreds of women, adult women, most of them veteran health professionals, **chanting** like they were attending Mass, "except in the warmth of mother's embrace." They erupted in applause when the talk was over, stampeding forward to meet Swedish Chef in person.

This wasn't a conference. It was an assembly for a cult.

I shied away from the madness for the next part of the morning, passing time in the exhibitor's room. I was amazed at the number of contraptions designed to help women perform a task they're supposed to do easily and naturally. Some of the devices looked more suited to the Tower of London torture chambers than a maternity ward. As I have a penis – though I couldn't be sure for how long - I kept my opinions to myself.

The session that brought me to the conference was right after lunch. It was a panel of managers from other health units relating their stories of implementing the Baby-Friendly guidelines. The question inevitably came up of how each health unit handled requests for information on bottle-feeding.

"When we have a woman at a prenatal class who asks about formula feeding," said the first nurse manager, "we'll take her aside to get to the heart of why she's asking. Sometimes the mom can't nurse with the medication she's taking, and that's understandable. Other times, though, we make sure the client understands what all her options are to support her breastfeeding."

Pull her aside for an interrogation? That seemed kind of...not nice.

"We don't keep that information on hand during our prenatal classes," said the second manager. "What we do is direct them to our website for directions on preparing formula. It's in the Food Safety section."

Seriously? Next to the information about what temperature to cook meat to? Or how to select a countertop cleaner? How was a pregnant woman supposed to find the information if she was looking for it on her own?

The panel continued as I mulled over how to phrase what I felt compelled to ask. *Enemy territory, Frank, watch your words closely.* It took five minutes, but I settled on what I thought was a milquetoast, roundabout way to word things.

"Thanks for calling on me," I said sheepishly. "One question: have you thought to ask new mothers about any problems they might be having in finding information on bottle feeding? We always worry about alienating nervous mothers."

The woman next to me raised an eyebrow. "Didn't you just open a can of worms," she said.

Why did I bother trying political correctness? I should have just come out and asked what I wanted: why are y'all being so fucking **mean** if a woman wants to bottle-feed?

Thankfully the panel was drawing to its time limit, so my verbal shellacking was short and sweet. One member of the planning committee, a woman who by appearances hadn't lactated since D-Day, took to the podium, waving her fist. "This is the thinking we have to put a stop to! It's time to stop promoting formula like it's an acceptable choice, and get society to raise children naturally!"

I avoided eye contact with anyone once the session ended, made a beeline for the parking lot, topped up my car with gas, and raced to the highway. I'd already learned everything I needed to. Did the Ministry shoving this program down our throats have any inkling of what these people were like? These zealots, these...Jehovah's Wet-nurses...were going to guide public policy?

I contacted my colleagues in other health units to describe what I witnessed, in measured but serious terms. The panel of managers, after all, put on a textbook display of groupthink, violently dismissing my naysaying without a whiff of open debate. The doctors at other health units were conscious of possible problems but didn't seem terribly worried. At the end of the day, they couldn't refuse what the Ministry demanded, given that the Ministry controlled the purse strings. I went so far as to offer Stavros my resignation if it would get the Ministry to back off, but the offer was turned down.

For the first time, I had real doubts about the culture, even the purpose of Public Health as an institution. There's no small conceit in telling mothers how to raise their babies, at least when there's no evidence of neglect. I was growing uncomfortable with all of it, but was surprisingly alone in my apprehension.

I needed the warmth of a mother's embrace.

CHAPTER THIRTY-FIVE

Hail to the Chief

NOT LONG AFTER the Baby Friendly conference the Public Health job was starting to leave a sour taste in my mouth, for reasons having nothing to do with breast milk. The culture bordered on sanctimonious, pontificating to the public on issues that were trivially related to the day-to-day work. Promote vaccines, sure. Fluoride in drinking water, absolutely. But violence in professional hockey? Farmer's markets selling wine? Were meetings and advocacy letters about this stuff a defensible use of time? Should doctors and nurses be telling society how to conduct its affairs, without obvious connections to the health of the population? I've always rolled my eyes at anti-"Nanny State" blarney on web sites or talk radio, but Public Health played the part of Goody Two Shoes too readily for my tastes.

The bigger problem was that once I wrapped up the projects I'd been working on in conjunction with my Master's degree, there wasn't much for me to do, apart from the sexual health clinic which I found increasingly nauseating. The truth is I was getting bored, a sad irony given that boredom with clinical medicine was my reason to explore Public Health in the first place.

Oddly enough, a major kerfuffle had erupted between the Ministry and the Board of Health regarding my role and hours. Saunders County, right in Adelaide's backyard, had been run and governed so incompetently, the Ministry seized control of its assets and dissolved its governing Board. The Ministry's long term solution was a shotgun marriage of sorts with Adelaide. Merged governance, merged budgets...almost certainly a bundle of bureaucratic and political headaches for all parties involved.

At the center of the plan was me. I would be the Medical Officer of Health covering both regions. It would mean many more hours in public health, a lot more time on my ass on the road, and a greatly expanded set of duties, independent of Stavros or whomever the CEO of the amalgamated health unit might be. To the Adelaide Board of Health, a group of appointed area politicians, my new duties and salary were first and foremost a big new line item on the budget. Without a guarantee of full funding from the Ministry, the Board considered the plan a non-starter.

I was in active practice when I started at Adelaide and this mess was still under the radar, so I didn't pay much attention to it at the time. After recovering from the surgery and nearing the end of the Master's program, however, my thoughts around my career evolved.

The Board remained flatly disinterested in bringing me on full-time, and reinforced it was not in the cards. I understood the Board's stance from the political-fiscal point of view, but the intensity of the opposition struck me as disrespectful, both to myself and the position of the province. Without hiring me on as the Ministry planned, Adelaide was unusually strident for a public health agency. The government continued to press the issue, culminating in a meeting of Board representatives with the Chief Medical Officer of Health, to be held in Toronto in time for winter. For reasons that elude me, I was asked to attend.

TORONTO IS A FINE city to visit so long as you can avoid the use of a car. Since the Board members and I had arrived by train, I had no complaints. I could grouse about the weather, though. It wasn't freeze-your-mucus-on-inhalation cold, but the wind was blowing with a bite.

I'd kept quiet for much of the train ride, still mystified that I was invited. The Board members - there were four of them, plus Stavros - spent a good part of the trip walking through their "strategy" for the meeting, whatever good it would do them. If the teleconferences were any indication, the Chief Medical Officer of Health and his Ministry of Health underlings rarely heeded the opinions of others. When two of the Board members threw back some drinks and mused about hitting a strip club, it didn't portend an overly successful meeting. Well, at least I'd get a story out of it.

We arrived an hour early for the meeting, and spent it killing time in the coffee shop on the ground floor of the Ministry building. Apart from some pleasant stone tile and inoffensive sculptures, the building was a tower of dull, dingy concrete, a Brutalist structure more suited to Mao's China than the heart of Canada's biggest downtown. The gloom continued through to the upstairs floors, marked by long, grey hallways and stained drop-ceiling tiles. Whatever the government could be accused of wasting money on, it sure as shit wasn't the architecture.

The warm fuzzies just kept on coming, as we fumbled with an intercom system linked to plexiglass security doors. This was the least welcoming place I'd ever been, combining the creepy silence of a funeral home with the poorly-lit ambience of a hospital basement. Once we finally figured out how to ring the doorbell, we were escorted past a maze of cubicles into a windowless, featureless conference room. Was this a meeting or a police interrogation?

Dr. All-Business, the Chief MOH, arrived in the room with an entourage. The Chief had three senior staffers, though after the exchange of greetings only one of them ever spoke. It reminded me of the 1980s *Newhart* show, with the lumberjack brothers Larry, Darryl, and Darryl (maybe this was Laura, Darla, and Darla?). That said, Dr. All-Business and the retinue greeted me with warmth and enthusiasm, then shook hands with the Board members so we could take our seats and begin.

Uh oh. The Ministry people thought I was the guest of honor. The Board most certainly did not. How in the hell was this going to resolve things? And what would I say if asked?

Dr. All-Business passed out an agenda. "I want to thank you for coming. As you can see, we are on a tight timeline, so I'd like to get started right away. Dr. Warsh has now completed his Master's degree, and therefore meets the requirements of a Medical Officer of Health under the law. We have sent the Adelaide County Board of Health multiple documents outlining our intentions and expectations with regards to the merger of the Adelaide and Saunders health units. It is the position of the Ministry that the Adelaide health unit needs to bring Dr. Warsh to full-time hours to comply with the plan."

I should have brought a flask of vodka.

The Chair was first to speak on behalf of the Board. The Chair made an odd first impression. She presented herself as an ultra-conservative schoolteacher, drab skirt and cardigan included. Once you got past that, though, she was self-effacing with a bone-dry sense of humor to boot. Not that it would matter at this meeting. Humor had no place inside these Ministry walls.

The Chair donned her reading glasses to complete the *Saturday Night Live* Church Lady look and read a prepared statement aloud. "The Adelaide County Board of Health is of the opinion that Dr. Warsh has been, and continues to be, our full time MOH regardless of his paid time commitment. He is on call any hour of the day, any day of the week. During his tenure, there has not been one public health crisis that got out of hand, nor one complaint with respect to his performance. This plan is of the Ministry's making, not ours nor Dr. Warsh's, and is ultimately the result of another health unit's performance failures. For Adelaide to hire Dr. Warsh full time, without a way to make up the difference in his salary, would constitute a financial hardship for our health unit, likely leading to front-line staff layoffs."

Dr. All-Business answered by rhyming off the list of duties expected of the MOH, independent of being the administrative CEO. "The duties we expect Dr. Warsh to serve, in our opinion, cannot be met in only one day a week, particularly once the health units merge." They were talking past each other. What word, I wondered, was being repeated often enough to make for a good drinking game?

Darla and Darla continue to scribble notes in unison, both staying silent.

The Vice-Chair of the Board, a longtime school trustee before running for town council, was more soft-spoken and motherly in manner than the Chair. "Well, I would just say that one size does not fit all," she said. That was insightful.

The Past Chair butted in. A roofer by trade, he was normally jolly and boisterous. Not so on this day. "We have lost hundreds, if not thousands of jobs in our County. There is no way we can pay a full-time doctor's salary with our current tax revenues. I don't like to make threats, but I will point out that the Health Minister is reachable by phone. The office won't return our calls to discuss this, but we will keep trying."

Did he just make a threat, then turn around and admit that the threat was hollow? So much for following through on a strategy.

"I assure you," said Dr. All-Business icily, "the Minister is in **full** support of the Ministry's position."

The New One chimed in. He was the youngest of the group, possibly younger than me, but already a veteran politician. "Dr. Warsh works at our local Community Health Centre. These are the neediest patients, and our region desperately needs doctors. We should not be forced to pull him out of serving our community that way."

Something about the entire scene was getting under my skin. It was like being a teenager, trapped at your parents' dinner party while they discussed *your* future with their friends. It was presumptive and more than a little patronizing. What would I say if they call on me to comment?

As if on cue, Laura spoke up. "I have to say, I feel very uncomfortable talking about Dr. Warsh while he's in the room. Can we ask you, Doctor, for your thoughts at this time?"

I've never been a good negotiator and have sold myself short repeatedly over the years. If I was going to make a play for a full-time job, this was the moment to do it. The Board's entire strategy was incumbent on me playing along with their wishes. I could blindside them, claim entitlement to a full-time job. It would piss the Board members off to no end, sure. But they're politicians, and that's politics. Why should I give a shit about their agendas?

But was it the right thing to do?

I'd been at the Community Health Centre for two years, albeit only part time. I was also the only doctor who had lasted there beyond a year. The CHC served the neediest of the needy, people so poor and damaged they simply could not get proper care in the busy family doctors' offices that looked after the mainstream public. Three doctors had been recruited just over a year prior - all young, talented "franchise players" the Centre could have built a team around - but all three of them left town for family reasons. I was the closest thing to a full-time doctor they had, and to leave the patients behind for my own ambitions didn't feel right.

Fuck.

Deep breath. "I have to confess this is rather surreal for me, and humbling. I have an obvious conflict of interest, so I recognize that I need to be careful. I would *like* to work in public health full time, and see myself as able to do much more than I've been doing...but I'm comfortable continuing my work at the CHC for now. I would hate to think that my increased presence would come at the expense of front-line staff or damage my working relationships with Stavros and the Board."

"If the sticking point is funding," said Laura, "perhaps we can work out a plan to help phase this in over a few years."

The Chair eyed Stavros, then her fellow Board members. "That is definitely something we can work on going forward."

The meeting ended soon thereafter and we made our way to the train ride home. We rode in the VIP car, and the Board members took advantage of access to free booze. I kept to myself, half-assedly reading, drifting in and out of a nap.

"I think that went well," said the Chair. "You have to work these things out in person, not in a letter."

"Look," said the New One, "it'll take months to work out a plan that we're all happy with. We've got an election coming up, maybe there's a new government...who knows what will happen or be expected from there?" The other Board members murmured in agreement, then drank themselves into giggle fits.

So *that* was the plan? Run out the clock if possible, stretch things over years if need be? They didn't want me as an MOH. They wanted me as a pet, a lapdog to put out fires and save their budget. Regardless of how well we got along, they didn't respect me, my role, my credentials, or the hell I'd been through. I was supposed to let a bunch of politicians decide my career? My future?

Not long thereafter I very nearly quit for the sake of my pride, but was talked into tabling my resignation by Stavros, at least until I could be presented with a plan for transition to full-time. Said transition plan never materialized. I was given a list of vague ideas for how things might work in the future. It was back-of-a-napkin brainstorming and little else. I had the unavoidable impression I was being played for a fool. I was outraged at the disrespect, and very, very hurt.

Then came the letter from the College.

Dear Dr. Warsh,

We acknowledge receipt of a copy of your Master's in Public Health pursuant to your application for a Change in Scope of Practice...The...Committee has reviewed your file, including the reports from your supervisor, and has determined that you now require a Practice Assessment before the College can sign off on your change in scope...

...Enclosed you will find the 10-page Inventory of Professional Activities to complete, which asks you to describe in detail your achievements in the various domains of work in Public Health. Please complete and submit it along with the following documents: an updated curriculum vitae; your academic transcript; the health unit's strategic plan and organizational chart; and the region's Health Status Report. These documents will aid the Committee in identifying an appropriate Assessor...We ask that the documentation be submitted to the College by [8 days from the date of this letter]...

...Although this Assessment is being forced upon you, we hope you will see it as an opportunity to demonstrate your skills and knowledge base...a learning exercise to identify gaps in your knowledge, and guide you in further training opportunities...

...Pursuant to College policy, you will be invoiced the full cost of the Assessment fee...

Sincerely,

...College of Physicians and Surgeons of Ontario...

What. The. Fuck.

CHAPTER THIRTY-SIX

The Right Party in Power

DR. KUMBAYA AND Nurse Platitude were shoulder to shoulder, beaming like ex-high school sweethearts falling into one another's arms after fifty years. Why did so many of these conferences start with a love-in? It's a health care meeting, not Mass.

"I kind of feel like we're Bert and Nan Bobbsey standing up here," said Dr. Kumbaya. Who? "I can't count how many years I've been saying this meeting of Public Health and Community Health Centre delegates was like unrequited love. I never thought this day would come, and I'm still in disbelief. It really is like a marriage made in heaven."

"Oh, I couldn't agree more," said Nurse Platitude. "And to get these two groups together, at such an important time for our health care system, when we really have so many synergies to be found in partnering to address the determinants of health. There really are no two groups more dedicated to community building and improving the lives of our neediest members of society."

Three minutes in, and I already wanted to stab myself in the eye. I should have backed out of this conference. Or skipped out for coffee, or gone to an indoor driving range, or brought my bottle of expired Percocet with me. Pop a pill each time someone spouts a buzzword...surely that would end my pain.

"...and the explosion of ideas," droned Nurse Platitude, "harnessing the passion of such dedicated front-line professionals...through our community-focused partnerships, and active engagement with stakeholders..."

I remember when I couldn't be bothered to think up a topic for my Grade 8 public speaking contest. No reason, just pure, indefensible laziness. When it was my turn to speak, I ad-libbed a speech that was literally about nothing - the word, the philosophical challenge of defining it - profound stuff from a 13 year-old, if I'd put in a lick of effort. The class voted me second place, a terrific outcome all things considered. To this day I wonder if I could've taken first place, had I gathered some blank index cards to use as props. I share this rather pointless anecdote to illustrate a point: that grade 8 speech was more entertaining, and had measurably more substance, than the gibberish I was hearing at this conference.

I *should* have been speaking at, never mind simply attending a meeting like this. My work straddled both the Community Health Centre and Public Health worlds, and I had unique insights into what each institution can and can't do well. Then again, I doubted I'd be straddling both worlds much longer.

The letter from the College put me in a foul mood about everything related to Public Health, a foul mood I struggled to contain. I swore constantly at work, and lost focus all too easily in the exam room with a patient. I sent the College the paperwork it demanded - like *Star Trek*'s Borg, resistance is futile - but refused to let their assessment go further until I had a sense of my future at the health unit.

So here I was, a poster child for the two health institutions working collectively, ready to shit on the day's proceedings. I needed to shake this attitude, and quickly, or I'd risk making an ass of myself.

I zoned out for the remainder of the welcome address and pored over my choices for the breakout sessions. I've always made a point of looking for offbeat seminars at conferences. Topics like immunizations and child nutrition are old hat, and I'm inundated with e-mails around the latest evidence anyways.

I picked a session on Aboriginal healing practices since I knew nothing about them, and had relatively few indigenous patients in private practice. The presentation started out rather dull. Hard to believe that people still read directly off PowerPoint slides in this day and age, but they do. I was thinking it might be time to jump ship when the presenters started passing artifacts around, telling folk tales and describing traditional healing rites. That livened up the session a great deal.

Then the speakers lit up sweetgrass and taught us how to breathe in the smoke. At a public health conference. I took glee in the awkward silence around the room. Nobody would **dare** point out the irony of community health nurses smoking grass in an enclosed room, for fear of political incorrectness. In fact, fuck political incorrectness...was this even legal?

After lunch and a trip to the liquor store with my CHC coworkers, it was time for a panel discussion around advocacy and politics. It was a lively chat, with a panel comprised of prominent physician-advocates and a former provincial cabinet Minister, Ms. Ornery. Things got heated for a moment between one of the advocates, Dr. TEDtalk, and the Honorable Ms. Ornery. Dr. TEDtalk laid out a vision for leveraging social media into some vague public purpose. Ms. Ornery pooh-poohed it out of the gate.

"This is just pie-in-the-sky," said Ms. Ornery. "It takes months, even years of hard work to get a government to change a policy. You need to mobilize supporters, apply constant pressure, and be willing to make deals.

"Moreover, you need to support the party that can get into power and implement what you're looking to change. I mean, we're what, 3-6 weeks away from an election? What are the polls saying? The people of Ontario might well elect a right-wing government that isn't interested in Public Health or solving poverty. Is that what you want? No. So get out the word to keep the right party in power."

The room *erupted* in applause.

Wow. Partisan politics is a ubiquitous topic of conversation around the office and kitchen table, and there's nothing wrong with that. But here was a gathering of ostensibly public servants, conferring in their capacities *as* public servants, showing open support for one political party over another. It was a fucking disgrace, crossing a line that should never be crossed. I can only imagine what the press would report if witness to this spectacle. It would've been sheer pleasure, mind you, to see someone call this out for what it was.

And that was it for me. The cartoon angel and the cartoon devil on my shoulders nodded in disgusted agreement, and my inner voice snapped. Fuck this. Fuck all of this. I spent all those nights neglecting myself, neglecting my family, stressing myself to the bone with studies, holding down two jobs...all for what? To burn dick warts off sleazeballs? To sign off on self-righteous letters? To chastise women for choosing not to breastfeed? To shill for a political party? To be a lapdog for self-aggrandizing politicians? To take it up the ass from the College on my own dime, and call it an "opportunity"?

Fuck all of this, and fuck all of them.

My blood was still boiling an hour later during the coffee and snack break. The Medical Officer of Health from another region, a veteran family doc taking the same path to Public Health that I did, bumped into me in line for a cookie. He was an affable, humble guy, and I forced myself to take a few breaths before greeting him.

"Hi," I said, shaking his hand. "You got roped into this as well?"

"Still getting my bearings around this whole Public Health world," he said. "And being back at school after thirty years, learning by computer...it's all new to me."

"Oh I know. I'm glad it's behind me, though it looks like it was nothing but a big waste of my time. You weren't there at the last regional meeting when I talked about this to the rest of the group. I was close to resigning from the health unit then, now I'm pretty set on leaving before the summer is out."

"I'm disappointed to hear that! And after all the work you've put it. Can I ask what happened?"

"I'm just getting fed up with all of it, you know? I've been doing nothing of interest at the health unit, I'm tired of the politics, and the College keeps moving the goalposts on me. Who needs the stress?"

The sanctimonious culture, the tedium of the work, the high-handed harassment of the College...I had any number of reasons to quit the health unit. It was Kylea that finally held up the mirror, asking why I was still bothering. I could summon no good answer for her. Time to cut my losses and move on.

I met with the Board leadership, asking that they either hire me on as per the Ministry's edict or cut me loose. I suspect the request came across as blackmail, and I'm honestly not sure why I did it. I resigned before the Board could even respond, cleaned out my office like a thief in the night, and ran out the clock until my successor was found a few months later.

I bumped up my commitment to the CHC to four days a week, the closest I could get to working full-time with patients. Three years after my own crisis, I still struggled to provide care as the week wore on. And however noble it was to tend to the poor and the disabled, the patients of a Community Health Centre are not the most straightforward folks to care for.

CHAPTER THIRTY-SEVEN

Katelyn

IT WAS JUST my second week at the CHC. The first week didn't entail much in the way of patient care, just a whole lot of orientation readings, forms, and futzing with the medical record software. I tried to convince the management team to let me fumble my way through things on the go, earning the money I was paid, but the CHC is a government shop. Process matters, or so I was told.

It's just as well I didn't start in the deep end, seeing patients from the word go. I was only working a few half-days each week for starters. My blood pressure was coming down and the rest had been a help, but I had no idea if or how long I'd last in patient care.

Nurse NewAge was bringing in my first patient. That gave me all the time I needed to squint at the computer screen and get a sense of where the patient was coming from. One more luxury of the CHC model of care: comprehensive intake interviews, covering anything and everything you'd ever need to know.

I was to see Katelyn, a 25-year old woman who needed a doctor for her breathing and her nerves. Katelyn worked part-time at a thrift store...lived with her boyfriend...only used asthma puffers once in a while...appendix and hernia surgery...single miscarriage...smokes cigarettes and marijuana, no other drugs...nothing exciting so far...

My God.

I reached Katelyn's family and social history, transcribed to the chart verbatim. She was the product of an unwanted pregnancy and reminded of it routinely by her mother. Katelyn's biological father had custody of her on regular weekends during her childhood, weekends on which he relentlessly molested and raped her. This went on for years before Katelyn finally broke down one day and told an adult. She endured the legal system and everything it entailed before her attacker was finally convicted and imprisoned.

It's rare that I'm a total loss for words as I walk into an exam room. I'm so accustomed to meeting new patients, I can figure out how formal or casual I need to be within seconds and adjust my banter accordingly. As I got to know someone, things would naturally change, but my instincts were usually spot-on. Not so with Katelyn.

I stepped in the room unsure of how to introduce myself. Katelyn was petite, thin, fair but not pale, and quite pretty. She had more tattoos than I would expect to see on a young woman, even nowadays, with more body art evident beneath her fraying clothes. She was trembling, likely on the brink of panic or tears every waking moment.

She was rejected by her mother and abused by her father in the most horrific way fathomable. How could it happen? A stepfather, a foster parent, an uncle, a neighbor...while just the thought of it disgusts me, I doubt it would surprise me. But a man's own daughter?

I assumed, rightly or wrongly, that Katelyn avoided contact with male authority figures, so I opted not to reach for a handshake. "Hi, I'm Dr. Warsh," I said. I hunted for something comforting or intelligent to say, still drawing a blank. "Look, I...I read the notes from the history you gave to my nurse at your intake. I won't make you go through your life story again. It's...it's honestly the most awful thing I've heard since starting practice."

A few seconds of silence ticked by. I hope she grasped that I wouldn't just force-feed her a pill. "You told the nurse a few things you needed to see a doctor for. Why don't we start with whatever symptoms are bugging you?"

She started with her breathing. Physical symptoms are a safe starting point. I asked all the routine questions, none of which yielded a worrisome answer. She allowed me to perform a cursory exam without signs of anxiety. I was probably overdoing it with the kid-gloves treatment, but the last thing I wanted was to chase her away. If she'd gone through the trouble of registering with the CHC, she either avoided primary care or had a hard time finding it. My goal was to get her in with either of our social workers. Both had specialized training in helping victims of trauma.

We finished up with her breathing, which sounded more like mild panic brought on by obnoxious customers at the thrift store. I renewed her puffer and asked about her nerves.

"I don't know if I'm bipolar or just a freak," she said. "I can snap and start crying at the drop of a hat. Some days my boyfriend can't handle me, and I'll just curl up in bed and cry. I'll smoke up and it'll settle down a bit, but the next morning it's the same. Then I'll be at work, things will be okay, and a customer will start haggling me over a price, and that's it. I get these vicious migraines that don't go away, I start throwing up and have to leave, taking a sick day. The store owner says I'm on the verge of being let go, but I can't go back on welfare. I use them for pills and stuff, but I can't live on that."

"Does your boyfriend work?" I said.

"He's apprenticing as an artist. He makes a little money doing odd jobs and keeping the studio clean. Not enough for us to live on." She broke down in tears.

My instincts told me to reach out and hug her. Then my experience kicked in. Was I just projecting my fatherhood to Chloe onto her? She was a stranger, and I reminded myself of what caused her symptoms to begin with. There was a risk of harm, even in the innocuous act of a hug. My rational side won the day as I reached to hand her the Kleenex box. I just sat, waiting in silence. She calmed down a moment later.

"This the kind of thing that happens at the store?" I said.

"Sometimes. Sometimes it's just the migraine," she said.

"You've got a lot going on. And again, I can't imagine the stress you've grown up with, or what you deal with each day. I've got a good idea of where we can go to help treat your symptoms, but I'm a terrible therapist." She grinned at that one while I shrugged my shoulders. It's the truth. "With your permission, I'd like to see if I can get one of the social workers in right now."

Katelyn nodded as a show of consent and I darted around the corner. Only one of the social workers was in, and she was busy with a client for the next hour. Shit.

"Katelyn, only one of our social workers is here today, and she's with a client for the next hour or longer. Did you want to follow me to the front desk and we'll book you an appointment for later this week?" We set something up with the social worker for two days later, plus a follow-up with me after a week.

Katelyn never showed up for the social worker and cancelled her follow-up appointment with me. When we tried to reach her by phone, her number wasn't in service. Shit.

CHAPTER THIRTY-EIGHT

Citizens and Denizens

MY FIRST FEW weeks weren't a fluke. Nurse NewAge took *forever* getting my patients into a room. I get that she prided herself on staying "mindful" every waking moment, but the CHC was already hopelessly below its performance targets. Would it be all that "mindless" to pick up the pace? Maybe sneaking some gluten into her tea would help. Besides, it was only Weed Man. It's not like there was any secret as to what he was seeing me for.

Weed Man wanted narcotic painkillers. He used to get them regularly, from me no less. That was before his social worker found him face down in a mound of crushed, half-snorted pills. Since then, he and I had danced the same dance every two to three weeks: he pleads that he's in chronic pain, I remind him of the damning incident, he denies his worker's credibility, I still say no, and life goes on.

Why this scene repeated itself with painful regularity escaped me. Weed Man had complex mental illness, so I suppose either his disease or his medication could be responsible for frying his memory. Then again, he *did* have a legitimate injury, suffered on a long-ago night of drinking. He might have been gambling that I'd cave one day and give him back the damn pills.

Or it was the weed killing his brain cells. Weed Man smoked *a lot* of it. Some days he'd smoke up minutes before arriving for his appointment, stinking up the exam room. If, on a given day, he didn't shave or brush his graying mane, he looked an awful lot like Moses returned from the heights of Sinai, minus the rugged manliness of Charlton Heston in *The Ten Commandments*.

"And how are you doing today?" I said. "Any change with the last dose adjustment?" I'd tried every non-addictive medication under the sun with Weed Man. We were tinkering with Lyrica this particular month.

"No, man. Just made me feel too sleepy," said Weed Man. He murmured when he spoke. "I just stopped it."

"Did you want to try one of the other pills I prescribed?"

"I just don't understand why we can't go back on the Percocets. I'm getting my medications delivered daily. There's no way I could abuse them."

Here we go again. There's no way you'll abuse them because there's no way I'll prescribe them. "We've been through this over and over again. I don't think you're safe to take these medications. You were found--"

"There you go, trusting some bitch who doesn't even like me. She's had it in for me since the day she became my caseworker. Why you're going to trust her when things were working fine--"

"Things weren't working fine. That's why I stopped prescribing the Oxys."

"Okay, you don't need to get rude. You're supposed to be a doctor, to help me, not get up in my face." Weed Man's voice grew louder. "Fuck, it's not like I'm threatening you. You don't have to be an asshole."

He was escalating. Weed Man had never threatened violence, but if worked up he frightened some of the other staff. I stood to open the door, trying to be firm but calm. "That's enough. I'm not giving you the narcotics. Stop asking for them. You're going to have to leave now. If you keep swearing at me, we won't allow you back."

"Fine, I'm fucking leaving." He rose and smacked the door on his way out. "You'll listen to some bitch you've never met, telling you bullshit, instead of your patient. Real fucking nice."

I'd seen Weed Man leave in a huff before, but this was the first time I could label his demeanor *menacing*. There was disquiet among the nurses and front desk staff as he stormed out. I wrote a detailed record on the incident, making a mental note to let the Management team know what went down.

Some days later I was stapling paperwork at the front desk when I spied Weed Man on the security camera. The CHC had a secondary waiting area out of view from the front desk, monitored by security cam only. Weed Man made a short call on our courtesy phone, stood up and started...dancing?

No doubt about it, the man was dancing to some song in his head. He reached into his pocket to produce what looked like a cigar, though Weed Man used it as a...make-believe mic? After another thirty seconds of the onscreen performance, he strolled right past the front desk, waving the cigar like a Marx brother.

I shook my head at his remarkable change in temperament. "You know," I said half-joking, "you can't smoke that in here."

"Can't smoke it yet anyways," he said. "Haven't put in the weed!"

WEED MAN WAS the prototypical Community Health Centre patient: poor and struggling with mental health or addiction, very often both. The classic medical model of care - patient describes their symptoms, doctor diagnoses and prescribes treatment, patient gets better - is nearly useless to these folks. Their problems are so deep-seated, so all-encompassing of their lives, only a team can look after them effectively.

It took some time, but the CHC eventually put together a damn fine team of nurses, nurse practitioners, doctors, and social workers. Nurse NewAge didn't last, but her successors were a delight to work with, and I made fast friends with just about everyone. It created a real family atmosphere among the CHC staff, and it was a fun place to work once the team found its groove.

Hang on...working with mental illness and addictions can be fun? Bullshit, you say.

Okay, I'll concede that people with intractable mental health problems are more challenging than fun to care for. And they often don't get better, which can eat away at your sense of accomplishment, even your sense of value to society as a doctor or nurse. It's why CHC work isn't for the faint of heart, and why so many practitioners - doctors, nurses, social workers - burn out in the job after a time.

But here's the thing: for all the misery that surrounds these folks, there's an awful lot of black humor in their lives and social circles. As with the ER and the Medicine wards, sometimes being able to laugh is the only way to make it through the day. In the inner-city atmosphere of a CHC, you look to the Denizens for comedy.

When you meet a patient at a Community Health Centre, the stuff that might seem important to a doctor - age, diagnosis, medications, allergies - isn't. There is one, and only one thing you need to know about the person across from you in the exam room, one question that will inform every doctor-patient encounter: Citizen or Denizen?

Citizens thrive on being productive, until such time as they can't because of illness or frailty. Denizens thrive on being unproductive, until such time as they can't because they don't qualify for disability. Citizens respond to treatment, or stop treatment because of side effects. Denizens don't respond to treatment, unless the treatment is addictive, in which case they can't get enough of it. Citizens abhor the thought of accessing the welfare system. Denizens know welfare inside and out. Citizens recognize that children are a blessing, but a blessing that demands incalculable hours of work and dedication. Denizens can't have enough kids, because it's the daycares and schools that raise children while they whittle away the hours on an X-Box from the pawn shop.

It's not that citizens are rich and denizens are poor. It's that the denizens have neither pride nor shame. None. Why save for a 20" TV when Rent-A-Center will hook you up with one twice as big *and* throw in a PlayStation? Why buy a phone when a doctor's note gets you one for free? Thinking of quitting school in grade 11? Eh, the girlfriend's cheque is enough to cover rent and smokes.

Denizens are drawn to the one-stop shopping of a CHC like a free membership to a spa. Get your pills renewed, your forms filled out, your ID replaced, and toss back a complimentary cup of coffee while making free calls in the waiting room. Step into the bathroom, and stock up on free tampons and condoms. If only they didn't put the toilet paper in a locked case...well, you can't win 'em all.

A citizen sees a doctor to get better. A denizen sees a doctor to get what he or she can. I met a good number of citizen patients in my four and a half years at the CHC. I met a *great* number of denizens in that time.

These are their stories.

IT WAS MID-MORNING on a lovely autumn day, and I had a last-minute cancellation. I was suffering with a grumbling headache that was unlikely to resolve without coffee. Trish, our office administrator, normally brewed a pot of Folger's or Maxwell House to start the morning, but she was late in arriving. Once upon a time I could make a pot of coffee, but once Kylea discovered the convenience of coffee pods, I couldn't remember the proper scoop-to-cup ratio anymore.

Trish was the last human being I would expect to see working in a medical clinic. Though happily married, she showed up to work up as the textbook definition of a cougar: hazardous heels, animal prints head to toe, and a skirt leaving all too little to the imagination. Not that your imagination mattered around Trish, because her stories swept away any mystery as to how she made use of her leisure time. Trish worked at a sex store before entering the less ribald world of health administration, and was versed in more techniques and paraphernalia than even I knew were out there. Her reaction to the *Fifty Shades* books? "Pfft...that's it?"

"Trish, my dear," I said, "did you happen to throw on the coffee when you came in?"

"Sorry," she said. "I can run to Tim's if you'd like." Tim Horton's, the coffee shop as important to Canadians as hockey and complaining about the weather.

"Don't worry about it. I have a cancellation and can use the walk."

I left through the CHC's front door. I gave a brief wave to Nearly-Homeless Ned, pacing as always in front of the clinic, cigarette in hand. We attended to Ned's health needs whenever he asked, but he didn't take well to unsolicited help.

Past Ned was a three-block stroll to Tim Horton's. This part of Fort Sussex, the west end of its main street, was an obstacle course of cigarette butts, potholes, and dog shit. The streetscape, if you can call it that, was a mix of empty storefronts, boarded-up windows, and people on route to, or returning from, their daily trip to the methadone clinic. One of the methadone clients fired a snot-rocket at my feet, and another belched as thanks for holding the door open at Tim's.

The town was in dire need of a drone strike.

Upon my return, coffee in hand, I was pulled aside by Vicki, the medical secretary at the CHC. Vicki split her time between the CHC and the local walk-in clinic. She was gruff, tough, and put up with no guff. You *need* a rock-solid backbone to work in either setting as a secretary. At a walk-in clinic, you face a deluge of patients demanding fast service, with a tendency to bitch and yell when they don't get what they want. You can get some of that at a CHC too. More often, though, it's not the number of people through the door so much as the patients not understanding why they could or couldn't see someone immediately on request.

"Dr. Warsh," said Vicki, "Methadone Marcus came in for his B12 injection, but wonders if he can see you briefly. I told him I would ask you, but I can book him in--"

"That's fine," I said. "I have the time and Marcus is usually quick."

I fetched Marcus from the waiting room. He was squat and moped instead of walking upright. He arrived with his girlfriend, looking frazzled and strung out as ever, perhaps due to lingering pain from her myriad tattoos of Boston Celtics logos. She had a full set of teeth, a surprise since she looked much more the addict than Marcus, and methadone rots the teeth more than Jolly Ranchers.

"How can I help you, Marcus?" I said.

"I'd like to see someone about getting my versectomy undone," he said.

"Your vasectomy? How long ago was it done?"

"My ex-wife made me get it done years ago, but we're thinking about having a baby."

"It just doesn't seem fair," said Bos-Tats, "that we can't have a kid because his ex was such a bitch. Did you hear why they split?"

"I didn't know you were ever married, Marcus," I said.

"Well," said Marcus, "I was let out of the jail early this one day in January, right? I get to the house and the girls are playing in the garage without their jackets on. I say, 'what's going on? Why no coats?'. They say, 'Mommy has a friend over.' So I go in the house and she's in bed with some guy. I didn't want nothing to do with her after that."

"Do you get visits with the kids?" I said.

"Yeah, but I couldn't get custody with the criminal background."

Right. "Okay, well, I can refer you to a specialist for the procedure. You know there's a cost, though, right?"

"It's not on OHIP?" said Bos-Tats. OHIP, or Ontario Health Insurance Plan, is Ontario's tax-funded medical insurance.

"We can save," said Marcus. "What is it, a few hundred bucks?"

"More like a few thousand," I said, "and it doesn't always work."

"Well, I guess if we start saving now..." said Marcus. "Thanks, Doc. I'll get out of your hair."

As they walked down the hall from the exam room, I overheard Bos-Tats ranting away. "We should go after that bitch for the money, after the house..."

I chuckled. Marcus was probably done having kids.

ROCKSTAR RICK! OKAY, he wasn't really a rock star, he just looked like one. Not an active, globetrotting rock star, mind you, nor a still-cool, cigarette-dangling Keith Richards rock star. No, Rick looked like a burned-out, washed-up rock star. He had a salt-and-pepper ponytail on a receding head of hair, stretch marks on his belly to complement the track marks on his arms, and impressive man-boobs thanks to years of heavy drinking.

Rick was in with his girlfriend to follow up on blood tests I'd sent him for. She had her own issues, but better someone to look out for him than no one.

"Okay Doc," said Rick, "let's have it. How bad was the bloodwork?"

"I've seen worse," I said, "but it's far from ideal. Your liver's in bad shape. That could be from the years of drinking, the Hepatitis C, or both. An ultrasound might help tease it out. Are you still drinking?"

"I'll have the odd drink now and then."

First year med school lesson: always clarify a vague answer from a patient, especially if it's about drinking or drugs. "What's now and then? Once a month? Once a week?"

"I guess a few days a week."

"So two days? Three? Four?"

"Be honest with him," said the girlfriend.

"Probably closer to four, maybe five," said Rick. "Some weeks I'll drink six days."

"Now how *many* is the odd drink?" I asked.

"Two or three."

"Two or three shots? Beers?"

"Mixed drinks. Rye and Coke, mostly." Another Canadian institution.

"And at least a beer," said the girlfriend.

"Rick," I said, "given your blood test results, I think we probably need to talk about you cutting down on your drinking."

"Done," said Rick.

"Done what?"

"I'm done drinking."

"You should probably start by cutting back a little. I don't want to see you--"

"Whatever you say, Doc."

Rick left, mumbling something about turning over a new leaf and taking control of his health. The girlfriend and I made eye contact, both of us skeptical of Rick's level of commitment.

Three days later, I got stacks of reports on Rick from the local ER. Delirium, hallucinations, dehydration...admitted for alcohol withdrawal? Seriously? The one time a patient takes my advice...

IT WAS MY second appointment with Jailhouse Jake. The first appointment was months prior, before his last stint in custody for violating something or other...it was honestly hard to keep track. It wasn't easy taking a history from Jake. His speech was preposterously rapid, like playing a vinyl LP recorded at 33 rpms on a turntable cranked up to 45. He probably stood to benefit from ADHD medication, but drug problems are what landed him in detention in the first place.

"What can I do for you, Jake?" I said.

"It's weird," said Jake, "because I didn't have this problem in jail, but my bowels are really, really loose, to the point where sometimes I've even been incontinent, which is really terrible, especially since I've got a new girlfriend, but I can't really see her if I might soil myself, unless--"

"Had you have had this problem before?"

"They told me I had Irritable Bowel, but a really bad case, which I don't really get because it's a serious problem, and even though I didn't have the symptoms when I was in jail, I tried to figure out what foods might cause it, or if it's an allergy, but--"

"Did you figure out what foods might bother you?"

"Not really, but as I said, the symptoms weren't there when I was in jail, and I don't think I ate anything different when I was in jail, except that the food in jail is shitty, but it's not like I can afford a lot to eat with what I get now on my cheque, but it isn't dairy, or gluten, or--"

"Sorry, I'm just trying to figure this out. So you're having very loose bowel movements since being out of jail, to the point of incontinence. But you had the same problem before jail as well?"

"Yeah, and I went through all these tests, but they just said it was Irritable Bowel, but I don't understand why if that's true that I wasn't bothered in jail, because now it's so bad I need to wear adult diapers, so--"

"Okay, okay, I get it. We'll do some blood tests, and I'll give you a kit to make sure you didn't pick up a parasite in something you ate. Once those are back, we'll see what I can prescribe to help you out." Like perhaps going back to selling drugs and getting caught. Some folks just aren't cut out for life on the outside.

"FRANK," SAID BILLY with a shit-eating grin. "I triaged this one straight to you." Billy was the CHC's homegrown Nurse Practitioner. He was a seasoned ER nurse before the grind and the shift work convinced him to go back to school. Fearless and spunky, Billy was my protégé at the CHC while he completed his qualifications, and still came to me for advice. Unlike the patients, he actually followed it most of the time.

"And what honor have you bestowed upon me?" I said.

"It's Hottie Heidi. She's got a sore bum."

Whatever my thoughts on religion, I'm a believer in karma. My entire life I've had a thing for asses, whether it be admiration of my own butt when I stayed in shape, micromanagement of my diet to produce a perfect poop, or ogling the backsides of women in yoga pants. It was karma, then, that all the patients with anal complaints would fall under my care.

"She has pain in the ass, you say?"

"Ha, ha. Yes. I'm not good with butts, and I've got some babies in my schedule that might take extra time. And Jumpsuit Jill is pregnant again, coming in for her checkup."

"Pregnant again?!? What's that, her third in as many years?

"It's her fourth."

"Jesus...put the dick down, Jill."

I escorted Heidi to the exam room. She was a slight thing, but warm and bright-eyed. A one-time small-time model, she'd struggled with alcohol and drugs for years. Just when she put part of her life together, she'd pick the wrong roommate and fall right off the wagon.

"How are you, Heidi?" I said.

"I'm okay," said Heidi. "I just have this bad pain around my hole."

"When do you notice it?"

"Mostly during sex. Sometimes when I go to the toilet."

I learned not to bother beating around the bush with CHC patients. "Do you get the pain when you have vaginal sex, or anal sex?"

"Oh, anal."

Of course. What would ever lead me to believe that a sore anus might be a cue to skip the anal intercourse? I motioned for Heidi to climb on the exam table, so I could have a look. Sure enough, she had an angry hemorrhoid right at 4 o'clock.

"Well, Heidi," I said, "you've got a pretty big hemorrhoid. I'll give you an ointment to help shrink it down, but you need to give the area a rest."

"Can I use lube? I need to have sex...a lot."

"You can have sex if it's not uncomfortable. Just please ask your boyfriend to try it the old-fashioned way."

Things you never picture yourself saying when you start off in med school.

ONE OF THE nurses left a gift on my desk. It was a patient application, reading like the world's least enticing personal ad:

I'm 6 feet and 150ish pounds. I smokes cigs and pot to stay recreational. I have fake HPV-- lots of small cysts on genatals and penis junk. Also crabs lice and body lice. I need a doctor to perscribe medical pot.

JAILHOUSE JAKE'S BACK! Well, sort of. He showed up to make sure his medications were up to date. He was headed back into custody to serve out a short sentence. Better to get it over with than prolong the fight and risk jail through the holidays, no?

"Good day, Jake," I said. "I'm not sure I understood what you told the nurse. We just renewed your prescriptions last month."

"I know you did," said Jake, "but I was hoping you could write a list of what I'm on so there are no mix-ups, even though they won't give me any of the pills that have street value like the Valium I sometimes take for sleep when I can sleep, and I was also hoping I could get a prescription for a special soap to help with my underarm rash problem, since it'll be covered for me while I'm in jail, but only if you write it on a prescription, at least that's what--"

"We already prescribed a lotion for that. It takes a few weeks to work, but it should work."

"I know it will, because I already itch less at night, but you can also prescribe me a soap that works against it, because the jail will cover it as long as it's on a paper from my doctor, even though it isn't covered by my drug card from welfare, which covers most of the pills, except for--"

"Wait...your medication coverage is better in jail than on welfare?"

"I think so, or I really don't know, since I'm not on any really fancy medication, and I suppose it would be different if I were taking something addictive, but they told me they will cover the soap, which is good because my armpits are still itching even with that lotion..."

Wow, he could look forward to his bowels *and* his skin improving. Jake needed to get off welfare ASAP, and go back to failing at crime full-time.

WEED MAN WORRIED he might have an STD. "Doc, when I had sex last time, my come was green." Charming.

His tests all came back negative, leaving me without a clear diagnosis. Can semen go green from smoking too much weed?

I NEVER KNEW what to make of Angry Abby. One of the CHC social workers described her as a textbook example of "failure to launch". She had no history of abuse but grew up with disabilities that made school and gainful employment non-starters for her.

Abby badly wanted to get pregnant but hadn't been able to conceive in the two years I'd been seeing her. The man she continuously tried to get pregnant by was Stand-Up Steve, a malingerer of the finest pedigree. Steve would hobble into the clinic, hunched over his cane with a "bad back and syattic", moaning and begging for relief, disability papers in hand. As soon as he stepped out of the building, however, his posture miraculously straightened, and he could be seen strutting down the road, twirling his cane like Charlie Chaplin. Thumbs up to the CHC architect that suggested a one-way mirror for the front desk.

And I mean it when I say Abby and Steve continuously tried to conceive a child. Their typical day consisted of three, and only three, activities: smoking pot, X-Box games, and sex. The most likely explanation for Abby's infertility was past STDs, but marijuana is famously unkind to sperm. Steve might have been shooting blanks, as the saying goes.

We had sent Abby to a gynecologist for a fertility workup a few weeks earlier, an appointment at which Abby was advised to take prenatal vitamins. She came to us with the prescription, asking that CHC pick up the tab. While we were known to foot the bill for scripts when patients couldn't afford them, it was almost always for a one-time thing like antibiotics. The money just wasn't there to subsidize long-term medications or vitamins. I tried pointing out that buying a bottle of prenatal vitamins wouldn't cost more than 10% of what she and Steve spent monthly on pot. Abby wasn't terribly pleased with me that day.

I brought Abby in from the waiting room and she stomped and huffed all the way to the exam room. She didn't even wait for me to close the door before barking at me.

"Well, I bought those vitamins," she said. "I even had to skip dinner last week to pay for them. I'm taking them every day, and I'm still not pregnant. How long is this supposed to take?"

I fought back my laughter. "They don't really work that way, Abby," I said. "You take them to make sure that when you *do* get pregnant, you have the best odds of carrying a healthy baby to delivery."

"That's not what the specialist told me!"

"Abby, I think you might have misunderstood. She can't give you the fertility medications until after your tests are back. Speaking of which, did you pick up the paper for Steve to get his semen tested?"

"No, he doesn't need it. The problem is with me."

"We don't know that for sure. The semen test is a routine part of the workup."

"He's fine! I know that he's fine! He's already had a kid with his last girlfriend, and he got another girl pregnant that had an abortion. So it's just me! It's so unfair."

"It is, Abby, but you never know what the specialist will find on the tests."

"Whatever. What do I do now?"

"Have you and Steve talked about cutting back on smoking weed? We did talk about how it can lower sperm counts and hurt the baby if you get pregnant."

"That's not true! Steve got both of his ex-girlfriends pregnant smoking just as much weed as now. Not only that, but this girl I know smoked weed all through her pregnancy and the baby turned out fine."

Man, was she ornery. "Does your friend still have custody of her baby?"

"She's not my friend. And no...but it wasn't because of weed. She was stupid and did crack or meth or some shit. I would never do that."

"You know, Abby, I've been seeing you for just about two years, and in all that time you've been focused on getting pregnant."

"Well, yeah, and you've been no help."

"I'm just wondering if you've given any thought to how you would raise a baby if you did get pregnant."

"I'll be fine! I will love that baby like nothing else on Earth."

"I'm sure you would, and I can tell that you would be a very loving mother. But you're not able to work with your learning disorders, and Steve doesn't look like he can work for now." Even though he can. "Babies are expensive, and take an unbelievable amount of time and energy."

"What would you know about it?"

"Well, I have two children. My wife and I both work, we have family not too far away, and we still find it a challenge to raise our kids healthy."

"Oh please...you're just the father. You don't know the first thing about caring for children."

I think I finally knew what to make of Abby. Note to self: marijuana does not cure Daddy Issues.

FUCK DID I HATE drafting lawyers' letters. Why, why, WHY do we have this insane appeals bureaucracy for people turned down for disability? Adjudicators, case workers, lawyers, tribunals, doctors, third party consultants...it never ends, just more and more money pissed away. It's not like going from the basic welfare stipend to the disability pension is winning the lottery. It's an increase from barely having the money to pay rent to barely having the money to buy food. Why not just approve everyone a doctor says is disabled? Surely it would be a wash in terms of overall costs. It sure as hell would have saved me a migraine every other week.

This particular letter was a tough one. It was for Bummer Barry, a pitiful guy trying to piece his life together but his own worst enemy. He'd take anti-depressants for a month, and then stop. He'd do a handful of counselling sessions, then stop. He'd get referred to a psychiatrist, then no-show. I never doubted the man's genuine misery, but he was only in his 20s. The bureaucrats don't easily buy a young man being disabled for the long run, especially a young man that won't buy in to getting better.

I didn't know Barry all that well. He was followed by one of the other CHC docs that had moved out of town months prior. I'd met him only a few times and briefly at that, but someone needed to complete his forms and draft the letters for his appeal.

I waded through his old chart, looking for anything of substance for better or worse. The chart was scanned into his electronic record, which was far more cumbersome to navigate than flipping through a paper chart. Whoever thought electronic medical records would be a health care panacea was a fucking fool. Nine times out of ten I needed to reprint the documents anyway.

Blood tests - nothing. X-rays - old broken bone, not helpful. Hospital reports - mostly ER visits, all for minor ailments. Wait...pathology report, surgery consult - this could be something.

This otherwise healthy man presented to the ER with rectal pain due to an impacted foreign body. He reports the foreign body as being needed to pre-dilate his rectum. This

would make room for drugs he planned on smuggling into jail while serving a sentence over a weekend. He was unable to remove the object on his own and could not be manually dis-impacted in the ER. **Under general anesthesia, the patient was prepped and draped...no blood loss, foreign body removed without complication. Foreign body appears to be a tennis ball.**

I left that one out of the lawyer's letter, but damn...gives a whole new definition to playing tennis as a moonballer.

IT WAS A BRIGHT summer morning, and Jailhouse Jake looked as chipper as I'd seen him. He was released from custody earlier than expected, just in time for the long weekend. Jake was now also a grandfather several times over, as his teenage sons impregnated multiple girls in the prior year.

"Jake, what can I do for you?" I said.

"I need my scripts," said Jake, "but I also have a question about concussions, because I'm worried I might have gotten one, and I just want to be sure I don't have brain damage or anything, with all the bad stuff I've done to myself over the years, with the drugs and--"

"What happened that makes you think you've had a concussion?"

"I was with a friend last Tuesday, and he wanted to let me try out his dirt bike, but we had to do it in the back woods because I'm not supposed to drive one of those things, and it was kind of dark, and I rode it and WHAM! - I hit the side of my head on a tree, and then I got back on the bike to ride again, and BAM! - I hit the front of my head on a tree, and I didn't get thrown from the bike, but--"

"You went dirt biking in the dark? Did you at least have a helmet?"

"It's funny you should ask, because I had this brand-new helmet to use when I ride my girlfriend's motorbike, but I didn't put it on, because it was new and I didn't want to get it scratched."

"I see."

"The good news is that I didn't black out, or at least I don't think I blacked out, even though my memory is a bit fuzzy from that night, but my friend said he didn't think I blacked out, but I just want to be sure that I don't need a cat scan in case I have some kind of serious brain damage, you know?"

"It sounds like you probably did have a concussion, but if you needed a CT you'd have ended up in hospital that night. In the meantime, wear a helmet from now on." As for brain damage, that train appears to have left the station a long, long time ago.

IT'S WEIRD TO get work-related messages on Facebook, to say the least. Most days I'd just assume it was a joke, especially since the message came from Jessica. Sadly, I happened to be carrying the on-call phone this weekend, so anything was possible.

OMG! You would not believe what happened with your patient!

Jessica was the nurse I worked most closely with. Was she an RN or an RPN? Or RNP? I can never keep track of what schooling gives a nurse what designation - RPN, RN, NP - but RPNs are paid the least of the three. Jessica was one of the funniest people I'd ever met. Whether relating the mishaps of her goofy pet cats or trading raunchy one-liners with me, she was always a hoot to be around. Perhaps I shouldn't think so well of her, because she *did* run me down with a golf cart at a charity event that one time. But in her defense, I was dreadfully drunk at the time...for all I know the incident was my fault.

The Facebook message included a link to the local paper's website, specifically the weekly recap of lesser police arrests. I was directed to read the second story down, about...holy shit, Molly Melodrama was arrested!

Molly had Histrionic Personality Disorder, on top of a tendency to chomp on Morphine pills like they were Skittles. Once all her tests turned up negative, I tapered her off the painkillers, but that didn't stop her shenanigans one bit. She'd come to appointments showing off more cleavage than a stripper taking the stage, go through emotional swings at the snap of a finger, and spew bad soap-opera lines in lieu of normal dialogue. When I cut her Morphine dose by something like 10%, her eyes welled up with tears as she announced that, "Of all the doctors I've known, Dr. Warsh, I've always thought that you were the one on my side. But now, you aren't the same doctor you were in the beginning. You've *changed.*" Who talks like that?!?

It turned out Molly and her new boyfriend visited churches at Christmas-season masses, the cloakrooms specifically, to raid coats for car keys. The two then took those keys and raided the corresponding cars for Christmas gifts. How much they absconded with was hard to say, but this criminal masterstroke was foiled by police without great difficulty.

The good news was twofold. Since she'd be spending most of it in detention, Molly would have plenty of company through the holiday season. More importantly, my children and grandchildren could forever boast that their Papa was doctor to The Grinch Who Stole Christmas.

CHAPTER THIRTY-NINE

The Community Cares

IF ONLY EVERY patient that came through the door of the CHC was a pot-addled jailbird. I could have happily spent the rest of my working days around these folks, documenting their every misadventure, then enjoyed my retirement relating their stories in a stand-up act. As you can imagine, that was not at all the case.

In fact, even among the rogues and delinquents flowed an undercurrent of tragedy. So many of the patients had been born in the wrong place to the wrong parents, doomed to a world where drug abuse ran rampant and physical abuse ran close behind. How do you survive, let alone thrive, when the landlord won't clean up the mold, your neighbors steal anything of value, and your best friend is too high to keep you from being raped by her brother?

I'm not naive to human nature and the awful things we do to each other. But trying to find a diagnostic label for human misery, trying to treat it with pills or a formulaic, scripted counselling session...it wore on me, broke down my spirit, my sense of hope.

It would be one thing if we acted like the downtrodden dregs of society simply weren't there, whitewashing how the lesser half live. Then helping the poor, the frail, and the disabled - housing, feeding, clothing them - would be an act of charity...God's work for people of faith. But we don't. We set up bureaucracies, and staff them with people whose job security is measured not by what service they provide, nor how satisfied the clients are, but by how much of the budget can be preserved. Then we pit one set of bureaucrats against the other, to piss away hours on end haggling over the same pot of funds. It's the most perverse way to structure social services and betrays the very clients the system is purportedly designed to serve.

"I WANT TO thank you all for coming here today - Dorothy, your daughter Cathy, Dr. Warsh, Jessica - and of course my own staff from Community Care. I'd like to open this meeting by looking at the broader context under which we're providing home care services to the local community. Over the next twenty years, the number of Canadians over the age of sixty-five is going to grow dramatically. Given the aging of the population, and the ongoing struggles of the broader economy, the province is facing enormous budgetary pressures to meet the health care needs of--"

I was putting a stop to this before it went any further. "I'm sorry to interrupt," I said, "but I've been listening to this kind of boilerplate since I started medical school. We are not here to discuss Community Care's ten-year budget forecast and strategic plan. We are here to discuss the needs of one client that your organization is not meeting, despite the very recommendations of your own staff."

Dorothy was in her early 70s. She used a walker without protest, but sciatica and worn out discs in her spine made it difficult for her to bathe and do housework. Dorothy was also the stubbornly devoted caregiver of her husband Charles, who had advanced dementia. Her grit reminded me of my own late grandmother. Just like my Nana, Dorothy was no fool.

Dorothy had been receiving home care once or twice a week to help her bathe, but the service was stopped just over a month earlier without warning or explanation. The Community Care office had already conducted two separate assessments of Dorothy's capacity for self-care, and both assessments reported she couldn't bathe independently. Nevertheless, the service was still stopped.

After a short time without regular baths, Dorothy developed an angry, infected rash on her back. She responded well to antibiotics and daily dressings by our CHC nurses, but she never should have had that rash in the first place. After weeks of unreturned phone calls, delays, and complaints to higher executives at Community Care, we were finally able to arrange this meeting to sort out what the hell was going on.

It took all of five seconds before Thing One - the frumpy, jargon-spewing middle manager from Community Care - raised my ire.

"I appreciate your point of view, Doctor," said Thing One, "but if I could, I'd just like to explain Community Care's new model going forward. We're making a paradigm shift, away from direct service provision and towards teaching and empowering the client to help themselves."

"That's all well and good," I said, "but I repeat: *your* own assessments, by *your* occupational therapists, say Dorothy can't bathe herself. It doesn't matter what 'paradigm shift' is going on. Dorothy is not physically capable. She needs the service. What's the holdup?"

"According to the criteria we use to evaluate service needs, Dorothy is a good candidate for facilitative training."

"Then your evaluation criteria need to be re-examined." Along with your fucking head, I thought, if it can be dislodged from your ass. "I don't see how this could be more straightforward. She needs the service. You have documented proof she can't physically do it on her own. Denying her the service has now caused clinical complications resulting in an ER visit, multiple medications, and daily visits to the CHC. The whole point of home care is to prevent these things from happening. How much does a support worker cost per hour? How many baths could Dorothy have had for the money spent on her health care in the past month? How many baths could she have for the money spent to have this meeting? I'm pretty sure that my sitting here costs more to the taxpayer than bathing Dorothy once or twice a week for **months**."

"It sounds as though there's a disconnect between our needs assessment and what Occupational Therapy has indicated. That's something we need to revisit."

Cathy, Dorothy's daughter, interjected before I blew my top. "Stop. Just stop. I'm going to tell you what I witnessed when Dorothy tried to shower. This is a proud woman - do you think she likes having someone else bathe her? Only once a week? She cannot lift her leg to step in the tub. She simply can't. She cannot clean her back that's covered in boils." Both Cathy and Dorothy fought back tears. "I had to personally help her undress, lift her legs into the tub, and wash her like she was my child.

"I'm self-employed and live more than an hour away. I gave up a day of work to drive for this meeting. It's luck - luck! - that I came early enough to see what she actually goes through, and to help her because you won't."

Thing Two, Thing One's overseer, chimed in. "We'll reinstate the support worker for baths. We can have that in place next week. We'll reassess Dorothy's needs sometime after that." She glared at Thing One. "And we'll put the brakes on the new Client Needs Tool until we get more client feedback."

In an ideal world Thing One would fall on her sword somehow, perhaps demoted or simply let go. She made the wrong call, putting meaningless paper guidelines ahead of the client in front of her face.

More likely, she'll get a raise.

CHAPTER FORTY

An Old Friend

"FRANK!" SAID BILLY, poking his head in the door as I pecked away at the keyboard. He had yet to write the final exam to obtain his nurse practitioner's license, but essentially ran his own exam room.

"Yeeeeeees?" I said, my eyes still fixated on the computer.

"I have a young lady in with a bladder infection. All the typical symptoms, urine dip went positive right away. She needs a script and I need you to cosign it."

"No problem. What's her name?" Time for the cumbersome click-fest of medical record software.

"I just need to get the spelling of her last name. Her first name is a spelling of Caitlin I haven't seen before: K-A-T-E-L-Y-N."

My head jerked up. "Did you say Katelyn with a 'K' and a 'Y'?"

"Yeah. Why?"

It had been - what? Two, maybe two-and-a-half years? I printed off the antibiotic script and followed Billy into the exam room.

"Well, howdy stranger," I said, my expression reflecting joy that she was okay and lament that she fell off our radar. "It's been a while." Billy stood off to the side as a witness.

"Yeah, I was kind of a mess the last time I was here," said Katelyn.

"How are you doing now? Apart from the urine, I mean. That's easy to fix."

"I've been okay. Still at the same job."

"Same problems with headaches and freaking out?"

Katelyn's eyes welled up. "Still there. Just trying to deal with it as I can."

"We can help with that. I mean it, and not just with pills. We...*I* was actually wondering about you."

"You were?"

"You missed some appointments, which happens, but your phone was out of service. We couldn't get in touch to follow up with you. Would you still be interested in talking about what's going on with you? No pressure."

"I would. Thank you."

"I'm glad to hear that. The good news is that even if you don't have voice minutes, we have a phone to text with." I scribbled the number on the prescription. "And next time, don't wait two years!"

Katelyn became something of a pen pal (or e-pen pal, specifically) to me in the ensuing year. I kept tabs on how she was doing every week or two by text. She had a brief period of emotional decompensation, triggered by her landlord's malfeasance. I felt a trial of medications was appropriate, but she didn't tolerate the pills at all. She met with a social worker once or twice, but her work schedule precluded a serious commitment to therapy. Ultimately, a pet dog proved more therapeutic than anything else.

It was heartwarming to hear that she was doing so well, given how unhappy and alone she was the first time we met. I don't take any credit for it, nor do I take any offence at a puppy proving more effective than my prescription pad. Unless the patient is at imminent risk of death, whatever works.

There's a flipside, though, to going the extra mile for a patient, and it's not the obvious risk of your efforts becoming a permanent expectation. That happens too, but I'm referring to something subtler. Once you give the extra effort, make the patient somehow feel more important, it erodes the objectivity that's essential to be an effective doctor. Something other than the medical needs of the patient drives your clinical decisions. That's not only ethically questionable, it can lead to bad medicine.

CHAPTER FORTY-ONE

Pill-Popping Penny

"HOW STUPID CAN you get?" I asked for the tenth or twentieth time that week.

"I know," said Jessica. She'd heard this tirade before.

"I'm serious! Your teenage child complains of a minor ache, so you pull them out of school for what, three days until you can get the kid to the doctor?"

"I know."

"I'd have to bleed, barf, or break something to get off school! Nicole really pulled her daughter out for a sore foot?!?"

"Toe."

"Can I write a doctor's note saying, 'please excuse Taylor's absence from school. Her mother's a moron.'?"

I couldn't decide if I was coming to my sell-by date at the CHC or just desperately in need of a vacation. Nicole the Nitwit, for all her incompetence at parenting, wasn't *that* difficult to care for. She dragged her kids to her appointments and asked that they be squeezed in, but that's low on the nuisance totem pole. She didn't even generate much paperwork. Come to think of it, why *did* I get so annoyed seeing her name on the schedule?

"You know what? Screw it," I said. "If that's all that they're here for, I don't even need to see the kid. God knows I could go a week without having to deal with Nicole." I clacked away on my office keyboard and hit PRINT. "Here's the note. Just give it to her and say I'm tied up on the phone or something. If she wants to wait I can see her." I suppose I needed to earn my salary at some point.

Another day, another day of people going nowhere. For all the talk about the "dignity in each of us", we had an awful lot of people that were tragically redundant to the run of society. Nicole was but one of many I saw in an average week. Was that why I was getting so cranky? No positive outcomes? Then again,

I'd been at the CHC over three years by that point, and maybe I was just coming to the end of my run. Every three years, like Kylea said. I leaned back in my chair, glancing to the ceiling for salvation.

A rap on the door. "Frank? Do you have a minute?" It was Amber, the third and youngest of my trio of nurses. Amber arrived on the scene not long after Billy but before Jessica. She was quieter than the other two, but no less funny or crass when the situation called for it. She put up with a lot of teasing on my part, as she spent each morning whining about the blandness of her paleo diet and her post-CrossFit muscle aches. Call it the Healthy Person's Hangover if you must, but I have no pity for such self-inflicted miseries.

"I do," I said. "Why?"

"Please don't shoot the messenger. I'm just covering the front desk for Vicki. Penny is here, wondering if she can be seen."

"She was supposed to come in yesterday."

"She says she messed up the date, but it's a really important reason for the visit. She'll understand if you can't see her but needs to see you as soon as possible."

Sigh. "It's okay. I dispensed with Nicole quickly. I can see Penny. Just ask her to wait a few minutes and I'll take her in myself."

Pill-Popping Penny. A woman of 30-something going on 60-something, medically speaking. She'd had diabetes for years, but it was impossible for us to keep tabs on it. Every accessible vein on her body was scarred from the sins of her younger days, years of drug abuse that left her broke and without access to her kids. When I first saw her, not long after I started at the CHC, she complained of non-specific pains that wouldn't go away without Percocet or one of its narcotic brothers. Her past problems were enough to disqualify her from narcotic pain medications, but I gave her the benefit of the doubt. It dawned on me - more than once - that I gave said benefit of the doubt more easily to women than men. Was I even capable of being objective anymore?

At any rate, I prescribed the pain killers to her, until she committed so-called "red flag" behaviors: ratcheting up the dose at her own discretion, repeated requests for early renewals, and lost prescriptions. I'd kept her on a pretty short leash to begin with - isn't that a dignified metaphor - with contracts, urine tests, and the like. But raising red flags was a no-no. I stopped prescribing her narcotics without hesitation, and she skipped town with her boyfriend, Pot-Pushing Pete, soon afterwards.

We didn't see Penny for over a year when she suddenly re-appeared at the CHC a few months before this day's visit. This time, however, things had changed. She had entered a treatment program to deal with her past problems. She reconnected with her kids and began the interminable process of earning regular visitation. She complained of pain, but this time it was - dare I say it - *believable*. She described diabetic neuropathy in vivid, accurate, and not memorized-from-a-textbook terms. I tried her on the typical medications that work (rather poorly) for neuro-pathic pain while we completed the diagnostic workup. Sure enough, she had nerve damage in her legs and feet thanks to years of poorly managed diabetes.

She wanted to revisit narcotic pain medication, and all the addictive risks those drugs entailed.

I escorted Penny into my exam room. "How are things, Pen-ny?" I asked.

"Not good, Doc," she said. "The last medications didn't touch the pain."

"What dose did we get up to?"

"Look, these pills aren't going to work. I know you don't trust me. I don't even blame you for it. I've done so much stupid shit in my life...I don't even know how bad my diabetes is, because my veins are so messed up. That's never going to get better. But I hurt, Doc. I hurt all the time. I have to find a new apartment, 'cause it hurts so much to climb the stairs. Yeah, I smoke pot, and yeah, I'm in treatment for addiction, but my days of screw-ing around are over. Pete...we're together, but I wouldn't let him go near anything you give me. I get it. You don't want to give me the pills, but please. Let me prove to you that I can be responsi-ble."

I let a minute of silence pass while I mulled things over. It would be so easy to say no. My colleagues, my nurse coworkers, the pharmacies...nobody would bat an eyelash. It was responsible, by-the-book medicine, the only way to handle prescription requests for dangerous, addictive medications. Who could fault me?

The patient.

The obsession over narcotics isn't about patient safety, nor is it about any high-falutin' dedication to public health. It's about not wanting your name on the bottle when a patient overdoses or sells their prescription on the street. It's about covering your ass, nothing more.

I had objective evidence her pain was real, and objective evidence she wanted to get over her addictions and on with her life. Then again, she was a *denizen*, girlfriend to a known drug-dealer and unrepentant malingerer.

Do I go by the guidelines or give the benefit of the doubt?

"Penny," I said, "I want to trust you. I really do."

"But you don't," said Penny.

"Let me finish."

"Sorry."

"We're going to try the narcotics again. Morphine, at a lower dose than where you were before, but we can bump up the dose if it works."

"Oh my God. Really?"

"Hang on. We'll start slow, with you going to the pharmacy every day to get your dose. I can't trust you yet, given your past...but I know that your pain is real."

"Thank you. Thank you so, so much."

"Don't mess up."

"I won't."

Penny stuck with the plan. It took a few weeks of playing with the dose before it worked. But no early renewals, no self-prescribed dosage increases, no overdoses...just a dose that worked and improved her quality of life, guidelines be damned.

Guidelines be damned, evidence be damned. What in hell was I doing?

Coming to the end of my run. Sigh. At least Penny's visits were pleasant from that day forward.

CHAPTER FORTY-TWO

Shrinking Violetta

I HAD A SINKING feeling about the day. Shrinking Violetta typically missed about half of her appointments, but she'd called and confirmed just an hour before. Though not the worst of the CHC troublemakers, Violetta was the only patient to revive my fantasies of faking my own death, this time without the chronic pain to fuel the fire.

Violetta first came to see me within days of my starting at the CHC. A spry but soft-spoken senior, she was a widow from rural Italy who immigrated to spend retirement with her children. Her early encounters weren't much more than secretarial for me...she was seeing some specialist her son had arranged for her in the States and needed me to fill out the authorizing paperwork. Normally I'd be put off by such demands, but the woman had a laundry list of complaints all related to her pelvis. Some of her symptoms didn't conform to accepted medical knowledge about the pelvic organs, and some of them didn't conform to logic either. Better to save myself the trouble and let the guru handle things down there.

Once the seas calmed in Violetta's nether regions, there was no end to her oddball complaints and requests for tests or referrals. She likely met the criteria for Munchausen Syndrome, which is psychiatrist-speak for an addiction to medical attention. When her bowels became the source of what ailed her - karma gets me again - she browbeat her gastroenterologist and me into ordering an upper GI series, barium enema, ultrasound, MRI, endoscopy, colonoscopy, and something called a defecating proctogram. In lay terms, that's a real-time X-ray of the patient's rectum whilst he or she takes a shit. How'd you like to be the technician performing *that* test? Not even Dr. Google can explain the diagnostic use of a proctogram, though its comedic value is pure gold.

Jessica shook her head as she relayed Violetta's complaints, caught somewhere between laughter and sympathy for what I was about to endure. "Doctor," she said in a mock Italian accent not far off from Violetta's, "I feel like my bottom is falling out."

"Say what?" I asked.

"I don't know," said Jessica with a shrug. "Her story's pretty messed up today."

I took a few huffs and trudged down to my exam room. On other days, I'd just hunker down and brace for the worst, but I could not find my game face. I issued one last sigh in resignation, knocked on the door and strolled in. "Hello, Violetta. How are you doing today?"

"Oh, Doctor," she moaned, "I feel awful. I barely make it here. So weak, so much pain. I no have strength anymore. I want to fly home, see my sister for a month. But I cancel plane. I no fly feeling like this."

"What's changed since last time?"

"It feel like something...something falling out of bottom, my rear."

"Like your bowels?" Prolapse of the rectum isn't all that uncommon. "Do you feel something pop out when you go to the washroom?"

"No, is not like that. Is like one side, one of the...the buttocks is falling. Like the muscle have no strength, maybe circulation terrible. I see physiotherapist, and she see it. She look shocked. She say, 'Violetta, things look awful. You have no muscle on this side. Maybe is a damaged nerve.' When I explain what I go through with American doctor a few years ago, she say I must to get this checked soon as possible, before it no work anymore."

Nerve damage only affecting muscles in a single buttock? I suppose it's possible. "All right, Violetta," I said, pulling on some exam gloves. "I'm not sure I've seen that before, but let's get you on the table and I'll do a buttock and rectal exam."

"I think you see more easy if I stand." And just like that, before I could raise a finger in protest, Violetta was directly in front of me, dress hoisted and panties around her ankles.

Me and my thing with asses. I hate karma.

"Well, Violetta, I, uh, don't see any obvious deformity to the muscle, and--"

"The physiotherapist, she say doctor need to feel himself." Before I could blink Violetta reached behind to seize control of my hand. She then had me grope her aged, sunken rear, convinced I would discover what ailed her. It was like feeling up a grandmother. Fuck I hate karma.

I stared at the heavens, or at least the corner where the wall met the ceiling. I thought back to my days as a resident, when a video camera adorned each exam room so faculty could evaluate our patient interview skills. If only there were a camera videotaping **this**. You could send that video to every bright-eyed, altruistic, aspiring med student, with the simple instruction, "Watch this. This is the life of a doctor. Think carefully before spending a dime on your application." That video would have changed my life. I'd be an accountant, or an engineer, or a chef. Or a piano tuner.

You might think that tuning a piano would be the most boring job in the world. Why? You work at your own pace, essentially and necessarily in quiet. The piano never talks back, never complains. When you're finished, you're rewarded with your fee plus Brahms, Mozart, and Beethoven.

I should have been a piano tuner.

"There's nothing, Violetta," I said. "Your backside is as healthy as it's ever been." Could some bolt of lightning strike me down? Please?!?

Violetta dressed and took her seat. She rambled on and on about her other body systems. By her account, she was on the brink of multi-organ failure. By all available data - and heaven knows there was a lot of it on her chart - she was healthier than me. I'd be lying if I claimed to be alert through her monologue, though. I just nodded absently, conceding defeat like a long-distance runner watching a rival pull ahead in the home stretch...sapped of strength, surrendering to the inevitability of defeat.

I hadn't been so despondent since the dying days of my private practice. I was close to the end and could feel it.

CHAPTER FORTY-THREE

Rachel

THE FIRST TIME I left practice, I was in the throes of a crisis...crippled, miserable, on the brink of a heart attack if I was lucky, a stroke if I wasn't. If I did it again, if I walked away, even with months of notice it would be a conscious decision. A choice. Why not take two weeks, three weeks, even three *months* off? What made me think it was time to walk away for good?

The patients would understand. They'll have been through it before, with other doctors in other clinics.

You keep telling yourself that, Frank.

I had reached a point of just spinning my wheels with the CHC patients. Many of them didn't want to get better, others just didn't no matter what I advised or prescribed. So much pain, so much misery in this town. The men unemployed or unemployable, no ambition beyond the next high. The women bouncing between panic and despair, victims of rape and abuse, unable to keep their daughters from suffering the same fate.

Hopeless or not, someone would still care for them. They were resilient, resourceful. Survivors. The CHC wasn't going anywhere. The other docs, the nursing team, the social workers...they were all dedicated to excellent care, and less lazy than me to boot.

You keep telling yourself that, Frank.

I knew the patients would take it hard. They might claim to understand, but's only one more reason to be angry - no, to hate themselves. *I had a good doctor, but I drove him insane and he quit.*

Rachel. Rachel would be the toughest.

Rachel was my age, give or take a few months. Sharp, tough, and motivated, she'd have been a force to be reckoned with in business or politics, had she been born to a different family and asked out by different guys. But like so many others, the what-ifs were cold comfort. Rachel had a life of horrors - sexual assault, chronic pain, drugs - and just couldn't seem to catch a break. Freeloading boyfriends, sleazy landlords...none of them make life easy when you're chronically pissed off at yourself, and trying to raise quirky boys with nary a dime to spare.

Rachel was a mess when I first met her. Her mood was wildly erratic, going from near-manic excitability to sobbing despair at the snap of a finger. She had uncontrolled full-body pain that wouldn't respond to any drug, narcotic or otherwise. She was desperate to come off methadone, to preserve the scraps of her failing self-esteem and give her some capacity to care for her children. She was on an ever-fluctuating cocktail of stimulants, sedatives, neuroleptics, and analgesics. Her working diagnosis was Dissociative Identity Disorder, a severe form of PTSD seen in victims of extreme childhood abuse.

By the time I knew enough about Rachel to take full responsibility for her medical care, she was thirty pounds below her target weight and falling. She was weeks away from metabolic shutdown, hospitalization, or worse.

Then some poor schmuck tried to rewire his own basement one night, and burned the local methadone clinic to the ground.

"FRANK, I HAVE Rachel on the phone," said Jessica.

"Does she want to come in?" I said.

"She says yes, and she's not going on the bus. Your day is pretty busy, though."

"Find a time. I need to see her."

You know a town's in rough shape when a fire at the methadone clinic is treated like a catastrophe on par with 9/11. Then again, dozens of addicts roaming the streets of Fort Sussex in withdrawal was a disaster waiting to happen by pretty much any measure. Maybe the state of municipal panic made sense. The interim solution was something to behold. Methadone clients were bussed in waves to the nearby clinic in the big city - a half hour drive each way - for their daily dose, at least until a new place could be set up in Fort Sussex. The nurses and I debated if it would be unbearable or funny as hell to ride the bus on that particular *Magical Mystery Tour*. Probably a little bit of both.

Rachel was worked in to my schedule and came in upset but not frantic. "I want off this," she said before I got a word in. "I'm tired of being talked to like a low-life junkie. I never took pain killers for anything except pain, never injected, and never wanted to get high. It makes me sick to see those other people getting their drinks. I know all of them, and they're fucking losers, and I don't want to see them anymore.

"I just can't go through the withdrawal." She sobbed, shaking her head in defeat. "I've been through it before. The sweats, the diarrhea, and the pain. It's going to hurt so much, and I can't eat, and I'm losing weight. I don't want to die! I don't want to die!"

There was no time and no point in asking for help. I knew what my coworkers thought about narcotic pain killers. And even if I could get a hold of a consultant, I'd hear nothing but the usual tripe about using my best judgement, consulting the guidelines, blah, blah, blah. It was my best guess, and her life.

"Rachel, I'm going to do what I can to get you through this. I've got an idea. It'll sound crazy, but hear me out. We stop it all - the methadone, the stimulants, the other junk--"

"No! I'm going to go through withdrawal...I can't handle it. I can't handle it."

"Hear me out. We stop it all. I give you hydromorphs and valium to reduce the withdrawal and prevent serious symptoms. We titrate the dose as quickly as we need to and worry about managing everything else down the road. I suspect some of the ups and downs you have every day are constant withdrawal from the methadone, but it might be the other crap you've been prescribed as well."

"I'm going to end up in hospital, aren't I? I'm going to lose custody of my kids. What do I do?!?"

"I can't promise you won't end up in hospital. Then again, we both knew you haven't been far from it since before the clinic burned down. All I can ask is to trust that I don't want anything but to see you feeling better."

"Okay."

Fuck, I hope I know what I'm doing.

It was a dicey few weeks that followed. I badly underestimated Rachel's tolerance for narcotics and needed to crank up the dose radically in the first three days. More frantic phone calls followed, and I did what I could to reroute any grief befalling the other staff onto me. It was my half-baked idea, and my responsibility for whatever came of it.

It was a month of twice-weekly appointments and constant back-and-forth phone calls to the pharmacy. Then something funny happened.

Rachel's need for opioids levelled off. There was still constant tinkering, with changes to the drug, changes to the dosage schedule, and changes to the daily dose at most visits. But three weeks into this little experiment, she stopped shedding tears on the spot during appointments. She avoided admission to hospital, and even escaped a trip to the ER. Then her weight started to climb.

Holy shit. It worked.

RACHEL STILL HAD her problems when last I saw her, but almost two years after coming off methadone she was thriving. Her relationship was far from perfect, her kids wouldn't get along with one another, and she remained just one bad break from disaster. But she was socializing again, returning to hobbies, and backing away from needing constant medical care. It turned out we both played music – though I use the word play loosely with regards to myself - and had similar tastes in television. It made for enjoyable banter at her monthly appointments.

The good news didn't stop there, either. She began cutting back on pain medication, with a long-term target of reducing her dose by half. To this day I consider Rachel one of my true professional success stories.

Should I?

Rachel still took addictive pain medication at high doses, and still smoked marijuana regularly. She was no closer to working full time, and no closer to getting off social assistance than the day she came under my care. Any way you push the paper or crunch the numbers, I went almost nowhere with her care after three intensive years.

And isn't it always the paper pushers and number crunchers that win the day?

CHAPTER FORTY-FOUR

The Bitter End

IMAGINE THAT YOUR child can't seem to get his or her math work finished at school, and the struggle goes on for weeks on end. The teacher asks for your help in rectifying the problem. Which of the following do you suggest?

a) See how well he understands the material, and hire a tutor if needed?

b) Make sure she's getting enough food and sleep, to ensure she's not sluggish when tackling the work?

c) Pay someone to time your child walking to and from the pencil sharpener, and report suggestions on how your child might improve homework efficiency by 15-20%, perhaps by investing in a mechanical pencil or erasable pen?

If you answered 'c', congratulations. You are now thinking like someone running a health care institution.

I can't speak to how other public sectors go about problem-solving, nor how other nations troubleshoot their health systems. In Canada, the health system is driven by and for the numbers, period. There are millions upon millions of dollars thrown at fast-talking consultants each year, all in the name of training doctors and nurses in the latest craze in industrial management to rein in costs, increase volumes, or reduce the almighty Wait Times. What was intended as a service for the poor and the sick somehow morphed into an unwieldy pseudo-assembly-line, treating the patient as something between an inanimate object and a fast-food patron.

But after the millions are spent and the shift in the numbers fails to materialize, the blame falls on the care providers. We're too rigid in their thinking, you see, to grasp the obvious benefits of management strategies that work perfectly well for Toyota or processed-meat plants. Even when the needle does move, never is there any scrutiny of whether the results come close to the opportunity costs. Sure, the consultant cost as much as hiring a full-time nurse, but we wouldn't have a 6% decrease in the median time to discharge!

Why rant about this here and now, so close to the end of my story?

Because the government bureaucrats in charge of the CHC budget started pushing **hard** on the numbers. And, as happens in every clinic and every hospital on every day, making it all about the numbers undermined the confidence and value placed on the work of the front-line staff. Morale among my coworkers and me went into freefall, and it was a matter of time before one of us snapped.

I WAS THREE days back from vacation, and the only one to show for his appointment was this guy? When had I seen him last? Two years...really? That long? I don't see a patient for two years and still can't stomach the thought of his next appointment? Now that's a personality disorder that leaves an impression.

The owner of said personality disorder was "Woe-Is-Me" Warren, an unrepentant do-nothing who had no interest in making his life any better. The first few times I dealt with him I could laugh it off, but this day I needed him in and out.

I'll take any accusation thrown at me - gender bias, arrogance, indifference - so long as the accuser spends ten minutes in a room with Warren first. Unlike Bummer Barry, Warren didn't even try to better himself. He came in, kvetched about his life, rejected every treatment plan offered to him, then bitched that I was an unhelpful, uncaring doctor.

Warren couldn't have picked a worse day to throw his bullshit my way. Kylea and I had taken the kids on an overseas trip the previous week, and I came back to a pile of requests for lawyers' letters. One office was particularly obnoxious, asking for multiple clarifications with next-day deadlines. None of my patients had shown up either, so I had nothing to distract me from the tedium of paperwork.

To top it off, the mood at the CHC had taken a turn for the worse. The government demanded that we roster two to three times the number of patients we were already seeing, irrespective of the intensity of care each patient demanded. The nurse practitioners were distraught, fearing sanction if they couldn't meet the government benchmarks. Two of my physician coworkers had been scaling back their hours for months and murmured about working elsewhere. And me? I was burned out and fed up as fuck.

"How can I help you, Warren?" I said.

"I came in hoping you could help me," said Warren. "The news had a story this week about physician-assisted suicide being legal. I wonder what your thoughts are."

Oh, for the love of... "Stop. Just stop. It doesn't apply to you."

"How can you say that? It's for people who suffer severe, debilitating illness, isn't it? I've been suffering with mental illness and unhappiness for years. I have no life."

"It will be at least a year before the laws and guidelines are clarified. In any case, I guarantee that you do not and would not qualify for assisted suicide."

"So I'm screwed. I'm just going to be depressed and miserable until I die of natural causes."

"Warren, do you know why it's called *assisted* suicide? It's for people that are so disabled they can't do anything for themselves! People with diseases like MS or AIDS or advanced cancer. You're young and perfectly able-bodied."

"There you go, practically making fun of me. Nobody here takes me seriously."

"Warren, we absolutely take you seriously, it's you that doesn't take *us* seriously. I offer you medication, you won't take it. You see our psychiatrist, you said you didn't like him."

"He called me a lazy piece of shit!" Okay, that I hadn't heard. Had to fight back a snicker on that one.

"So I referred you to a different psychiatrist," I said, "and you didn't show for the appointment, nor did you rebook. You saw our social worker but turned down counselling. Medication, specialists, second opinions, counselling...what else do you imagine I can do for you?" Wave a fucking magic wand?

"I guess I'll have to make an appointment with someone who listens and cares."

You do that.

The next day was no better. A couple of people showed for me in the morning, but I was still going back-and-forth with this paralegal pest. Had I really just come back from holidays? It felt like I never left.

I was grumbling at the computer when Dana knocked on the door. "Frank, do you have minute?" she said. Dana was the recently appointed Manager of the clinical team. Before coming to the CHC, she was a liaison nurse that I knew from my days at the health unit. Though reserved and soft-spoken when you met her, Dana was married to a hockey coach and had worked the ER for years before moving on to other challenges. The woman was deceptively tough. With the push from the provincial bureaucrats to up our numbers, the CHC needed someone to wield the hammer, and Dana was a perfect fit.

"Fuck. I hate these fucking letters," I said. "Yes, Dana, I do have a minute. What's going on?"

"We have to go over the new privacy procedure. There's a form that we need to fill out whenever we get a third-party request."

"We talked about this at the last staff meeting. This is fucking absurd. It does nothing except waste time. It's bureaucracy for its own sake."

"I know, but this comes straight from the Boss and the Privacy Officer."

"Why? WHY?!? Do they understand what this is? A form for every fucking information request... are you serious? I get four or five requests a week. You're asking me to fill out a fucking permission form for my paperwork. How is that remotely fucking sensible?"

"Frank, you need to calm down--"

I'm often complemented, or at least known for being easygoing. In some ways, I've always been laid back, probably to the point where I come across as disinterested at times. I have a long fuse, but once it goes off it goes *off*. In my younger days, some of my old pals would intentionally push my buttons...piss

Frank off and watch the fireworks. It was probably entertaining, watching me rant and scream like the love child of The Incredible Hulk and Daffy Duck. I wouldn't know, since I'm rarely conscious of what spews from my mouth in that state.

"I don't fucking believe this. I come back from vacation. We're hearing all this shit about increasing our numbers, increasing our numbers. Three-fucking-quarters of my patients don't show this week, and now I need permission to do my fucking paperwork? Why? Why the fuck did I go into medicine?"

"Frank--"

"This is such irritating fucking crap. Our patients stand in the waiting room, broadcasting every detail of their dick rashes and sexual exploits to anyone within earshot...*they* don't give a fuck, but we need to fill out a form so our 'Privacy Officer' can sign off on every piece of paper coming across my desk?!? Fuck!"

"I agree, Frank. It's complete bullshit. But this is Management's decision." She shrugged her shoulders and left.

I plowed through the last of my paperwork, still fuming. With no patients calling in to be seen, my work for the day was done thirty minutes before my usual quitting time.

I knocked on Dana's door. "I'm leaving. My paperwork's all done, and nobody's coming to see me. I'm not in tomorrow anyway, but I have no fucking clue if I'm coming back Monday. If I'm fired, so be it, and God knows I wouldn't blame you. If not, well...I might just fucking quit."

SURPRISINGLY, THE EPISODE didn't spoil my weekend, but I cheated by doubling up on my blood pressure pill. It's hard to be angry and dizzy at the same time. But there I was again. Miserable in my job, struggling to give a shit about anyone that came through the door, bored as hell, and plain fed up. Without the excuse of Master's studies or working two jobs or kids in diapers or chronic pain.

I could rationalize it any number of ways. I was damaged goods when I came to the CHC...I stuck it out longer than anyone else, longer than I'd ever expected...I hated the paperwork...I was frustrated with "the system" working against

the patients...everyone gets burned out working with mental illness and addictions...I was angry at the bureaucrats...blah, blah,
blah. None of it changed the cold, hard truth:

I didn't want to practice medicine anymore, and never truly
wanted to in the first place.

Once I was over my issues with pain and took a solid chunk
of time to recover from my first bout with burnout, I honestly
thought it was all behind me. The anger, the bitterness - the foul
animal tormenting me had been caged then put down for good.
It wasn't naive, Pollyannaish thinking on my part. Kylea and I
hadn't argued about anything important - bickering over money
doesn't count - in years. The kids were thriving in school and in
their friendships. I even found myself able to enjoy golf while
sober.

But the Beast never died. It was there all along, lying in wait
as I tackled the needs of the poor and abused. Now it was breaking through its bars, eating away at me with a vengeance. I was
sullen around my wife, irritable around my kids, and avoided
keeping in touch with friends. Medicating the stress with a drink
or two was becoming part of my daily routine.

My life wasn't big enough for my family and a job that I no
longer enjoyed. I'd already tried my hand at going back to
school, shifting gears, all to invigorate – no, *resuscitate* - my unhappy career as a doctor. I put Kylea and the kids through it
once, on my ill-fated sojourn into the mixed-up world of Public
Health, and had little to show for it beyond unused qualifications and a paperweight as thanks for my service. I had no right
to put them through it again.

PENNY WAS MY first appointment the following Monday.
Wearing an unflattering sun dress, she was younger than me but
could easily pass for my aunt. She was muddling along with on
her painkillers, part of the toxic cocktail I was prescribing her
alongside sedatives and an inestimable quantity of pot.

As I booted up the computer to navigate the electronic record, we engaged in the typical doctor-patient banter. How was
she keeping cool during the heat wave? How was her pain this
week? Was she checking her sugars?

"Is everything okay?" she said. "You seem annoyed or irritated."

"Sorry," I said, caught off guard. "Really?"

"Yeah. You look angry or pissed off or something. Did I do something wrong?"

"No, uh, not at all." Was it that obvious? "Maybe it was the pile of paperwork on my desk when I came in that made me cranky. I'm sure I'll be fine after a coffee." We both smiled and the visit went on without incident.

Penny left the exam room and I finished my note. I strolled down the hall to grab a coffee from the staff kitchen but found myself stopped in my tracks halfway. *Your patient just called you out on your demeanor. A woman who spends her days gorked up, sedated, and high(!) picked up on your non-verbal cues. Still think you're doing much good around here?* I hate my inner voice some days.

I turned around and knocked on Dana's door, asking for a minute of her time. She invited me in and I closed the door behind me.

"If it's about last week," she said, "it's really not a big deal. We need you to sign a letter acknowledging the bad behavior, but it's not a formal warning."

"It's not that," I said. "I'm a big boy. I should know better than to throw a tantrum when I'm pissed off. The truth is I'm burned out, and have been for months. I should have seen this day coming when I started here, and certainly after I left Public Health."

"The Boss told me she thought you were close to burning out." Dana had sat with me on a committee in my last days at Public Health and knew what was coming without needing to say a word. "Is there anything we can do change your mind? Time off?"

"I wish there was, but I'm kidding myself if I think that would do anything but put off the inevitable." Sigh. "Please accept this as my three months' verbal notice. Effective the end of this year, I'm resigning my position here as a doctor."

CHAPTER FORTY-FIVE

Reefer Madness

THE ROOM FILLED with tepid, nervous applause as the Family Medicine Forum keynote speaker concluded her words of discouragement. Every year, at this annual meeting of the Family Medicine establishment, the keynote address throws cold water on an audience of thousands. One year the speaker presented a vision of primary care wholly incompatible with how most doctors earn their living. Another year was a dire warning against nurses and pharmacists encroaching on traditional doctors' turf. I looked forward to these unintentionally deflating speeches as a running joke.

This year, the keynote speaker was a nationally celebrated nun. She went over the exalted (if romantic) Four Principles of Family Medicine, then proceeded to **shatter** any illusions that said principles were being met by today's doctors. Only family doctors are self-effacing enough to sit through a scolding to open a conference. A room full of alpha-type surgeons would be full of piss and vinegar, and the big-money specialists would be dialing for a last-minute tee time.

It was an expensive conference to attend, even before the costs of hotel and parking in Toronto. Since I'd given my notice just weeks prior, I'm not sure why I didn't just eat the cancellation fee and stay home for the weekend. Okay, I did know. I needed to see what non-clinical work might be out there, because Kylea probably expected more of me than dinner and the "honey-do" list once I was unemployed.

Moreover, I wasn't giving up my license just yet, but had been slacking off on my professional development credits. These big conferences offered more than the same old lectures on high blood pressure or asthma. I flipped through the catalogue of sessions. What could I learn this year? 'The Healing

Power of Song', 'Experiencing Touch in Family Practice'...well, maybe I'd bump into some old classmates.

And I did! Three of them, in fact...a perfect group for exchanging war stories and laughing at the sillier things on display at the exhibitors' booths. The most popular booth this year belonged to a medical marijuana company.

Growing up, my friends only ever smoked one kind of weed: whatever they could get their hands on. Wow, had things come a long way since the 90s. This corporate booth looked like something between a pharmacist's dispensary and those loose-leaf tea shops at the mall. A set of shelves was piled high with double-zipped aluminum bags, small jars, bulk bottles, and medication scales, each adorned with color-coded computerized labels. It was all so...*clinical.*

I was inspecting the items on the shelf when the sales rep came over for the pitch. "Welcome, Doctor," he said, "have you been given the demonstration of our various delivery devices and formulations?"

"Like what, a sample joint to smoke?" I laughed.

"Very funny, Doctor. No, I mean the different ways by which the cannabis can be delivered to your patient. There's the traditional loose leaf, plus the liquid extract for our vaporizer--"

"You mean you put cannabis in one of those e-cigarettes?"

"It's a similar principle, just a different proprietary technology. We are selling a pharmaceutical product, after all, not something to be smoked recreationally."

"Of course." Perish the thought...how dare I even suggest such a thing?

The rep put a coffee pod in my hand. "Here, Doctor, you can see that we also have K-cups with the different strains."

"I'm sorry...K-cups?"

"Yes, Doctor, for seniors or lifelong non-smokers. You know, an elderly lady who would take this in place of her evening tea."

I stared in slack-jawed disbelief. "Wow. Oh, wait...it doesn't have the black dot on top."

"I'm sorry, Doctor?"

"You know, the symbol on the cover...the pods don't work in the newer machines without it." Being a smartass is always fun.

"We're working on it. We have to wait for the government to approve the coffee pod anyways."

Later that day, I tried to get in on a lecture outlining the evidence for medical marijuana (spoiler alert: the evidence barely passes the laugh test), but was barred from entry by security.

"I'm sorry, Doctor. The session is standing-room only. If we let in any more people, we'll be in violation of the fire code."

Standing room only for a talk on weed? Good grief. What else to see? 'Water Birth', 'When Mom Goes to Prison', 'Vulvar Dilemmas'...eh, I'd had my fill of vaginas, clinically speaking, for one lifetime. I suppose I'd have plenty of time to play guitar after leaving the CHC. Maybe I could still get into one of those music-and-medicine sessions.

I wandered back through the exhibitor's hall. I was stunned. There were at least a dozen new foundations, organizations, and businesses promoting the health effects of meditation and yoga...and that was just in this one conference hall on this one day.

It was two and a half thousand years since Hippocrates scratched out his oath, and cutting-edge medicine now entailed lighting up a joint and mumbling a mantra in the lotus position. We traded textbooks and tablets for Cheech and Chong.

I didn't know whether to laugh or cry.

But I knew I picked the right time to get out.

CHAPTER FORTY-SIX

Erica

"SO ARE YOU excited?" asked Jessica.

"About what?" I said, gobbling the last of a chocolate chip cookie.

"You're done in like, three weeks! We should have a party, go out for drinks...you need to celebrate!"

"Celebrate what? Unemployment? Career suicide?"

"Frank, you could work anywhere if you wanted."

"Or I could stay right here, though not if I want to avoid becoming an alcoholic to cope. I don't want a party, because there's nothing to celebrate. I'm not retiring after forty years or accepting a more prestigious position somewhere. I'm fed up, burned out, and crawling my way to the finish line. It's an inauspicious end to a thoroughly be-shitted career."

The last few weeks were proving to be murder. I barely slept, ate pure shit, and chose scotch over exercise in my leisure time. I kept awake by guzzling enough coffee to give my eyelid a constant twitch. My only discernible feeling was guilt: guilt about leaving, guilt about not earning a living as of the next month, and guilt about not keeping up with the kids' schooling or the housework.

I shouldn't have cared what my extended family or colleagues thought, but I did. They all said, "you just need some time off, then you'll be back." I don't think they understood. Or maybe they did, and the platitudes were an attempt to get me feeling upbeat about my professional future. I hadn't the heart to tell them it was wasted effort. My pain was gone, my degree was done, my blood pressure was fine...it was just me in a career I found no joy in any longer.

The rapid-fire beeps of the CHC security sensor heralded the end of lunchtime and the arrival of afternoon patients. Most of the patients were saddened by my imminent departure, a few annoyed but understanding. My chronic pain patients were in a panic upon hearing the news, as I'd expected. I worked out a treatment plan with just about all of them, Rachel and Penny included, reinforcing that my departure didn't equate to their abandonment. The one exception was Erica, my second patient that afternoon.

Erica's and Rachel's respective histories were virtually interchangeable. Both suffered repeated sexual assaults starting at a very young age. Both experienced horrendous PTSD symptoms and chronic pain every day of the week. Both struggled to raise kids on inadequate support from the government and ex-partners. Both wrestled with addiction, and both had received intensive service by the doctors and social workers of the CHC. The difference between them, apart from hair color? After two years of regular visits, medication adjustments, tests and referrals, we simply couldn't find Erica a way forward in her care.

I'd seen more than my share of lost souls since starting practice, but by and large they were older. The folks in their 50s or 60s, the ones kicked around since forever by family, betrayed by supposed friends, and stymied from a normal life by red tape...I can see how they might give up, seeing life as something of a curse. But Erica was young, intelligent, and despite her insistence, there wasn't much physically wrong with her. I suppose my failure, or the health system's collective failure, was getting her to accept that fact. If she came around to acceptance, at least the team could help her adapt to her symptoms and build a life for herself.

My first afternoon appointment went by without incident, and I escorted Erica to my exam room. We were to be joined by Jewel, one of the CHC social workers, but she was with a client for the time being. The goal of the visit was to devise a plan for Erica once I was gone, including who would "play quarterback" and assume responsibility for her primary care. Jewel had been lured from a CHC elsewhere in the province, when her predecessor left to start a private practice. I have the deepest, enduring respect for social workers that work with these patients. As a doctor - even at a CHC - you still see bread-and-butter, diagnose-and-adios medicine that doesn't tax your coping skills. Social workers don't have that luxury, but somehow have the resilience to thrive in the job.

Before I could say a word, Erica produced a stack of reports from her handbag, and slapped them one at a time on my desk. "Complicated endometriosis! Adrenal fatigue! Abnormal spots on my MRI! Prolapsed heart valve! You have never been interested in any of my conditions. You haven't believed for a day that there's anything wrong with me. You have been condescending since day one and dismissed everything I've ever told you about my medical history."

"Erica--" I said, trying to get her attention.

"You didn't believe me when I told you I had Post-treatment Lyme disease. You didn't look into my swollen joints. In two years, you haven't looked into **any** of this. You've been obsessed with getting me off pills like I'm a junkie! Now you're going to leave?!? Not before my heart tests are followed up on, before my MRI is followed up on--"

Jewel knocked and entered, interrupting Erica's outburst. Notwithstanding her demands, Erica's theatrics were transparent. She was enraged by my departure, and I'd been expecting an episode like this for more than a month.

Like so many people I'd seen over the years, Erica had amassed a mountain of data and opinions on her clinical condition but couldn't discriminate signal from noise. I would never expect a patient to possess that ability, since that's what doctors and nurses are trained to do. But the Age of Google made it a challenge to elicit the symptoms and impacts of a disease without inspiring the patient to self-diagnose or self-medicate.

Erica simply didn't know what was important and what wasn't. The test findings she was up in arms about were incidental and didn't require follow-up. The word she used to describe her joint problems meant something different to the chiropractor she heard it from than it meant to a medical doctor. Her claim to various diseases was based on specialists' musings, not the results of conclusive tests. Not that it would matter if the diagnoses were accurate, because no known treatments exist for most of them. Others weren't even accepted diseases.

Jewel seized control of the appointment to acknowledge and diffuse Erica's rage. I spent a moment just observing in silence. Maybe Erica was in withdrawal, since she admitted to taking her medication inappropriately at times. Her mood and speech pattern flipped like a toggle switch. She went from monotone to fury in a snap, like a wounded animal.

And that's what Erica had become, hadn't she? Savagely abused time and again, she was a cornered animal, guarding her wounds that refused to heal. She never let down her guard, because that only ever led to deeper wounds, to more long, lonely nights of pain. If she were a dog she could be euthanized, put out of her misery. As things were, I guessed she'd spend the rest of her days treading water in the health system. She'd bounce from clinic to clinic seeking something to make her feel whole, never finding it without the trap of addiction. I could only hope I was wrong.

Jewel was almost ready to turn things back over to me. I sensed that Erica was no closer to being satisfied, and no further from hating me. I mulled over the many things I could say, the myriad directions I could steer the conversation, when a terrifying reality hit me.

This is what it meant to play god.

I don't mean God...the vision of a transcendent, benevolent being that decides who lives and who dies, an all-seeing, all-powerful entity capable of miracles. No, I was playing the part of a lesser god, a pagan god...ancient, even primitive. Purveyor of wonders perhaps, but fickle, needy, possessed of human weaknesses: jealousy, pettiness, vanity, spite.

I could tell Erica I wouldn't tolerate her abuse and throw her out of the office once and for all. I could call her a fool for clinging to fantasies of an exotic disease and send her away in a fit of laughter. Or I could give her a hug and total reassurance, gaining her forgiveness at the expense of being forthright and honest.

I could acquiesce to her demands and make the referrals she coveted so dearly. I could send her to the kindest, sweetest consultants I knew, that would order any test and dole out any drug. Or I could send her to a cold-hearted prick, someone to label her an addict and send her scurrying to a bottle of whatever was around.

I had sole control of the only record there would ever be of the conversation. I could play up her theatrics and play down her misery. I could craft words of outrage or words of umbrage, all in the name of making myself look good. If ever things should come to a College complaint or lawsuit, it was her word against mine...and mine was the only word put down in writing.

I'd almost certainly committed each of these acts at some point over the years, some likely more than once. I'd wielded the power of a god, toying with the lives of others while facing neither sanction nor censure. Had I landed in trouble, anything short of sexual contact could almost certainly be justified by some study or some guideline, all in the name of what I thought was "best for my patient".

Intoxicating as it was, this was power I'm not sure anyone has a right to wield over another human being, regardless of education, credentials, or an oath to some ethical code. It was power I had no interest in ever wielding again.

"I'm truly sorry this is how you feel, Erica," I finally said. "Your endometriosis? Maybe I prescribed the wrong treatment or made the wrong diagnosis. I make mistakes, and I'm relieved that it improved after you saw the specialist. The other things you're upset about? I haven't followed up on them because I didn't need to. There might be statistically abnormal numbers or unusual findings on a report, but they don't mean anything to your longevity or your health. If you don't believe me or trust me, I understand. I can only go by my education and my experience.

"I can also tell you that you aren't being abandoned. Jewel will still be seeing you, and we'll figure out which of the nurse practitioners will take over your care. If you need a prescription the NP can't write, like Valium or whatever, I give you my word it will be written."

I wrote my chart note while the appointment was still fresh in my thoughts. The note was as plain and objective as I could make it, colored only by a lament for the hostility in the room.

Garbage In, Garbage Out

I WISH THAT a reflection on my career could end with a proc-
lamation like, "I have no regrets", or, "I wouldn't change a thing",
but the only people who get to say that are retired athletes, rock
stars, and billionaires. I have countless fond memories from the
thousands of patients I saw, but also harbor countless laments
and regrets. If I didn't, I'd be either delusional or a sociopath, or
perhaps both. The truth is, after 15 years of practice I'm no closer to understanding the purpose of medicine than I was on that
fateful Tuesday morning I dragged my ass out of bed to answer
the phone.

I entered medicine with a preconceived notion of a *calling*...a
noble, even divinely inspired mission to "help people", though I
don't think I ever truly heard the call. Still, it was sold and treated as a privilege, an undertaking of the highest purpose, that
only the brightest, most compassionate, and most altruistic need
apply. I seized the brass ring of an offer to attend medical
school, sacrificed my 20s at the altar of studies, toiled in the
punishing crucible of residency...

...only to emerge exhausted, nearly bankrupt, and drifting
rudderless like flotsam in an ocean of piss and shit, blood and
bureaucracy, and above all **boredom.**

I suppose for me that was the bottom line. For all the glory
and prestige ascribed to it, medicine proved to be an intellectu-
ally mundane job. It was more pattern recognition than
detective work, and more playing with a treatment recipe than
inventing something truly novel. That's a good thing, mind you -
we can't be experimenting on our patients willy-nilly - but it
begs the question of whether the job *duties* still match the job
description. With medicine plowing full steam ahead towards
screening and management of chronic disease, at least outside
the OR and ER, is a doctor still doing the job of "doctor"? Or

should the vocation be more accurately labeled "patient health janitor"?

Yes, you need to be smart, observant, and a decent critical thinker, but above all medicine is people working with people. The intellect has its place, but it's the *heart* that matters most. You don't need to sweat sympathy or fart altruism, but you need a sense of when to give the patient a pill, and when to give the patient a hug.

Nobody I've ever met has the boundless patience and compassion to treat everyone with equal importance, especially when the patient lacks the capacity or insight to return the sentiment. It's why so many doctors burn out from working with the poor or the mentally ill. The greater the patient need, the greater the drawdown on your emotional reserves. Without some way to replenish your energies - the surgeon's thrill of operating, the obstetrician's shared joy when a patient gives birth - it's a matter of time before there's just nothing left to give. The superstar doctors, the ones with boundless passion that inspires patients and students alike, simply get a charge out of caring for others. Kylea fits that description, and it makes me as envious as it does proud.

Me? It turns out I had a needier intellect than I'd thought, with an insatiable appetite for new knowledge and new perspectives. I never found it for very long in medicine, and personal time is hard to come by. There are only so many hours left in the day for brainy indulgence, after the grind of work and my day-to-day duties as husband and dad.

I think that line of reasoning can help clarify the distinction between normal fatigue and the more perilous state of burnout. Everyone needs time off and away from their jobs, not just doctors. But medicine is busy, tedious, stressful, full of sadness, and replete with stuff that's just plain gross. If you couple that with a deep dissatisfaction in the basics of the job, you start down a darker, despairing path, the path to true *burnout*. Bitterness, resentment, and anger poison your thoughts. If you're lucky, with a good support network and enough self-awareness, you get out while you can or find some way to right the imbalance. If you aren't quite so fortunate, well, things can only end in tragedy.

As a reader, you might wonder why I haven't brought up money, except in the context of onerous student debt. Surely with the constant news reports about doctor-government conflicts, discrepancies in income between family doctors and specialists, and health care systems all over the planet nearing bankruptcy, frustration over pay must have played a role in my decision to leave early, right? Actually, no. At the risk of professional heresy, there were many days I felt *overpaid* for the job I was doing, because the work was so mindless relative to the money. But I speak only for myself on that one.

My other reason for setting money aside is that doctors earn different incomes in different parts of the world at different times for treating different diseases. But all doctors face the same headaches whether they practice in Alaska or Algeria: fatigue; bureaucratic meddling; patient apprehension; unclear ethical obligations; and the fragile balance between the needs of the individual patient and the comfort level of the individual doctor. Perhaps money can make some of the problems more palatable, red tape in particular, but that's a judgement for each doc to make for him- or herself.

You've probably gathered that I think very little of bureaucracy. Some of that stems from my experience with the College of Physicians, so I can't dispute a charge of selfishness. My bigger problem, though, lies with bureaucracy that's dysfunctional to the outside observer, and serving artificial purposes at the expense of real people. Is it more sensible to provide intensive, effective care to a few, or superficial, pointless care to an arbitrary benchmark of many? Health care providers - doctors, nurses, social workers - aren't inanimate drones or expendable soldiers. Sometimes ideas and policies just aren't worth the paper they're printed on, and the naysayers should be taken at face value and trusted to do their jobs conscientiously.

I'd be remiss if I didn't end things with an idea for how to keep doctors thriving in their jobs. My suggestion, or pardon the pun, *prescription* is a simple one: get prospective doctors to understand what they're getting into, and what it is society - not just medical school - expects of them. A doctor doesn't need to ace organic chemistry; she needs to *grasp* organic chemistry. A doctor doesn't need to produce scientific research; he needs to *digest* scientific research. A doctor doesn't need to save lives in far-flung corners of the world; she needs to embrace the community in her backyard.

For my money, it's the insistence that only the absolute cream of the crop need apply that lies at the heart of the problems in medicine. Elite overachievers should be left to overachieve, not toil in hospitals tending to the nearly deceased, nor dispel young parents' neuroses, nor piss away time filling out forms. To take academic sensations, that have padded their resumes with overseas volunteer work and excellence in athletics or the arts, only to task them with a lifetime of the banal...is it any surprise doctors can have inflated egos? Or seem preoccupied with how much they're paid?

Instead of taking the brightest young people out there and trying to mold them into caregivers, start with people passionate about people, then ensure they can handle the subject matter and rigors of the job. Let's disabuse everyone of medicine's mystique, and help society understand that stuffing a workforce with lifelong perfectionists is no guarantee that they'll work to perfection. Dial down the culture of hyper-achievement before and during training, and the growing obsession with performance metrics during a doctor's working years. It's not only to prevent doctors from burning out and calling it quits. Sometimes disease, suffering, and human misery are beyond anyone's control. It will drive everyone, above all the patients, to *madness* trying to force things otherwise.

Who knows? We might just end up with a kinder, more dedicated, longer-lasting, and cherished generation of doctors. If we're lucky, we might even stop the rapists and sociopaths from getting a foot in the door.

I could be completely off the mark. Maybe there's some grand, imperceptible logic to everything that doctors think and do. I just don't *get* it because I never *had* it. Let's face it, I wasn't a "blue-chip first-round draft pick" to med school. I landed my spot on a fluke, was a misfit through much of my training, and a journeyman through my lamentably short time in practice. Maybe I was simply destined to be a dud...garbage in, garbage out.

But I do know a thing or two about burnout, and what it does to a doctor. I'm a shadow of my former self, with almost no capacity to handle stress. I get pangs of anxiety at the thought of returning to practice and fits of overwhelming guilt that my former patients are the ones worse off because I quit. With so much of a person's identity defined by his or her career, to say nothing of pride at being a family breadwinner, I'm still very much adrift. I wonder if I've done more net good than harm as a doctor, and I'm puzzled as to how I'm supposed to fill my days beyond blogging my opinions and housework. The sum-total of these emotions isn't depression or panic or self-pity or anger. They've just left me feeling humbled and numb.

More alarming is the number of doctors, even medical students, that feel somewhat the same way. I'm incredibly lucky to have a supportive spouse, understanding friends, and above all, forgiving former patients. Not everyone struggling out there can boast of the same, which means other doctors' stories won't end tidily like mine.

Laughter and tears, pain and recovery, an anthology of anecdotes and a catheter clogged with come...life as a doctor, (genital) warts and all.

ACKNOWLEDGEMENTS

I Owe You One

This book could not have been possible without the help of countless people over the years: family, friends, teachers, coworkers, colleagues, employers...I could fill another forty chapters naming everybody, but there are folks that warrant special mention.

Thanks to my deeply adored wife Kylea, for our equally adored children, for our home, for standing by me in my darkest hours, and for keeping me around, what with the insurance on my head and all.

Thanks to Julie Devaney, for invaluable feedback to get me past my own ego and take my writing to the next level.

Thanks to Brenda, Megan, Michael, Christine, and Karen, my "beta testers", for advice on fine tuning.

Thanks to my awesome son Ben and irresistible daughter Chloe, for being straight-up amazing kids and teaching me how life works.

To the thousands of people that have sought my professional opinion or allowed me to take part in their care, I humbly thank you for your trust, and the privilege of being your doctor.

And to the singular person without whom none of this story would be possible - the guy or gal one spot ahead of me on the McMaster wait list - thanks for getting yourself admitted elsewhere. If ever we should meet, your first round is on me.

ABOUT THE AUTHOR

Dr. Franklin Warsh is an Investigating Coroner and retired Family Doctor from Toronto, Canada. His blog and podcast on all things related to health care and medicine can be found at http://drwarsh.blogspot.com. *The Flame Broiled Doctor* is his first full-length book.

Hailing from Toronto originally, Franklin now lives in London, Ontario with his wife, children, and adorable but malodorous pets. If he can steal time from the laptop and the laundry, he perseveres in the quest to bake a patisserie-quality macaron.

Manufactured by Amazon.ca
Bolton, ON

10602006R00157